Language Rights and Cultural Diversity

Center for Basque Studies
University of Nevada, Reno
Conference Papers Series, No. 9

Language Rights and Cultural Diversity

Edited by Xabier Irujo and Viola Miglio

Center for Basque Studies
University of Nevada, Reno
Reno, Nevada

This book was published with generous financial assistance from the Basque government

Conference Papers Series, no. 9
Series editor: Joseba Zulaika

Center for Basque Studies
University of Nevada, Reno
Reno, NV 89557
basque.unr.edu

Cover and book design: Kimberly Daggett and Daniel Montero

Cover illustration: Chumash Rock Painting, uknown source, subject matter unknown. In the collection of the Museum of the Mission of San Luis Obispo de Tolosa. Photo by Xabier Irujo.

Library of Congress Cataloging-in-Publication Data

Language rights and cultural diversity / Edited by Xabier Irujo and Viola Miglio.
pages cm. -- (Conference papers series ; no. 8)
Includes bibliographical references and index.
ISBN 978-1-935709-47-3 (pbk. : alk. paper) 1. Language policy. 2. Linguistic minorities. 3. Minorities--Civil rights. 4. Language and culture. 5. Sociolinguistics. 6. Linguistic demography. I. Irujo Ametzaga, Xabier, editor of compilation. II. Miglio, Viola, 1966- editor of compilation.
P40.5.L56L36 2014
306.44'9--dc23

2013046194

Contents

The Lack of Legal Status as the Main Challenge for Endagered Languages

Xabier Irujo and Viola Miglio

Even in a highly domesticated, often industrial, modern, and regulated geographic area such as Europe, linguistic diversity is nothing short of phenomenal. Concentrating on Europe, we would like to point out some considerably striking numbers that bolster the well-known adage popularized by Max Weinreich that "a language is a dialect with an army and navy," and propagated by linguists, sociologists, and minority rights activists alike.

To name but a few, in 2012—as we write—the European Union now has twenty-seven members and twenty-three official languages, however, the most widely spoken languages are English, French, and German. A tally of actual documents issued by the EU, however, shows that their vast majority is in English and that German may be ousting French from second place as the most widely spoken language in the EU.[1]

Vying for second place might not seem of great importance if one considers another set of striking facts: 23 may be the official languages of the EU, but the number of European languages, dialects, and varieties considered together is an order of magnitude greater, the estimates varying from a conservative 113 to 230 or even as many as 300.[2] Thus, taking the middle ground, only about

1. Arzoz, *Respecting Linguistic Diversity in the European Union,* 48–57.
2. See UNESCO Red Book of Endangered Languages, but many regional dialects and varieties are missing from that count (Basque dialects, for instance). Ethnologue had 239 for Europe (see Krauss, *The Vanishing Languages of the Pacific*

10 percent of languages have some official status in the EU, and this is only possible if the state within which these national languages are embedded has already granted some official recognition to the language under consideration. Usually this excludes dialects or varieties.

One more striking fact is that at least ten languages have become extinct in Europe over the last two hundred years alone, and hundreds have become endangered. Moreover, dialectal varieties are quickly losing ground—an example from Italy might suffice: when Italy was unified in 1861, only 2 percent of the population spoke "Italian," 98 percent spoke other dialectal varieties or languages exclusively. In 2000, those who spoke dialect only (although it is unconceivable nowadays for these speakers not to be bilingual with the standard variety)[3] comprised 19 percent of the population, whereas those who spoke Italian only made up 46 percent of the entire population.[4]

We maintain that there is a correlation between these trends—language loss, dialect attrition—and the lack of legal protection and therefore official representation afforded to minority languages. This makes the *need* for the political accommodation of linguistic diversity in Europe (and elsewhere) an urgent task.

Historical Context for the Extinction of a Language

Languages are becoming endangered at an alarming rate, a fact that has been attracting the attention of linguists and international institutions like UNESCO only in the last twenty years or so. Michael Krauss calculated that 20 to 50 percent of the world six thousand languages would become extinct during the twenty-first century and only 5 to 10 percent (i.e., three hundred) were to be considered "safe."[5] However, if we consider the number of

---

Rim, 6).

3. A variety is a specific form of a language, including dialects, registers or other sociolinguistic variations. The standard variety itself is often chosen to be the "standard language" and, legally, the official language of the state administration and education. As a consequence, the term variety is used as opposed to the terms language, usually associated with both the standard and the official language, and dialect, associated with non-standard varieties "thought of as less prestigious or 'correct' than the standard." Schilling-Estes, "Dialect Variation," 311–41.

4. De Mauro, *Storia linguistica dell'Italia unita;* ISTAT, Notiziario: Lingua italiana e dialetti in Italia.

5. Krauss, "The World's Languages in Crisis," 4–10. See, also, Krauss, "Keynote-Mass Language Extinction and Documentation: The Race Against Time."

languages that have been known to become extinct historically, at least from Charles Voegelin and Florence Voegelin's classification, we find around 370.[6] Krauss observes that the number is surely higher since historical times, but probably not much higher than four hundred, although from now on that number could go extinct every decade.[7]

The main factors that Krauss isolates as contributing to making a language "safe" for the current century are the sheer number of its speakers and the language's prestige. As for the number of speakers, Krauss maintains that 1 million is the safe number that will make sure that these languages are still spoken by children in 2100—this is an even more alarming number than the one quoted in the 2010 edition of *UNESCO Atlas of the World's Language in Danger*, which maintains that a hundred thousand speakers already constitutes a safe number.[8] The even more conservative number quoted by Krauss, however, 1 million speakers, is the number that usually defines what are referred to as "small languages"—regardless of whether they are minority languages or national languages. Krauss's justification for using a million speakers to judge a language safe is important: as a case in point he mentions Breton in France and Ryukyuan in Japan (both with over a million speakers in living memory at least) and Greenlandic or Faroese with around forty thousand speakers each. Breton or Ryukyuan are more likely candidates for extinction despite the number of speakers because of the type of linguistic policies that have been implemented in France and Japan respectively, which have severely endangered those two languages, whereas—as Krauss comments—Greenlandic and Faroese enjoy "geographic isolation and the relative lightness of the Danish yoke."[9]

We estimate that some two hundred to three hundred languages have over a million speakers; however, according to the 2010 *UNESCO Atlas of the World's Language in Danger* this number is offset by the 230 languages that have become extinct since 1950.

The study of extinct languages (languages that have disappeared without evolving or giving rise to new varieties) or are in danger of extinction suggests that it has occurred in the context

6. Voegelin and Voegelin, *Classification and Index of the World's Languages*.

7. Krauss, "Keynote-Mass Language Extinction and Documentation: The Race Against Time."

8. Moseley, *Atlas of the World's Languages in Danger*, see http://www.unesco.org/culture/languages-atlas/.

9. Krauss, "Keynote—Mass Language Extinction and Documentation," 8.

of a political conflict that produces the collision of two or more cultures.

UNESCO's FAQ answer to "How do you define an endangered language," can in fact also be the answer to "How does a language become extinct":

> A language disappears when its speakers disappear or when they shift to speaking another language—most often, a larger language used by a more powerful group. Languages are threatened by *external* forces such as military, economic, religious, cultural or educational subjugation, or by *internal* forces such as a community's negative attitude towards its own language.[10]

For small languages to survive, Krauss mentions some necessary minimal conditions "viable literacy, and social conditions favorable enough to support . . . maintenance of that language."[11] In this view, languages are only safe under those conditions if they "enjoy recognition and support as national languages of nation-states or at least as regional languages thereof."[12] Very few languages enjoy those conditions even among those that do count a hundred thousand or more speakers, since there are about two hundred countries in the world, and six thousand languages. Those top three hundred "safe" languages account for 90 percent of the world's population. Of the about 3,000 languages considered endangered, Krauss mentions that 229 have ten or fewer speakers—of those 229, 105 are in Australia and 48 in the United States.[13] Although it is tempting to draw a political and historical conclusion about language policy in those two countries, it may well simply be due to a better understood distribution and documentation in those two countries than in parts of Asia or Africa.

In an intriguing article in *Nature*, Daniel Abrams and Steven Strogatz explain their mathematical model of the dynamics of language death.[14] They envisage languages as fixed entities competing with each other for speakers on the basis of the "attractiveness" of the language itself: the factors contributing to attractiveness they mention are number of speakers and perceived

10. UNESCO, FAQ website, response to question "What are the causes of language endangerment and disappearance?" See www.unesco.org/new/en/culture/themes/endangered-languages/faq-on-endangered-languages/ (last accessed October 21, 2013).
11. Krauss, "Keynote—Mass Language Extinction and Documentation," 8.
12. Moseley, *Atlas of the World's Languages in Danger*, 82.
13. Ibid., 11.
14. Abrams, "Modelling the dynamics of language death," 900.

status—that is, the social or economic opportunities afforded to its speakers. They give the example of Quechua, which, despite its large number of speakers, suffers from low status compared to Spanish and a shift in favor of the higher-status language is quickly taking place (at least in the community of Huanuco, Peru, that they modeled). How can we explain the existence of bilingual societies then? The explanation is sinister: usually, these societies come about because their histories involved split populations that had no significant interaction and lived de facto as separate, monolingual populations, and have begun to mix only relatively recently, which is when language competition began. They maintain that only by "policy-making, education and advertising" can a language increase in status and therefore its attractiveness for speakers and reach a steady-state as part of a bilingual society.

Factors Leading to Attrition and Extinction

If one looks at the examples of extinct and moribund languages contained in the European section of the *Red Book of Endangered Languages*[15] one encounters thirteen extinct languages (no surviving speakers), nine nearly extinct (only tens of speakers, most elderly), twenty-six seriously endangered languages (no transmission to children, mostly elderly speakers), and thirty-eight endangered languages (some children among speakers but losing ground).

Among the extinct or nearly extinct and seriously endangered languages are ten Sami languages, seven languages that arose from the Jewish diaspora as well as Mozarabic, extinct in the early modern period, Old Prussian—a Baltic language with two varieties, one of them that went extinct in the thirteenth and the other in the sixteenth century.

In the same group we also find many languages that were lost from the territories they were spoken in the Russian area of influence. Some fell victim to the expansion of the Russian empire (and died out in the from the seventeenth to nineteenth centuries), and of the Soviet Union later (Baltic states, for instance), or were spoken in some of the Republics of the Russian Federation (Southern Mansi, Livonian, Votian, Ingrian, Ludian, Vepsian, Western Mari, Karaim, Crimean Tatar) and became extinct or seriously endangered in the twentieth century.

---

15. The indexes do not include ancient languages known to have become extinct. www.helsinki.fi/~tasalmin/europe_index.html#extinct.

If some diversity in the modality or time of extinction or endangerment can be seen among the European extinct languages, the thirty-one East Asian extinct languages unfailingly ceased to be passed on to further generations over the past two hundred years, many of them since the mid twentieth century.

In some cases language death literally meant the death of its speakers: for Eastern Kamchadal, Juha Janhunen[16] reports that the Kamchatkan population used to form a coherent cultural group numbering about fifteen thousand people and covering the whole of the peninsula in the early eighteenth century; however:

> The greater part of this population was massacred by the Russians, who first arrived on Kamchatka in 1697; the colonization of the peninsula was completed during the 18th century, and the remnants of the Eastern and Southern Kamchadal speakers were incorporated into the Russian-speaking immigrant population.[17]

Languages can also be lost when their speakers are split into separate groups and forcibly relocated: this is the case of Crimean Tatar,[18] most speakers of which were deported from the Ukraine to different areas, mostly to Central Asia after World War II and few have returned to their original homeland.[19] This mass deportation was ordered by Stalin in 1944 under the pretext of Crimean Tatar collaborationism with the Nazis and resulted in the death of 46 percent of the Crimean Tatar population from starvation, disease, and poor planning of such mass resettlements. The Crimean Tatars were forced to work in the Gulag systems. Considering that around 110,000 people died as a consequence of this forcible resettlement, it is perhaps more appropriate to describe it as genocide.[20]

Although ethnic cleansing, mass murder, and mass relocation are of course drastic manners of accelerating language death, they are also not the only ones. There are other factors that can be as damaging for the language and result in language attrition and death. The applied mathematicians Abrams and Strogatz hit the nail right on the head: prestige is key—if we subsume a whole array of factors under prestige, among which, an unfailing presence is the competition from a bigger, more prestigious "bully"

16. See www.helsinki.fi/~tasalmin/nasia_report.html#EKamchadal.
17. Ibid.
18. See www.helsinki.fi/~tasalmin/europe_report.html#Crimean.
19. Grünthal and Salminen. *Geographical distribution of the Uralic languages.*
20. Pohl, *Ethnic Cleansing in the USSR, 1937–1949,* 4, 112–117.

language at hand.

A few further examples will make some of these factors clear: many of the Sami languages are endangered and some extinct—this in part has to do with the limited number of speakers in each group and the difficulty of maintaining a nomadic lifestyle in post-industrial Europe. Under the many varieties of Sami—those that are still marginally spoken, that is—we regularly find this type of assessments: "speakers possibly not fully competent," or "younger speakers may be less competent and prefer Scandinavian (Swedish-Norwegian)."[21] When the group of speakers is small and not completely competent in the aboriginal language, it is even more difficult for the group members themselves to distinguish between the language they speak and the ethnonym as part of their identity. Chuvan, for instance, which was originally a Yugakiric language of Eastern Siberia is now extinct, although of the 1,400 members of the ethnic group, 300 claim to speak the language, but in fact they speak an archaic variety of Russian.[22]

Small numbers, historical violent confrontations, diseases brought from contact with outsiders, and political events are also the background of the extinction of the Ainu languages, spoken on the Kuril islands, Sakhalin (Karafuto), and Hokkaido in northern Japan. Since Karafuto/Sakhalin and the Kuril islands have been disputed between Russia and Japan for over two centuries,[23] Ainu speakers were forcibly moved (Karafuto Ainu were moved to northern Hokkaido after 1945 when the island became part of the USSR), or left voluntarily to avoid becoming part of a different political entity (some Kuril Ainu are known to have moved to Kamchatka after the Kuril islands became part of the Japanese kingdom in 1875—but the population was estimated to be by then already down to about a hundred individuals—after repeated encounters with Russian hunters and traders since the eighteenth century. Even Hokkaido Ainu is, in all likelihood, extinct (the few remaining speakers were elderly in the 1990s when this study was completed thirty years ago) according to Grünthal and Salminen, although Ethnologue cites ten living speakers[24]) and the Ainu

21. Grünthal and Salminen, *Geographical Distribution of the Uralic languages.*
22. Information *on Endangered Languages: Northeast Asia.* Available at www.helsinki.fi/~tasalmin/nasia_report.html (last accessed July 6, 2013).
23. Patrie, *The Genetic Relationship of the Ainu Language.* 5.
24. Grünthal and Salminen, *Geographical distribution of the Uralic languages;* www.ethnologue.org/show_language.asp?code=ain (last accessed February 24, 2014).

population had essentially shifted to Japanese over the preceding two generations or more. Ainu never had a written standard although katakana and Latin script had been used to write down some texts in Ainu.

From the preceding examples, it seems clear that ethnic minorities composed of small numbers whose lifestyle does not "agree" with the majority of the population in the area where they live are often absorbed or forcibly assimilated into the majority culture. Moreover, small groups of native speakers find it of course hard to maintain a language in competition with a much more widely spoken language on the same territory, whose mastery offers many advantages to improve one's social and economic position. The situation is made even more difficult if the ethnic group is divided across different areas, and by different languages or many dialectal varieties, especially if the language has no standard or more than one, or is mainly/only a spoken language: its speakers, at least the younger generations, will be drawn to the prestige of the majority language, just as younger Sami speakers find some form of Scandinavian a more attractive language for future prospects. Krauss's number of 1 million speakers for language sustainability—or isolation and some form of legal status in the case of smaller languages (Greenlandic, Faroese)—and the "lighter yoke" of a neighboring more prestigious linguistic community are amply justified by the existing evidence.

Clearly, political and legal factors contribute to a language's fate, as well as social prestige in the broadest possible sense as the status of a language in so far as it provides its speakers with the opportunities it provides its speakers for economic and social advancement. Bluntly put, the social prestige of a language is directly proportional to the degree of legal recognition and protection that language is given by the community, and legal status is an essential condition for its survival. A newly recovered legal status for a language that was ignored and vilified for decades or centuries, however, cannot work miracles: the recovery of lost prestige may take decades to spread positive emotional attachment to that language throughout the community and thus change deeply engrained opinions. In these terms, therefore, one should heed Krauss's justification of a million speakers as a "safe number" to guarantee transmission of the language to future generations, since even for widely spoken languages, a conflict of (economic, social, political) interest with a world-wide spoken language may spell attrition and eventual death. Given the change from isolated, sedentary, rural populations to industrialized urban communities in the context of the creation of the officially mono-cultural nation-states in most parts of Europe and many areas of Asia, as well as the competition for speakers of languages representing former colonial, and/or expansionist powers (Spanish, French, English, Russian, Japanese, Mandarin), it is hardly surprising that the rate of attrition of minority languages has greatly increased in the last two hundred years.

The Ideological Basis of Cultural Monopoly and the Rise of the Nation-State

As previously mentioned, the rate of extinction of languages has increased very rapidly over the past century—and many examples of languages and varieties that became extinct in Europe and Asia did so starting from the eighteenth century onward. It is naturally tempting to establish a parallel between language attrition and death in these areas and shifting ideological and political concepts promoting the territorial expansion of certain ethnic groups and their language—as in the Asian expansion of the Russian Empire—or the consolidation of hegemonic power of a certain group over all regions and other groups within a state.

In order to understand the ideological import of language in the building of the nation state at the end of the eighteenth century and throughout the nineteenth, it is important to highlight the philosophical discussions concerning the nature of language that had started in France in the seventeenth century. The view of traditional grammarians in France before the Port-Royal enterprise embodies an aristocratic concept of language based on usage, but the usage of the upper classes: those are the only repositories of "*bon usage*"—as we find in Claude F. de Vaugelas's *Remarques* (1647).[25] The hoi polloi (*peuple*) can only be masters of "*mauvais usage.*" As Ulrich Ricken points out, the Port-Royal enterprise and its *Grammar* (1660) point to a newly found "self-confidence of the bourgeoisie," which questions the predominance of the *bon usage* of the Court, and introduces the ability of urban, cultivated French speakers to be masters of good usage—Parisian speech as the norm in opposition to Versailles.[26]

25. Ricken, *Linguistics, Anthropology and Philosophy in the French Enlightenment*, 5–7 and 191–225.
26. Ibid., 6.

Other philosophical tendencies have to be taken into account to understand the ideological climate surrounding the discourse on language in the seventeenth and eighteenth centuries, beyond the socioeconomic considerations mentioned above. The secularization of thought that rationalism brought about with Descartes and the Enlightenment had wide-reaching implications. It was conservative and aristocratic thinking that saw language as being based on the *bon usage* of the Court. In turn, the aristocracy's hierarchic system made use of the support of the Catholic Church, as well as of the ideological stance of God-given rights. Religion also justified man's dominance over the animal world—man has a soul, animals do not. It is unsurprising that while Descartes still maintains the distinction between man and animal in that man is capable of thought, other thinkers of a more empirical nature (Pierre Gassendi for instance) see man as one of the extremes in a continuum of animals, just as language is a refined way of communicating with more abstract abilities than other existing systems of communications of which animals are also capable.

It is unsurprising that the Port-Royal enterprise was born out of a Jansenist circle, at odds with the cadres of the Catholic Church, and with the Jesuit Order in particular. Its grammar is not based on "good usage," but rather on "reason," and in clarifying principles of language not peculiar to any one specific language, but rather to all languages, Port-Royal clearly aims at finding universal principles of language. Just as in Chomskyan grammar three centuries later, the Port-Royal logic places great importance on syntax and word order as the basis for the expression of thought through language.

The rationalistic ideology vis á vis language can be summarized with a sentence culled from Beauzée's *Grammaire générale*, where it is clear that "pure thought" lies at the basis of all languages, despite the changes in word order—since the connection between ideas can still be deduced:

> The analysis of thought is the work of the pure understanding; and the invariability of the original prescribes unchanging rules for the copy . . . without differences of time, place, climate, and language: "raison" is at all times and everywhere the same for all languages.[27]

Word order was a key point in establishing the superiority of French over other languages, but it should be kept in mind that

27. Ibid., 127.

this position can only be understood as an extremely rationalistic stance born out of the debates over the sensual origins of thought, human essence as opposed to animal nature, the dichotomy of body and mind, and between mechanism and metaphysics.

Word order embodied in a tangible way the logic of thought expressed in language, whose essence was supposed to be universal, but whose several, multifarious manifestations were undeniable. How could the rationalists of the Enlightenment reconcile language diversity and universality, while simultaneously maintaining the superiority of French? The evolution of language was teleological for these thinkers, thus if it was true that Latin had a very flexible word order, French had distilled the most logical sequence for sentence components: subject-verb-object (SVO). Du Marsais, for instance, justified it by maintaining that when Latin started a sentence with the direct object, it was because the verb was already conceived of, and even before the verb, its subject, thus making the most linear word order SVO.[28] It should also be mentioned that these views were not unchallenged—Diderot, Condillac, and Batteux, using elements argued by the first two thinkers, proposed very linguistically up-to-date objections to Du Marsais. For instance by maintaining that even if a (transitive) verb started the sentence, that would already imply the presence of a direct object, thereby invalidating any claim to a specific hierarchy of one part of speech over one another. Batteux correctly observes, for instance, that Latin word order is much more flexible than French because Latin has a much more complex morphology with endings that mark the function of the word in the sentence and wonders how precisely is Latin's flexibility deviating from Nature's "natural order", embodied by French SVO. Moreover, with an intuition worthy of modern pragmatics, Batteux maintains that word order in language is not a given higher metaphysical order, but that it rather depends on the interest of the speaker in a certain topic over others in a specific sentence. It is not dependent on abstract concepts that only a grammarian, that is, "a minority within the larger linguistic community"[29] would know, but not the majority of language users. Batteux also understood grammaticalization: he understood that independent particles can coalesce with other words and develop into a complex system of inflection, but that French does not belong within

28. Ibid.
29.Ibid., 128.

this category, and that therefore it uses word order in order to express the function of the word in the sentence.

Batteux summarizes sensualistic and rationalistic oppositions vis á vis language understanding that what we see from Latin and Greek texts is the sum of general linguistic usage. If this goes against the "natural order" established by the rationalist thinkers, from Port Royale to the Enlightenment, it is because the grammarians extracted from (French) usage some very abstract rules and then proceeded to assume that those rules (created by them on the basis of one language at a specific point in time) were the rules that Nature herself had established for language in general. Ergo, anything that deviated from those rules, did not conform to the natural order, even when those rules blatantly do not explain or correspond to the wide linguistic diversity that exists. Batteux's modern reasoning could be applied to much of modern generative grammar too, since it "revealed that the rationalistic theory of word order rested on the fatal tendency of the human mind to absolutize its own abstractions and afterward to view them as a priori principles."[30]

Unfortunately, the good faith philosophical debate was quickly sharpened by national prejudices whereby French—the language of culture of the eighteenth and nineteenth centuries—became de facto the superior language to all others. It is in this climate that Antoine de Rivarol won the prize awarded by the Berlin Academy of Sciences in 1783 for his (in)famous essay "*De l'universalité de la langue française.*"[31] The essay answered the question about the reasons for the universal superiority of French, basing his logic on the embodiment that French represents of the "natural order." De facto, Rivarol establishes a theory of the inequality of languages and cultures by defending that the French language stood above the rest of the European languages by its "genius" or "inner spirit," which gives ideas expressed in French more clarity, rigor, rationality and power of expression and thus makes it the ideal language to express the ideas of human reason.

We have seen that there were dissenting voices, such as Batteux, but unsurprisingly there were also many respected thinkers that approved of his theory, such as Voltaire, who believed that the preeminence of French literature was based on the naturalness of the word order of the language. Voltaire saw in the clarity

30. Ibid., 129.

31. Rivarol, *De l'universalité de la langue française.*

of French the ideal means to propagate the ideas of the Enlightenment, and even Diderot agreed that the clarity of French could best communicate abstract ideas. It would not be long until these views were instrumentalized for political reasons.

Rivarol had criticized the convoluted syntax of other languages as the carrier of passions and sensations, the imprecise and sensualist enemies of reason. However, a journalist and grammarian advocating revolutionary ideas, Thibault de Laveaux,[32] criticized Rivarol's in 1784–1785—maintaining that language can only be as rich as the ideas of the people that speak it. Criticizing also Court de Gébelin's theory of the relation between climate and language, therefore, he maintains that "religious despotism" and its political manifestations (presumably the monarchy), "stultifies people more than climate or poverty."[33] Quite the opposite of Voltaire and Diderot's penchant for the clarity of French, Laveaux maintains that if the structure of a language is not flexible enough to express the diversity of human feelings, it is actually imprecise and unclear.

In all of these discussions, it is clear that eighteenth-century thinkers equated the written word and the structures that a long written tradition enable the language to develop with superior clarity and precision. As an extension, the success that French culture and literature had in the Age of Enlightenment was taken to be a proof of the superiority of the French language—again, in written form. This mentality clearly differs from modern linguistic thought that gives priority to spoken language. In fact, only one third of the world's six thousand languages has a written form, and writing is considered to be a subsidiary activity that is "learned" through schooling, not "acquired" as all normal human children acquire their native language. The so-called superiority of the written word only deepens the prejudice against languages, dialects, and other linguistic varieties that have no written form or that are predominantly oral—Rivarol himself, after all, came from the Languedoc region.

Some basic human rights were undoubedly first articulated during the tumult of the French Revolution,[34] such as the princi-

32.Ricken, *Linguistics, Anthropology and Philosophy in the French Enlightenment*, 130.

33.Ibid.

34. Through the Declaration of the *Rights of Man and the Citizen* of 1789 (see avalon.law.yale.edu/18th_century/rightsof.asp).

ple of legal equality, the assumption of innocence, the abolition of torture to exact confessions or as punishment, and the respect basic human dignity.[35] Specifically, article 11 addresses free speech:

> The free communication of ideas and opinions is one of the most precious of the rights of man. Every citizen may, accordingly, speak, write, and print with freedom, but shall be responsible for such abuses of this freedom as shall be defined by law.[36]

Therefore, it is not surprising that the rationalistic ideals of the universality of language—regardless of social origin of the speakers—were adopted by the French Revolution. In part it is because of their distance from the aristocratic views of language as the *bon usage* of the Court, because if language is universal it affects all castes of society, and because it was established as part and parcel of human nature, independently of a gift given by God and subject to religious reverence. In fact, Laveaux and the Enlightenment praised language as the vehicle for abstract and rational thought, conceded that a language could only be considered superior to another because of the ideas that were born out of that linguistic community, and condemned religious dogmatism as stultifying.

What is surprising is that in the aftermath of the *Declaration of the Rights of Man*, and considering article 11 above, the rights of speakers of *anything but French* in the post-Revolutionary French State should be trampled underfoot in the name of the national unity. If language was a universal characteristic of man, in all its facets, why didn't human rights translate into linguistic rights in post-Revolutionary France? The answer lies in the idea that equality can only be truly established through uniformity.

The nation-state-building process of the modern era sought to create its own legitimacy. Before the eighteenth century, religion was one of the main factors that expressed community identity in European monarchies; after the eighteenth century and especially in the nineteenth century, language started emerging as the symbolic factor of uniformity of the new nation states. In this, post-Revolutionary France was no different—and it is important to underline that many of these thinkers—indeed, those who most vehemently opposed the use of regional languages and dialects—were born and raised in bilingual or multilingual regions (Rivarol

---

35. Hunt, *Inventing Human Rights: A History*, 137–145.
36. Verpeaux, *Freedom of Expression*, 16.

in Languedoc, Bertrand Barère de Vieuzac in Gascony, and Henri Grégoire in Lorraine).

Following the American and French revolutions, we witness the inception of nationalism in the modern sense of the word, as patriotism to one's abstract idea of state rather than one's nation (or culture), which unsurprisingly goes hand in hand with the birth of the nation-state. Two of the political principles that underpin the modern notion of nation-state are the "unity of the state" and the "indivisibility of the state". The unity of the state is promoted by slogans (*E pluribus unum*, "one nation, one state, one language"), and rituals such as the singing of the national anthem, the pledge of allegiance, and the national flag. Unity is only possible if there are no language or cultural differences between citizens. The democratic concept of "equality before the law" was and is often confused with the political principle of "cultural standardization." This type of cultural standardization is at the root of the incendiary form of nationalism advocated by Barère de Vieuzac. A lawyer from the rankandfile of the small nobility (the "de Vieuzac" he would keep added to his name came from the small town on his father's side of the family in Gascony), he proved his unquestioned loyalty to the principles of the Revolution by advocating for a quick execution for Louis XVI, maintaining famously that the tree of freedom grows from the blood of tyrants.

Barère's idea of nationalism was developed thusly:

> Each nationality should constitute a united, independent state, and every national state should expect and require of its citizens not only an exclusive patriotism, but also unshakable faith in its surpassing excellence over all other nationalities and lofty pride in its peculiarities and its destiny.[37]

He is not advocating for a federal state for France, in fact he is not even seeing the multilingual and multicultural reality of the post-Revolutionary French state. There is no room for a multicultural doubt in the patriotism that believed was required of the state's citizens. Quite the opposite, for the sake of national unity and superiority over other states, internal differences must be quashed or ignored.

Although the result is the same as Rivarol's justification of the superiority of the French language, Barère's and Gregoire's premises are quite different: where the superiority of French was

37. Cook, *American Institutions and their Preservation*, 700–1. See also, Gershoy, "Barère, Champion of Nationalism in the French Revolution," 421.

argued on the basis of its terse syntax and ability to express abstract thought, as well as on the basis of its written tradition, Barère does not argue for any *intrinsic* superiority of French—its superiority comes from its status as the national language, as a unifying principle for the newly minted post-Revolutionary state. Barère does comment on the supposed inferiority of the other languages present on the French territory (*jargons barbares, idiomes grossiers*, see below), claiming that they must be sacrificed in the name of national unity and internal coherence, that is, cultural standardization. Gregoire also argues for the superiority of French and the leveling of other dialects and linguistic varieties on the basis of their inferiority toward the written terseness of the national language. But once again, he subordinates linguistic pluralism to the importance of all citizens having access to government, and if de facto, the documents issued by the Republic are only in French, education in French must be mandatory for everyone to be a fully functional member of the state.

In a statement that resonates with the prejudices of the place and time in which he lived, Barère stated on January 27, 1794 that:

> Federalism and superstition speak low Breton, emigration and hatred of the Republic speak German; counter-revolution speaks Italian and fanaticism speaks Basque. Let's destroy these instruments of injury and error.[38]

There had been a proposal by Bouchette to translate the laws of the state into the different regional languages, but because of its impracticality (and lack of real solid intentions toward the maintenance and status of these languages), the project was abandoned in 1790, although it was still discussed in 1793. Barère was a staunch supporter of universal education, since that would allow all citizens to participate in the government of the Republic. Unfortunately, regional languages and varieties were considered remnants of feudal divisions and associated with the ancien régime. Thus Barère states:

> The monarchy had its reasons to resemble the Tower of Babel; in democracy, however, leaving citizens in the ignorance of the national language, incapable of controlling power, means betraying the motherland. . . . In a free nation, the language must be one and the same for everyone.[39]

38. Gazier, *Lettres à Grégoire sur les Patois de France (1790-1794)*, 94–95. Also, Kjaer and Adamo, *Linguistic Diversity and European Democracy*, 46. Translation by authors. Unless otherwise stated all translations are by the authors.
39. Gazier, *Lettres à Grégoire sur les Patois de France (1790–1794)*, 94–95. Also,

And, he explains that:

> Moreover, how much have we spent translating the laws passed by the first two national assemblies into the various languages spoken in France! As if it were up to us to keep up these barbaric jargons and coarse idioms that serve no purpose but for fanatics and couter-revolutionaries![40]

The same views were shared by Henri Grégoire, better known as Abbé Grégoire, constitutional bishop of Blois, a Catholic priest with Jansenistic sympathies, born in a bilingual region of France (Vého, close to Lunéville in Lorraine) and a fervent supporter of revolutionary ideals. In 1794, he published his notorious *Rapport sur la nécessité et les moyens d'anéantir les patois et d'universaliser l'usage de la langue française.* To his dismay, when he set out to chart the use of French across the post-Revolutionary state, he found that only a small minority of French citizens knew or used French. To dismantle all remnants of feudal allegiances and regional identities, the administrative provinces of the ancien régime had been redrawn and ethnic, linguistic, and cultural groups had been parceled out into different administrative units. Despite this institutionalized geography, Gregoire found that less than 3 million citizens of 25 spoke French, the national language, that is, those of fifteen of the new administrative départements out of eighty-three. After his survey he found that despite the thirty provinces that had been dismantled, there were still thirty dialects (*patois*) whose names reminded their speakers of their former regional identity. This was clearly unacceptable and the jargons and dialects had to be extirpated because:

> Thus local dialects will gradually disappear, the dialects of those six million French people who do not speak the national language. I cannot repeat it often enough, in fact, that it is of much political importance to eradicate this diversity of coarse dialects that prolong the childhood of reason and maintain the maturity of prejudices.[41]

It is clear that the concept of linguistic right, that is, the right to express oneself in his/her own native language, as part of basic human rights has no place in the post-Revolutionary concept of a militant democracy, which is keenly focused on stomping out "prejudice" and cultural traditions as remnants of the ancien ré-

Kjaer and Adamo, *Linguistic Diversity and European Democracy*, 46.

40. Ibid. See also, Stephens, *The Principal Speeches of the Statesmen and Orators of the French Revolution, 1789–1795*, 41–42.

41. Ray, *Réimpression de l'ancien Moniteuri*, 358–60.

gime.

While undoubtedly these ideas are, in part, a logical progression of the rationalistic views from Déscartes onward and later serve the purposes of post-Revolutionary France, no doubt they also reflect social prejudices current at the time. Gregoire refers, for instance, to Corsican and Alsace German as "highly degenerate" dialects. There is in fact a desire to belittle regional languages, defining them as inferior, boorish, and uneducated, diminishing their status even further by referring to them exclusively as "barbaric idioms," "local jargons," "uneducated idioms," whereas the proper name of language was reserved exclusively for French, "notre langue"—everything else, be it a Romance language or variety like Provençal, Normand, or Picard, or another language family like Breton (Celtic) or Basque (isolate), are all defined by Gregoire as *patois* or *idioms feodaux*.

A proposal by Charles M. de Tayllerand advocates for public primary education in all municipalities, and reflects the institutionalized prejudice against regional languages harnessed for the advantage and consolidation of the state:

> The language of the Constitution and the laws will be taught to everyone, and the multitude of corrupt dialects, the last remnants of feudalism, will be forced to disappear: it is in the nature of things.[42]

Consequently, on July 20, 1794, the French National Convention, after hearing these reports on language, passed a law (2 Thermidor II) that, in essence, prohibited the use of vernacular languages within the administration: "no public document can be written in any other language but French in any part of the Republic' territory."[43] The law was suspended a few weeks later, but French as the language of instruction was there to stay, confirmed by a decree dated November 17, 1794, which read as follows: "In all parts of the Republic, instruction must be carried out exclusively in the French language."[44] In the second half of the nineteenth century, still 7.5 million (among a population of 38 millions) citizens of France did not speak French. The message contained in a letter from a prefect from Côtes-du-Nord and Fin-

42. *Archives parlementaires de 1787 à 1860: recueil complet des débats législatifs et politiques des chambres françaises*, 467–73.
43. Irujo and Urrutia, *A Legal History of the Basque Language (1789–2009)*, 130.
44. *Décret 27 Brumaire an 3 (17th of November 1794) relatif aux écoles primaires* (1, Boll. 90, nº 465; B 48, 188; Mon du 27 Brumaire an 3, Rap. Lakanal). In Irujo and Urrutia, *A Legal History of the Basque Language (1789–2009)*, 132.

istère to the minister of public Education, M. de Montalivet, reflects the beginning of a cultural genocide or linguicide, especially in Brittany, Occitania, Catalonia, and the Basque Country:

> [It is necessary] by all possible means, to promote the impoverishment and the corruption of the Breton language, to the point that from a town to another, the speakers won't be able to understand each other. . . . Because, then, their need for communication will lead the farmers to learn French. We must absolutely destroy the Breton language.[45]

This became the program of the central French government and a whole series of practical measures to destroy regional languages were set in place, from Brittany to Occitania, often with the help of the clergy. For instance priests were required not to give communion to children who spoke no French. Teachers and public education were the main instrument of repression: despite the fact that systematic linguistic discrimination in France is still a taboo topic, and many people refuse to accept that it ever existed, there are clear proofs of the role of schooling in the demise of regional languages, such as the following official statement by a sub-prefect to public school teachers in Finistere, Brittany, in 1845: "And remember, Gents: you were given your position in order to kill the Breton language."[46]

The practical measures implemented were similar in all regions, and consisted of constantly detracting prestige from the regional languages, so that their speakers would feel ashamed of speaking anything but French: carrying a clog or a sign indicating the pupil spoke Occitan or Breton in class (called *le symbole* or *la vache*), signs in public schools that read "Be clean, speak French" or "Don't spit on the ground or speak Breton."[47] Pupils were encouraged to accuse other pupils of the same wrongdoing in order to rid themselves of the mark of shame that speaking a regional language entailed. At the end of the day, the offending pupil was punished with staying in school longer and having to write sentences such as "I will never again speak Breton" fifty or one hundred times. All of these measures actively discouraged the use of anything but French, and de facto interrupted the handing down of the language from generation to generation, as parents did not want their children to get in trouble because of the regional language. In Occitan, these discriminatory measures are collectively

45. Abalain, *Le français et les langues historiques de la France,* 113.
46. Labouysse, *Histoire de France,* 90–92.
47. Morin, *La situation linguistique en France,* 15.

known as *Vergonha*, or “shame”—as shame was indeed an important means of annihilating the little remaining prestige of regional languages.

French rationalistic ideas on language and the Enlightenment were fundamental in the creation of the notion of the unity of the state through monolingualism, thus it was necessary to draw examples from the linguistic policy of France, but these cases are by no means isolated to France, or the eighteenth and nineteenth centuries. Very similar cases and numbers can be quoted for the Spanish state and its repression of regional languages such as Cat-

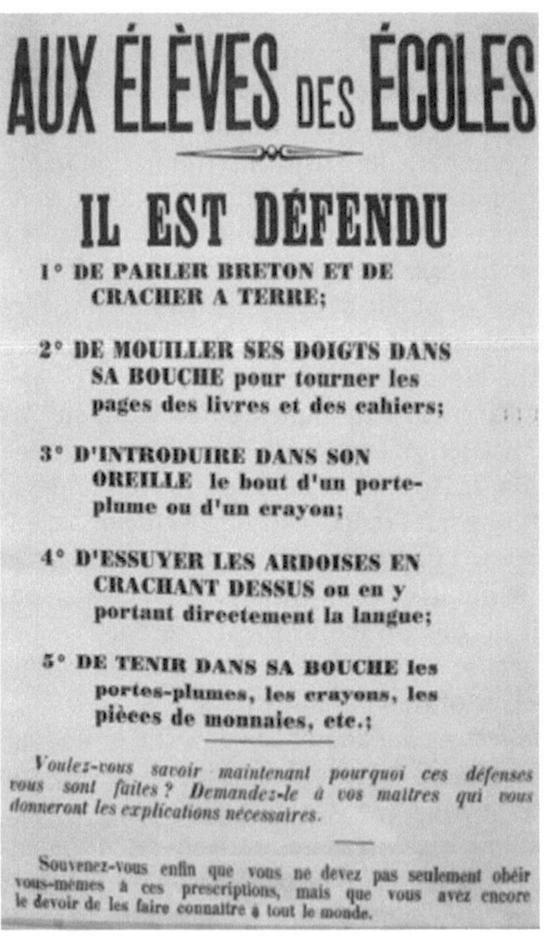

Figure 1. “It is prohibited to speak Breton and to spit on the floor.” Source: Author’s files.

alan and, especially, Basque.

When one of the cultures in conflict for the management of the state administration is in a position to impose a monopoly, for instance the imposition of a single official language, the process of regression of the rest of the cultures that are incorporated within the state begins. As early as the reports by Barère and Grégoire, the best strategy indicated to destroy regional languages was to create a monolingual administration and a relentlessly monolingual school system. If according to the report by Henri Grégoire in 1794 only 11 percent of the citizens of France were French speakers, the strategy was highly effective, since today the whole population of the nation-state of France is essentially French-speaking. A similar process can be seen in the creation of the Italian State in the nineteenth century, as can be seen in figure 0.2—where dialect attrition is clearly highlighted. Compared to 98 percent of the population who spoke something other than the "national language" at the time of Italian unification, less than 20 percent did so in 2000.[48]

While the means of suppressing regional language and dialects as pillars of subsidiary sub-national identities are the same, the vehemence and violence with which they are applied can vary: In the Italian case the mechanism was the school system and the compulsory military service, as well as the absurd enforcement of moving civil servants (including school teachers and draftees for the military) from their original region to other regions as far away as possible, to more severe threats and enforcement of corporal punishment, marginalization, shame, discrimination, imprisonment, and death in the Basque case. Perhaps the obsession of the French and Spanish states, and, indirectly, the resilience of their regional languages can best be seen in the amount of decrees and laws concerning language over the past two centuries. From 1789 to 1946 in the French state and from 1812 to 1975 in the Spanish state, nearly five hundred regulations were passed on the prohibition of using the Basque language in both states. From 1789 onward, thousands of laws have been passed on the exclusive use of both official languages—in both states, no less than thirty-one languages have been declared endangered.[49]

48. De Mauro, *Storia linguistica dell'Italia unita* ; ISTAT, Notiziario: Lingua italiana e dialetti in Italia.

49. Irujo and Urrutia, *A Legal History of the Basque Language (1789–2009)*, 17–23.

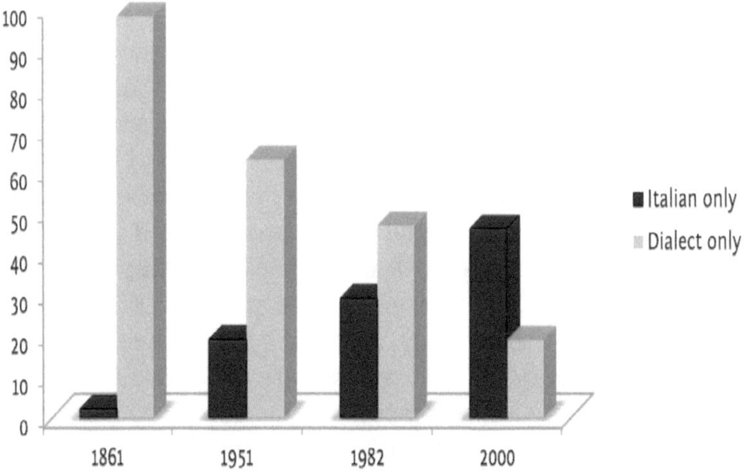

Figure 2. Dialect attrition in the Italian state.
Source: ISTAT, Notiziario: Lingua italiana e dialetti in Italia.

Language as Identity

The war against regional languages during the creation of the nation-state was dictated by a tacit recognition that language is an important part of ethnic and cultural identity. Regional identity was considered to be detrimental to national unification, because recognizing (and the mere recognition also meant "privileging of") an ethnic group over others denied the brotherhood that united all citizens, who were to be equal, and by extension homogenous.

If we return to the *Declaration of the Rights of Man and Citizen* of 1793, the basic human rights mentioned are "liberty, property, security, and resistance to oppression." (art. 2), whereas art. 11 says:

> The free communication of ideas and opinions is one of the most precious of the rights of man. Every citizen may, accordingly, speak, write, and print with freedom, but shall be responsible for any abuse of this freedom in all cases defined by the law.[50]

To a modern mind, this would imply an extension "in his/her own native language," because surely if the citizen does not know the language s/he is supposed to express him/herself in, s/he cannot "speak freely, and this "droit les plus précieux de l'Homme"

50. Asbeck, *The Universal Declaration of Human Rights and Its Predecessors (1679–1948)*, 50.

would turn into a blatant form of oppression. However, the revolutionary fathers of human rights hardly shared that opinion. Officially, as we saw above, the reasoning behind the extirpation of the barbarous regional idioms was that if the citizen was to participate in the governance of the state, and reap the benefits of knowing its laws and his rights,[51] he had to speak the official language of the state, in which all laws and decrees were written. In part, we saw above, that there was a cultural bias, and possibly a political bias, since foreign enemies of the Revolution had tried to infiltrate the newly established state through regional opposition and incitation to revolt.

The fundamental notion, however, was the need to dismantle any possibility of regional identity through language as separate from a national identity that would forge a citizenry loyal to the ideals of the revolutionary state. There is a natural connection between language and identity insofar as language often defines membership to a specific group to the exclusion of nonmembers. Through language the group manifests "personal strength and pride" and a "sense of social importance and historical continuity,"[52] and most of all belonging to an "imagined community" that shares a common worldview and that commands allegiance to it, hence competing with the state for citizens. It is not surprising, therefore, that the rhetoric of revolutionary thinkers, from Barère to Gregoire, set out to strip regional languages of their prestige, hence their "social importance" as an identity factor, by debasing them to mere "jargons" and "dialects," not in the sense of linguistic varieties, but rather of barbaric forms of expressions of uncivilized communities, remnants of a feudal order that perpetuated social privileges for an elite (in essence the ancien régime) to the detriment of others members of the community, and the languages of catechism, that is, that made communities dependent on religion—again an ally of the ancien régime and an entity vying for an allegiance of a potentially more devastating nature for a lay state.

Degrading these languages into incomprehensible jargons divided by numberless varieties, limited in scope, essentially oral, not represented by any institution (government, judicial, and ed-

51. The masculine possessive pronoun is used on purpose here, since women—and men with no property, one could add—were not represented by this charter.

52. Kramsch, *Language and Culture*, 65–66.

ucational), not buttressed by tradition and cultural history, but rather portrayed as enemies of progress that relegate their speakers to the Middle Ages had a concerted result. The inevitable loss of prestige caused by this systematic propaganda operates on two levels: members outside the community believe that extirpating such tools of stagnation was doing the members of the community a favor, and the speakers themselves abandon their own language of regress and stagnation to better their chances for social improvement.

These are typical methods that lead to language abandonment and loss, and in very similar formats we find in very different contexts (from the France and Spain of the past two hundred years, to the Ukraine and Georgia of the post-Soviet era). It works in the same way as dehumanization: "a psychological process whereby opponents view each other as less than human and thus not deserving of moral consideration,"[53] by debasing fellow human beings so that there can be no identification and no empathy with them for political or military manipulation. Dehumanization is in practice used against two targets: the victims, i.e. the ethnic group against which the ruling majority wants to unleash ethnic violence, genocide (Jews in Hitler"s Germany, Tutsis in a Hutu-dominated Rwanda, Hazaras in a Pashtun-dominated Afghanistan), who had better renege or hide their identity for their safety, and the perpetrators (militias, neighbors turning against neighbors, army recruits), who need to push past moral concerns to be able to inflict physical harm to what are, in fact, other fellow human beings.[54]

Dehumanization leads to genocide, just as debasing a language and by extension its speakers can lead to "linguicide." For them to work, the psychological impact of debasement, dehumanization, or in the case of languages, of loss of prestige and the conviction that one's own language no longer represents a positive part of the community's identity is crucial: language becomes a ball and chain to be gotten rid of and not to be associated with—not unlike Chicano speakers denying they speak Spanish nowadays because the majority identifies Spanish with the language of the laborers and the poor, or immigrants refusing to speak the language of the country of origin to their children so as to give them a social and economic advantage in their new country.

53. Maiese, "Dehumanization," online.
54. Boudon, "The Cognitive Approach to Morality," 83.

In the 1920s, after the massive immigration to the US from Mexico after the Mexican Revolution, English was clearly perceived as "the most potent weapon...to imbue the foreigner with American values",[55] not in the sense of giving the Mexican workers the necessary tools to communicate with Americans, but rather for cultural assimilation and homogeneity, through the perception of acquiring social and economic advantage:

> In 1917, California's Commission of Immigration and Housing recommended, "that employers of immigrants be shown the relation between a unified working force, speaking a common language, and industrial prosperity."[56]

Therefore, assuring mutual intelligibility can hardly be taken as the main goal of those political platforms (the US English Movement or the English-only movement for instance) that propose constitutional amendments to make English the official language of the federation. Assimilation and flattening of cultural distinctions are the real goals of these movements. As Kramsch pointed out in 1998, "in periods of social fragmentation and multiple identities, each clamoring to be recognized, language takes on not only an indexical, but a symbolic value," a way of delineating loyalty of a specific group to specific political affiliations, to foreign entities, to polarize the fears of the state's majority ethnic group for a political agenda (curb immigration, vote conservative, etc.).

Loyalty to the Nation-State, from Barère to the daily American Pledge of Allegiance relies on the citizens' participation in rituals devoted to cult of the nation's symbols: the national flag, the national anthem, festivals (Independence Day), national heroes (Presidents' Day), commonly practiced sports. It is not surprising, therefore, that the declarations of official languages are commonly carried out by the Constitutions, and are usually very close to the articles that identify the symbolic elements of the States.

We see for instance in the French Constitution of 1791, and the Spanish one of 1812, that languages and symbols are defined close to the concepts of Nation (as sharing one nationality, one culture, one language), and Sovereignty (the authority that emanates from the *nation*, as the abstract entity comprising a physical territory and its citizens. Next, Citizenship is defined, including its rights and obligations, as well as the Territoriality of the

55. Sánchez, *Becoming Mexican American*, 100.
56. Ibid.

State defining its boundaries. Then follow more general rights, as the right to vote and be elected, freedom of expression, etc., and more general duties (the right to know the official language of the state through education).

Discouraging Multi-National Identity by Imposition

Following the creation of the French (1789-1804) and Spanish (1812-1876) states, a monolingual political system was established according to the following precepts. There was to be only one official language of the state (French or Spanish in each of these cases). Only one language was to be the language of the state administration and of the administration of justice, and more importantly: only one language was to be the language of education, which from the nineteenth century on becomes compulsory. Compulsory schooling is part and parcel of the nation state: in 1859 (Casati Law), reiterated by the Coppino Law in 1877,[57] Italy also sanctioned the obligatory study of Italian, religious and civic duties—Mazzini, and Garibaldi, as well as other important figures of the Italian Risorgimento agreed on the importance of compulsory education to form the citizens of the new state, and that knowledge of Italian,[58] the closest direct descendant of Latin, was a way to reproduce the national unity achieved in the ancient Roman world.

Where monolingualism is imposed, persecution is never far behind: fines, exile, corporal punishment or even the death penalty have all been imposed, at some time or other, to speakers of minority languages after the establishment of the nation-state. One of the most popular methods in the nineteenth and beginning of the twentieth century was the use of the "Iron Ring" in schools (widely used in the Basque Country and several other countries), and the "*vache*" (mentioned above, in Brittany or Occitania)—any symbol of linguistic transgression, a wooden tablet, a clog, some sort of implement around the neck or visible on the body that

57. Stewart-Steinberg, *The Pinocchio Effect*, 312.
58. There was of course no consensus as to what Italian actually was or was supposed to be: where Manzoni favoured the imposition of Tuscan as the national language, because of its historical and literary associations, whereas Graziadio Ascoli, the linguist, favoured universal education as a means to improve the conditions of the poor and, he maintained, linguistic unification—in the form of dialectal leveling—would follow the pursuit of a common humanitarian goal toward the progress he believed would be delivered by universal schooling.

caused shame to the student wearing it and forced him/her to tell on other students that spoke their native language at school, and not the official language of the state. *De facto* the rules pertaining to the administration of the state in only one official language spelled exclusions for all other minorities.

The importance of language as an identity marker, the historical imposition of monolingualism and the rise of the nation-state help explain why languages die out. Violent persecution and psychological weapons, such as stripping of prestige, and debasing the importance of minority languages as an identity marker, are the means to achieve language attrition and death—often in the name of lofty national unification, at the expense of ethnic minorities. Language attrition and death do not simply occur because the older generation stops speaking the language and does not hand it down to a younger generation that does not learn it.

As we have seen, the actual reasons are of a very different nature, sociological, cultural and even economic, but all of these factors have their origin in political manipulation at the hands of one linguistic community (usually a majority) over others (usually the minorities).

This fact alone explains why based on the data provided by the UNESCO *Atlas of the World's Language in Danger* over 90 percent of extinct languages in the last fifty years had no official status, and why no official language is extinct as yet—only in very rare cases certain co-official languages are endangered (in most of the cases after a long process of segregation and lack of legal status).

Conclusions

The number of living languages on our planet is around 6,000, but as we write, in 2012, less than 4 percent of the world's languages have some kind of official status in any of the 196 existing states.

The idea of the nation-state, i.e. one nation occupying a well defined territory and speaking one language is a very rare case indeed, given the enormous disproportion between the two figures (6,000 languages vis-à-vis less than 200 states). Obviously, an approach based on the essentially monocultural and monolingual nature of the different states is clearly not in line with the existing linguistic diversity, the importance that UNESCO attributes to linguistic diversity, nor with the cultural and linguistic identity of individuals and groups speaking those 6,000 languages.

In recent years, several European constitutions have incorporated or extended their linguistic provisions adopting an official language while asserting the existence of other languages within the boundaries of the state: France, Portugal, Switzerland, Finland and Belarus. From the analysis of the 48 constitutions of the European States, it may be concluded that there are only nine states that do not mention at all language as a subject in their constitutional rules: the Netherlands, Iceland, the Vatican, San Marino, the Czech Republic, Serbia and Montenegro, Denmark, Luxembourg and the United Kingdom. However, the last four countries include provisions regarding languages in other different basic political regulations and, more importantly, none of them is officially bilingual.

On the other hand, international law has only been able to garner weak international support: although there are a series of charters and international covenants that specifically mention the protection of linguistic rights,[59] these are from a juristic point of view, part of cultural rights, rather than fundamental human rights. They are, therefore, so-called "third-generation rights" (after political and social rights)[60] and are less developed than other human rights. Moreover, states with vested interests in denying any rights to their linguistic minorities have the power of not signing or not ratifying these covenants and, even where there are legal provisions for the protection of cultural and linguistic rights, lack of funds for their implementation often nullifies the goal of the legislation.

The idea and the implementation of a monolingual state is clearly detrimental to language diversity, as represented by the fact that there are five endangered languages in the Spanish state, twenty-six endangered languages in the French state, and 191 languages in the United States. Reducing a language to the brink of extinction implies a lack of legal status, because legal status

---

59. For instance the following: International Covenant on Economic, Social and Cultural Rights (UNO, 1966/1976). Convention written in French, English, Russian, Spanish and Chinese (China has signed but not yet ratified it). African Charter on Human and Peoples' Rights (OAU, 1981). The African Union (AU) adopted the Constitutive Act in 2000. Article 25 states that the working languages of the AU are Arabic, English, French and Portuguese, "and if possible, all African languages." European Convention on Human Rights (1950). European Charter for Regional or Minority Languages (European Treaty, 1992). Framework Convention for the Protection of National Minorities (European Convention, 1995). Universal Declaration of Linguistic Rights (non-governmental organizations, under the auspices of UNESCO, 1996).

60. Ishay, *The History of Human Rights*, 245–325.

is one of the main guarantors of social prestige. The status of endangerment of a minority language is mainly due to its lack of officiality (or recognition of legal status) in the past and its level of endangerment is directly proportional to the level of legal recognition that the language has now and has had in the past.

Consequently, a certain degree of legal representation (officiality or co-officiality) is the only way to avoid further attrition or at least to limit the damages. This entails: bilingual administration, and a school system with immersion in the minority language—in other words, to make use of the same legal weapons that have contributed to the emergence of monolingual states and to the attrition of regional and minority languages can now reverse their fate, or at least delay the inevitable extinction of a given linguistic variety.

This, however, is only possible if we encourage the acceptance of cultural diversity and multilingualism as a positive outcome for the whole population of the state, not just for a minority within it. We should abandon the idea of the monolingual mono-cultural nation-state, and encourage the population of each country to adopt the concept of a multi-cultural state.

Bibliography

Abrams, Daniel M. and Steven H. Strogatz. "Modelling the dynamics of language death." *Nature*, vol. 424 (Aug. 21, 2003): p. 900.

Arzoz, Xabier (Ed.). *Respecting Linguistic Diversity in the European Union*. Amsterdam & Philadelphia: John Benjamin's Publishing House, 2008.

Asbeck, Frederick Mari van. *The Universal Declaration of Human Rights and Its Predecessors (1679–1948)*. Leiden: E.J. Brill, 1949.

Boudon, Raymond. "The Cognitive Approach to Morality." In Hitlin, Steven and Stephen Vaisey (Eds.). Handbook of the Sociology of Morality. New York: Springer, 2010.

Bradley, David and Maya Bradley (Eds.). *Language Endangerment and Language Maintenance*, London and New York: Routledge Curzon, 2002.

Cook, William W. *American Institutions and their Preservation*. New York: Norwood Press, 1929. Vol. 2, pp. 700-701.

Crystal, David. *Language Death*. Cambridge: Cambridge University

Press, 2000.

De Mauro, Tullio. *Storia linguistica dell'Italia Unita*, Bari: Laterza, 1963.

De Mauro, Tullio. *Storia linguistica dell'Italia unita* (Second Edition), Roma, Bari, Berkeley: Laterza, 1970.

Gazier, A. (Ed.). *Lettres à Grégoire sur les Patois de France (1790-1794). Documents inédits sur la langue, les mœurs et l'état des esprits dans les diverses régions de la France, au début de la Révolution*. Genève: Slatkine Reprints, 1969.

Gershoy, Leo. "Barère, Champion of Nationalism in the French Revolution." Political Science Quarterly 42, 3 (September 1927): 419-430.

Grenoble, Lenore A. and Lindsay Whaley (Eds.). *Endangered Languages: Current Issues and Future Prospects*. Cambridge and New York: Cambridge University Press, 1998.

Grenoble, Lenore A. and Lindsay Whaley. *Saving Languages: An Introduction to Language Revitalization*. Cambridge and New York: Cambridge University Press, 2006.

Grünthal, Riho and Tapani Salminen. *Geographical distribution of the Uralic languages*. Helsinki: Finno-Ugrian Society, 1993.

Hunt, Lynn A. *Inventing Human Rights: A History*. New York and London: Norton & Co, 2007.

Irujo, Xabier and Iñigo Urrutia. *A Legal History of the Basque Language (1789-2009)*. Donostia: Eusko Ikaskuntza / Society for Basque Studies, 2009.

Ishay, Micheline. *The History of Human Rights: From Ancient Times to the Globalization Era*. Berkeley: University of California Press, 2004.

ISTAT, 2000. Notiziario: Lingua italiana e dialetti in Italia (12 March). Available at: www3.istat.it/salastampa/comunicati/non_calendario/20020312_00/testointegrale. pdf

Kjaer, Anne L. and Silvia Adamo. *Linguistic Diversity and European Democracy*. Farnham: Ashgate Publishing, Ltd., 2011.

Kramsch, Claire. *Language and Culture*. Oxford: Oxford University Press, 1998.

Krauss, Michael E. "Keynote—Mass Language Extinction and Documentation: The Race Against Time." In Miyaoka, Osahito, Osamu Sakiyama and, Michael E. Krauss (Eds.), *The Vanish-*

ing Languages of the Pacific Rim. Oxford: Oxford University Press, 2007. pp. 3-24.

———. "The world's languages in crisis." *Language* 68, 1 (1992): 4-10.

Lorenzo Coveri. *Linguistica Testuale. (Atti del XV Congresso Internazionale di Studi, Genova–Santa Margherita Ligure, 8-10 maggio 1981)*. Roma: Bulzoni, 1984.

Maiese, Michelle. "Dehumanization." In Burgess, Guy & Heidi Burgess (Eds.), *Beyond intractability*. Boulder: Conflict Research Consortium, University of Colorado, 2003. Available at www.beyondintractability.org/essay/dehumanization.

May, Stephen. *Language and Minority Rights*, Harlow: Longman, 2001.

Morin, Séverin. *La situation linguistique en France*. Paris: GRIN Publishing, 2007.

Moseley, Christopher, ed. *Atlas of the World's Languages in Danger*, third edition. Paris: UNESCO Publishing, 2010 (3rd edn.). Interactive Online version: www.unesco.org/culture/languages-atlas/.

Mufwene, Salikoko S. "Language birth and death." Annual Review of Anthropology 33, (2004): 201–222.

Mühlhäuser, Peter. "Ecological and non-ecological approaches to language planning." In, Marlis Hellinger and Urlich Ammon (Eds.), *Contrastive Sociolinguistics*. Berlin: Mouton de Gruyter, 1996. pp. 205-212.

Nettle, Daniel and Suzanne Romaine. *Vanishing Voices: The Extinction of the World's Languages*. Oxford and New York: Oxford University Press, 2000.

Patrie, James. "The Genetic Relationship of the Ainu Language." In Papers in Linguistics vol. 15 no. 4 (1982): pp. 317-20.

Pohl, J. Otto. *Ethnic Cleansing in the USSR, 1937–1949*. Westport: Greenwood Publishing Group, Inc., 1999. Pp. 4 & 112-117.

Ricken, Ulrich. Linguistics, Anthropology and Philosophy in the French Englightenment: Language Theory and Ideology. New York: Routledge, 1994.

Rivarol, Antoine de. De l'universalité de la langue française: Discours qui a remporté le prix à l'Académie de Berlin. Berlin: N.p., 1784

Sánchez, George J. *Becoming Mexican American: Ethnicity, Culture, and Identity in Chicano Los Angeles. 1900-1945*. New York: Oxford University Press, 1993.

Schilling-Estes, Natalie. "Dialect variation." In Ralph W. Fasold and Jeff Connor-Linton (Eds.). *An Introduction to Language and Linguistics*. Cambridge: Cambridge University Press. pp. 311-341.

Tollefson, James W. *Planning Language, Planning Inequality*, London: Longman, 1991.

Voegelin, Charles F. and Florence M. Voegelin. *Classification and index of the World's languages*. New York: Elsevier, 1977.

1
Endangered Language and Self-Determination

Viola Miglio

Linguistic diversity, that is, the rich cultural heritage connected to the different languages that several ethnic or cultural groups speak as their native tongues, even within the same state or other political entity, is undeniably important from a number of viewpoints. From an anthropological one because language embodies (or Sapir-Whorfians would say "shapes") the mental categories that a specific group uses to make sense of the world it lives in; from a linguistic one because each language, while sharing many common, general characteristics pertaining to structure, meaning, and sounds, also selects certain ways of expressing meaning that are unique to it or shared with other members of the same language family, a certain sound system and intonation that is peculiar to it and to no other language in that form, and therefore gives it a special, exclusive recognizable identity; from a cultural and historical point of view, because traditional stories, and myths of ethnogenesis may trace cultural information about location, characteristics, and movements of the ethnic group in former times, or preserve traditional knowledge, which may still have considerable importance, and at any rate had a historical importance for the people who originated it. Diversity is also important because it is a fundamental part of creativity: different thought processes, or ways of understanding the world around us can be born out of cultural tradition, and lead to future innovation. And finally, diversity in the form of cultural characteristics, language, and specific knowledge of the environment the socio-cultural group lives in are a fundamental pillar of identity, and therefore crucial for the well-being of the individual as well as of the group. UNESCO (the United Nations Organization for Education, Science and Culture) agrees on the importance of cultural diversity in the following terms:

> Cultural diversity is seen as part of humanity's common heritage, which, as a source of exchange, innovation and creativity, is as essential for humankind as biodiversity is for nature. It should therefore be protected for the benefit of both present and future generations and be considered as a basic human right.[1]

While there has been some relative neglect of economic, social, and cultural rights,[2] after the Vienna Declaration adopted by the World Conference on Human Rights in 1993, it was suggested that these rights should be protected at the regional, national, and international level. Of course there has been considerable discussion as to the fact that given the conditions of abject poverty many human beings live under in many different parts of the world, economic rights are clearly at odds with the desires of part of the population.[3] However, the UN rightly maintains that—because such a large part of the world population goes to bed hungry and has no access to the most basic living conditions, such as safe drinking water—social, economic, and cultural rights must be made a priority.[4]

As has been pointed out on numerous occasions, ignoring these rights has often led to ethnically driven conflict and bloodshed and provides another clear reason why linguistic rights need to be protected and fulfilled. This was the case behind the establishment of the UNESCO-sanctioned Mother Language Day. The celebration commemorates Ekushey February or *Shaheed Dibas* ("Martyr's Day," February 21, 1952). On this day, the Pakistani government of what was then East Pakistan (and is now Bangladesh) violently repressed student-led demonstrations to claim language rights for majority Bangla speakers. Pakistan had declared that Urduwas to be the sole official language of East Pakistan, hence the prestige language that would give access to government jobs.

1. UNESCO, Cultural and Linguistic Diversity in the Information Society, 8.
2. UN, Economic, Social and Cultural Rights, vii.
3. Chapman and Russel, *Core Obligations;* Couret Branco, *Economics versus Human Rights.*
4. UN, Economic, Social and Cultural Rights, vii.

Bangla speakers, says DeVarennes[5] were essentially reacting to a discriminatory policy, hence highlighting a linguistic right as a fundamental human right.[6]

The manual issued by the UN points to one of the reasons why social, economic, and cultural rights have possibly been neglected, that is, because:

> Persistent false distinctions between civil and political rights, and economic, social and cultural rights, and lack of understanding of the legal nature and content of economic, social and cultural rights have undermined effective action on economic, social and cultural rights.[7]

Which this UN document maintains are part and parcel of human rights as a unit, and are therefore universal. Again in a footnote on the same page:

> These fallacies often centered on distinctions such as the purportedly positive versus the negative nature of the rights concerned, the allegedly cost-free nature of civil and political rights compared to the invariably resource-intensive content of economic, social and cultural rights, the capacity of civil and political rights to be implemented immediately and the purely progressive characteristics of economic, social and cultural rights, or the debate concerning the justiciable versus the non-justiciable nature of economic, social and cultural rights. Overcoming the falsehood of these arbitrary distinctions has been a major task of economic, social and cultural rights advocates for the past few decades—a task that has now in many respects been overtaken by the need to improve measures of enforcement and implementation of these rights.[8]

---

5. DeVarennes, "Les droits linguistiques en droit international," 189.

6. In this case, we can agree with De Varennes that a movement born around the need to defend and uphold linguistic rights had very wide-reaching consequences: On May 7, 1954, the Pakistani government recognized Bangla as a state language; on February 26, 1956, the Constituent Assembly passed the first Constitution of Pakistan recognizing Bangla as a State Language; on March 23, 1956, the first Constitution of Pakistan came into effect; on March 26, 1971, Bangladesh became an independent country. See sources quoted on www.virtualbangladesh.com/history/ekushe.html (last accessed July 14, 2012). It is significant that a Swiss National Research Program project on Diversité des langues et compétences linguistiques en Suisse mentions specifically the importance of legal representation of all official languages at the federal level as the key to linguistic peace: Le plurilinguisme de l'administration fédérale repose sur un large consensus et contribue à la paix des langues en Suisse, see www.nfp56.ch/f_projekt.cfm?Projects.Command=details&get=26&kati=3 (last accessed February 18, 2014).

7. UN, *Economic, Social and Cultural Rights*, viii.

8. Ibid.

Clearly a manual aimed at institutions of any state across the globe, with the intent to make the existence of these "third generation rights" known, with a view to their implementation cannot split juristic hairs as to the different nature of cultural rights (grouped with social and economic rights). We can afford to take a closer look, however—albeit concentrating on cultural rights only, and specifically on linguistic rights. There is a fundamental difference between civil and political rights—which are universal because they are connected to the nature of man as a human being, and linguistic and cultural rights. While the former have indeed a claim to universality, the latter are necessarily group-related, therefore it may seem that where human rights can be upheld for the benefit of all and to the detriment of no one, upholding rights—such as cultural and linguistic rights—that benefit one group to the exclusion of another makes them different from basic human rights.

Incidentally, retracing one's steps to the French Revolution and the Declaration of the Rights of Man and of the Citizen (1793) as the first legal source of basic human rights, it is clear that the incredible modernity and novelty of the document also rests on the concept of human rights as universal, that is, valid everywhere and at all times for any human being, exactly because they emanate from the nature of man as such, as a human being—and therefore worthy of respect and justice, and of access to the institutions that govern him (civil and political rights). It should be highlighted, as Pierre Encrevé does in a document where he assesses the nature of the "Declaration of the Rights of Man" vis à vis sign language,[9] that the democratic period of the Revolution also saw the translation of revolutionary documents and decrees into the different regional languages and that the Republic saw itself as multilingual, in opposition to the monolingual use of French by the king and the aristocracy. The (in)famous speeches by Bertrand Barère and Henri Gregoire belong to the Terror Time—*La Terreure*—when the creators of the new nation-state could only see fit to equate "a republican nation with a monolingual one."[10] Barère in his address on behalf of the Committee on Public Health (January 27, 1793) maintains that "the language of a free people must be one and the same for everyone,"[11] as a solution he ex-

9. Encrevé, "A propos des droits linguistiques de l'homme et du citoyen," 4–5.
10. Ibid., 5.
11. Encrevé, "A propos des droits linguistiques de l'homme et du citoyen," 5.

horts his fellow-citizens by famously stating that:

> Federalism and superstition speak Low Breton; emigration and hatred for the Republic speak German; counter-revolution speaks Italian and fanaticism speaks Basque. Let us break those instruments of damage and error.[12]

The same kind of reasoning is found once again, only a few months later (June 6, 1794), in Gregoire's rapport "Sur la nécessité et les moyens d'anéantir les patois et d'universaliser la langue française" ("On the need and means to destroy dialects and make the French language universal"). For Gregoire, all languages and dialects, even Romance ones—which had been spared (or ignored) by Barère, a speaker of Bearnese Occitan himself—must disappear. He restates the creed of Revolutionary monolingualism:

> The French people should be keen to consecrate as quickly as possible, within a united and indivisible Republic, the unique and invariable use of the language of freedom.[13]

Whatever the prejudices current at the time, and the fear that the border regions where regional languages were spoken would be a cradle of antirevolutionary sentiment, or whether the Revolutionaries really saw the local languages and varieties as remains of the Ancien Régime and instruments of error and feudalistic thinking, we can clearly retrace their vehemence against the linguistic rights of minorities in the French state back to the fundamental reasoning that all citizens must take active part in public life and know the laws of the state—if the official language is one to the exclusion of all others, all citizens must minimally know that language. The way to do it is to marginalize all other regionally used languages and varieties—of course the sinister project of constructing the model French citizen entailed the destruction of all regionally marked identities[14]—and language was in this case a fundamental pillar of those identities. At the same time, indoctrination in the new way of republican thinking, and teaching 25 million citizens who spoke no French the mandatory and unifying language of the nation-state could only be done through public education, that is, universal schooling—not for the democratic principles of universal access to knowledge, but rather for the

12. Ibid. All translations are mine unless otherwise stated.

13. Ibid.

14. Gregoire speaks of 'destroying'—*anéantir*—the regional languages and dialects, which he calls generically patois, depriving them of status and prestige.

political purpose[15] of unification through uniformity and cultural and linguistic flattening.

Of course, denying public voice to those citizens that spoke no French, a vast majority in 1793–1794 (approximately 90 percent of the population), in modern juristic thinking would be considered an immediate infringement of a fundamental human right, that of freedom of expression:

> Without our language there is no freedom of speech, as it is not possible to communicate and communication is carried out in the language with which each individual is familiar. Identically, languages are not separable from the right to a legal tutelage as without communication there is no defense.[16]

Thus, Iñaki Lasagabaster maintains the importance of being able to use the language with which one is most familiar (he is referring specifically to the legal status of Basque in that passage).

There are a number of texts that establish the importance of social, economic, and cultural rights, the main ones being the following: the *Universal Declaration of Human Rights* (1948); the *International Convention on the Elimination of All Forms of Racial Discrimination* (1965); the *International Covenant on Economic, Social and Cultural Rights* (1966); the *Declaration on Social Progress and Development* (1969); the *Convention on the Elimination of All Forms of Discrimination against Women* (1979); the *Declaration on the Right to Development* (1986); the *Convention on the Rights of the Child* (1989); and the *International Convention on the Protection of the Rights of All Migrant Workers and Members of Their Families* (1990).[17] And more recently, two more important documents have

---

15. Neither Barère nor Gregoire perceived sign language as a minority language that would impinge on national unity, quite the contrary: they thought it necessary for the benefit of making young deaf people part of the citizenry (Ecrevé, "A propos des droits linguistiques de l'homme et du citoyen," 6). This is undoubtedly due to the fact that sign language at the time was perceived not as a separate, fully fledged language, but rather as a means of communication, and a way to teach deaf people French.

16. Lasagabaster, "The Legal Status of Euskara in the French and Spanish Constitutional Systems," 118.

17. UN, *Economic, Social and Cultural Rights,* 3. There are also many regional instruments, such as the following: the African Charter on Human and Peoples' Rights (1981); the Additional Protocol in the Area of Economic, Social and Cultural Rights to the American Convention on Human Rights (Protocol of San Salvador) (1988); the European Social Charter (revised 1996) and the Additional Protocol thereto (2005), and many conventions and recommendation adopted by other organizations such as the International Labour Organization (ILO), the United Nations Educational, Scientific and Cultural Organization (UNESCO),

been added to the list, the 2003 *Convention for the Safeguarding of the Intangible Cultural Heritage* and the 2005 *Convention on the Protection and Promotion of the Diversity of Cultural Expressions.*[18]

The compilers of the UN manual maintain that economic, social, and cultural rights are not different from other basic rights, although they have been brought to the forefront of juristic discussions much more recently and that these three are specifically indivisible and interdependent. This means that they "apply to all individuals on the basis of equality and without discrimination, that they create specific governmental obligations, that they are justiciable and that they can and should be claimed."[19]

UNESCO has been at the forefront of the protection of third-generation rights, as the conventions on the intangible cultural heritage and the promotion of cultural expressions above show. UNESCO includes the right to education, linguistic rights, and traditional culture and folklore, and cultural diversity among cultural rights.[20] Despite the fact that recently there have been many more instruments addressing cultural rights, they remain problematic and not developed as precisely as political and civil rights. Because the above instruments are rather abstract as to what the protection of cultural rights consists in has caused this area of human rights to lag behind the others. Francesco Francioni spells out the "familiar argument" that was refuted in the opening section of the UN document mentioned above, for example:

> Cultural provisions contained in the existing legal instruments do not establish real rights, with corresponding precise and unconditional obligations, but rather political commitments of a programmatic character that create at most legitimate expectations but not true rights.[21]

The real crux of the matter, however, lies in the very essence of cultural rights as based "on the perceived uniqueness of the legacy that binds a group or community to a shared memory

---

the Food and Agriculture Organization of the United Nations (FAO) and other inter-governmental organizations, which have "established specific standards recognizing various economic, social and cultural rights. The 1951 Convention relating to the Status of Refugees also contains specific economic, social and cultural rights for refugees." (ibid., footnote 11).

18. Both available at www.unesco.org.

19. UN, *Economic, Social and Cultural Rights,* 4.

20. Francioni, "Cultural, Heritage, and Human Rights," 2.

21. Ibid., 3.

upon which the powerful sentiment of belonging and identity is built,"[22] for example, on claims of exclusivity, in contrast with the universal nature of basic human rights, which can also foment a certain imperviousness, lack of cultural exchange, and entrenchment around a "jealously guarded tradition,"[23] as well as the fact that in the name of bringing civilization first, and democracy later, these exclusive rights have been trampled since states and hegemonic groups have been engaged in expansionistic and colonial enterprises.

The second problematic issue Francioni points out in the nature of cultural rights is their being conceived as "group rights" or "community rights"—as opposed to other human rights, which are conceived of as individual rights.[24] Essentially, if they are community rights, they may conflict with individual freedoms, that is, if the cohesion of the group is to be kept, the group may resent the choice of any of its members to leave, return, speak a different language, marry exogamically. Cultural rights may also clash with other individual rights, for instance property rights. A community may want to enforce the rights to preserve its artistic patrimony and demand the return of valuable works that were removed from its territory, only to find that its cultural rights cannot be upheld because they clash with the property rights of the individual who bought said artistic treasures.[25]

A more fundamental clash between individual rights and the cultural rights of a community can be seen in the threat of violence and actual violence perpetrated in the name of religious extremism invoking the protection of a form of cultural right against the individual right of freedom of expression. Thus we can see that the problematic nature of cultural rights also lies in the fact that the rights of the community to preserve its traditions may infringe on basic human rights against women, or freedom of speech (the *fatwa* toward Salman Rushdie, the violent death of Dutch director Van Gogh, and the violent consequences of the Jyllands-Posten Muhammad cartoons).

However, there is a clear link between cultural heritage and human rights, as recognized by the 1954 Hague Convention, which states that "damage to the cultural property of any people

---

22. Ibid.
23. Ibid.
24. See also Pariotti, "Human Rights, Minority Rights, Women's Rights," 88
25. Francioni, "Cultural, Heritage, and Human Rights," 4.

whatsoever means damage to the cultural heritage of all mankind, since each people makes its cultural contribution to the rest of the world."[26] Francioni reminds the reader, for instance, of the horror the international community felt at witnessing the mindless destruction of the Buddhas of Bamiyan at the hands of the Taliban regime in 2001.[27]

Perhaps the exclusivity of cultural rights, as rights that inherently apply to a specific community and not to the individual, can be reconciled within the context of cultural diversity: if all cultures contribute to the cultural patrimony of mankind, then the preservation of all cultural heritage is everyone's duty, regardless of belonging or not to any one specific community or to the state within whose boundaries that community is found.

The Protection of Linguistic Rights and Language Revitalization: The Basque Case

While we have seen that cultural rights have only recently been worthy of discussion and protection as fundamental human rights within the provisions of international law, linguistic (and cultural) rights have not been the object only of dedicated conventions and other legal instruments. The UN *International Covenant on Civil and Political Rights* of December 16, 1966 (in force since 1976) mentions cultural rights in its preamble:

> In accordance with the Universal Declaration of Human Rights, the ideal of free human beings enjoying civil and political freedom and freedom from fear and want can only be achieved if conditions are created whereby everyone may enjoy his civil and political rights, as well as his economic, social and cultural rights.[28]

The same covenant also devotes article 27 to linguistic rights:

> In those States in which ethnic, religious or linguistic minorities exist, persons belonging to such minorities shall not be denied the right, in community with the other members of their group, to enjoy their own culture, to profess and practise their own religion, or to use their own language.

And yet, as Dinah Shelton observes,[29] despite a broad interpre-

---

26. Ibid., 10.
27. Ibid.
28. Available at www.ohchr.org/en/professionalinterest/pages/ccpr.aspx (last accessed February 18, 2014).
29. UN, *Economic, Social And Cultural Rights.*

tation of this article issued in 1994,[30] minorities have been unsuccessful in obtaining its implementation by the United Nations Commission on Human Rights (UNCHR), for instance because (1) cases are inadmissible when local legal resources have not been exhausted first (although these may be very expensive or hard to uphold), or because (2) states can simply "file a reservation to Article 27, effectively excluding the minority rights contained therein."[31] Shelton mentions the case of France, which at the time of ratifying the covenant also filed a "declaration" maintaining that Article 27 was inapplicable in France, since its national laws guaranteed equality and nondiscrimination. Hence the UNCHR declared itself with no jurisdiction on any case against France brought by Breton language speakers in view of Article 27 of the covenant.

We are brought back to the French revolutionary ideas on whose solid base the French nation-state rests: to be equal (vis à vis the law) one must not be (culturally, linguistically) different. This is uniformity enforced through monoculturalism/monolingualism, and using the individual's universal rights to justify the denial of the existence of cultural and linguistic minorities—the right to be citizens of the state, but also to be members of a smaller community within that state.[32]

The Basque Country is a very interesting testing ground for linguistic rights. De Varennes highlights several cases where, recently, the use of an official language does not trump linguistic rights before international courts: very similar cases have occurred at some time or other in the Basque Country. For instance:

- Use of a language in private cannot be prohibited to protect freedom of expression (Comité des droits de l'homme de l'ONU, Ballantyne, Davidson et McIntyre c. Canada, 1993)
- The family name and first name of a person are protected

30. Its text is available at www.unhchr.ch/tbs/doc.nsf/0/fb7fb12c2fb8bb21c12563ed004df111 (last accessed July 14, 2012).

31. Ibid.

32. Shelton points out in the same article that the UN HRC also considers claims to self-determination not part of its jurisdiction, since complaints can only be filed by individuals, whereas those claims are inherently a whole community's concern. She concludes in fact by stating that 'Thus, despite the Committee's broad definition of cultural rights in General Comment 23, it has chosen to limit claims of autonomy by minority groups, thus upholding the sovereignty and territorial integrity of states.' (2005, section 3).

by the right to one's private life (including one's name's original linguistic form) (*Coeriel et Aurik c. Pays-Bas*, Comité des droits de l'homme de l'ONU, 1994, et *Burghartz c. Suisse*, Cour européenne des droits de l'homme, 1994)

- The refusal of administrative authorities to use a nonofficial language with the public is considered discriminatory if there is no reasonable justification to do so (Comité des droits de l'homme de l'ONU, *Diergaardt et consort c. Namibie*, 2000)
- The right to education can include the right—in some cases—to be taught in one's own language within public schools (Cour européenne des droits de l'homme, *Chypre c. Turquie*, 2001)

Franco's dictatorship enforced many discriminatory laws similar to these: when the Basque Country was occupied (Bilbao was conquered on June 19, 1937, for instance), its legal codes and the economic and tax agreements were revoked,[33] books in Basque were publicly burned, Basque newspapers closed, and Basque civil servants and teachers in schools substituted with non-Basque-speaking personnel, loyal to the dictatorial regime. Other books that were clear instruments of propaganda became obligatory instead, such as the *Patriotic Spanish Catechism*,[34] where one finds the following statement on page 11:

> Spanish will be the civilized language of the future because English and French, which might have joined Spanish in this capacity, are such used-up languages that they are already on a path to extinction. So we speak other languages in Spain other than Spanish? It may be said that in Spain we only speak Spanish, since aside from it there is only Basque, which, being such an isolated tongue, is spoken only in a few Basque villages and has been reduced in function to a dialect due to its linguistic and philological deficiencies.

This was the first of several attacks aimed at the destruction of the Basque language, and consequently of Basque identity, as separate from Spanish. On May 18, 1938, Basque names (excluding only those of religious shrines, Aranzazu, Itziar, Begoña—all common female Basque names) were banned from the Official Registries because:

33. Irujo and Urrutia, *A Legal History of the Basque Country,* 215.
34. Menéndez-Reigada. Catecismo Patriótico Español, 3rd. Edition. Quoted in Irujo and Urrutia, *A Legal History of the Basque Country,* 219, 406.

> [They] are not only in a language other than the official Spanish, but that also imply defiance to the Unity of the nation. Such is the case in the Basque provinces, for example, with the names Iñaki, Kepa, Koldobika, and others that indisputably suggest separatist sentiment.[35]

This order was confirmed by a ministerial order dated August 12, 1938, article 2, which stated that "Inscriptions made in a language or dialect other than the official Spanish are to be considered null and of no legal value."[36] Thus it was also required that Basque names be erased from tombstones and replaced with names that were more respectful of the regime's linguistic policies, this would have to be done by the family of the deceased, who had to remove the headstones and replace them with new ones.[37]

These prohibition clearly also infringed on the private sphere of Basque individuals. In April 1937, the military governor of Donostia-San Sebastián) issued an edict that stated:

> SPEAK SPANISH!
>
> His Most Excellent Military Governor of this Locality has issued the following edict:
>
> It should be the concern of every branch of authority to eliminate causes that tend toward the disunity of the people. . . . To this end, one of the best ways to demonstrate mutual understanding and the exchange of kindness and ideas is to employ a common language.[38]

And in a much more sinister and threatening way, the circular issued as a Proclamation of the Military Governor on May 29, 1937, said:

> Any person who infringes on the prohibition against speaking languages or dialects other than Spanish will be reported . . . to the highest local Military Authority. . . . To repeat my warning, if, by some misfortune, offenders should surface, they should not be surprised to suffer the full force of the punishments imposed by His Most Excellent Military Governor.[39]

Simply speaking Basque was punishable by fines (one hundred to five hundred pesetas) or by imprisonment.[40] In Estella, even the use of the word *agur* "goodbye," common among Basque and

35. Irujo and Urrutia, *A Legal History of the Basque Country,* 220.
36. Ibid., 221.
37. Ibid.
38. Ibid., 222.
39. Ibid..
40. Ibid., 223.

non-Basque speakers alike was prohibited already in 1936, and so was the possession of any material in Basque, or even garments "of a separatist character," as well as portraits and statues of Sabino Arana, "or any other separatist ringleader."[41]

Thus began the relentless campaign that Basque was to die a natural death, because it was a relic of prehistory, inadequate for progress, barely a "dialect" (in the sense of a jargon, limited in use and distribution, with no written literature). The campaign aimed at robbing Basque of its role as preferred means of expression of the Basque people, a fundamental pillar of their identity. It was important to diminish its status indefatigably from the earliest years of a child's life, nowhere better than in school, where the teacher had the authority to dismantle the children's view of their native language. Schooling in such negative conditions, as well as the repression on all levels of the cultural, political, and private lives of the citizens would ensure the interruption of the chain that hands down a language from generation to generation. Parents after all want the best for their children, and if speaking to them in their native language meant they would be singled out and punished, then Basque had better be forgotten until better times. Little did people imagine that it would take forty-one years to see Basque recover its legal status.

A Linguistic Recovery?

The role of education in the Basque Country—especially in the Basque Autonomous Community (BAC)—has been fundamental in reintroducing, in part, a language whose chain from older to future generations had been severed by decades of violent repression and systematic loss of status, despite its very deep historical roots in the territory of the Basque Country.

Despite the clear advances, especially in the numbers of the "new Basque speakers," that is, those speakers who do not come from Basque-speaking homes and learn the language at school, it should stressed that Basque is still in a recovery phase.

While the number of original Basque speakers has stayed approximately the same, at about 20 percent of the population between 1986 and 2006 and hovers between five hundred and seven hundred thousand speakers (depending on sources).[42] What has

41. Ibid., 224.

42. Eusko Jaurlaritza, 1997, suggests that 22.5 percent of the population aged over fifteen is fluent at least orally in Basque.

changed significantly is the number of *euskaldun berriak*, the new Basque speakers, that is, those people who did not learn Basque from their parents, but rather from the school system.

This recovery among the younger generations of Basque people of their ancestral language, or at least the standardized variety, has increased the number of people who speak Basque adequately fluently, if not natively.

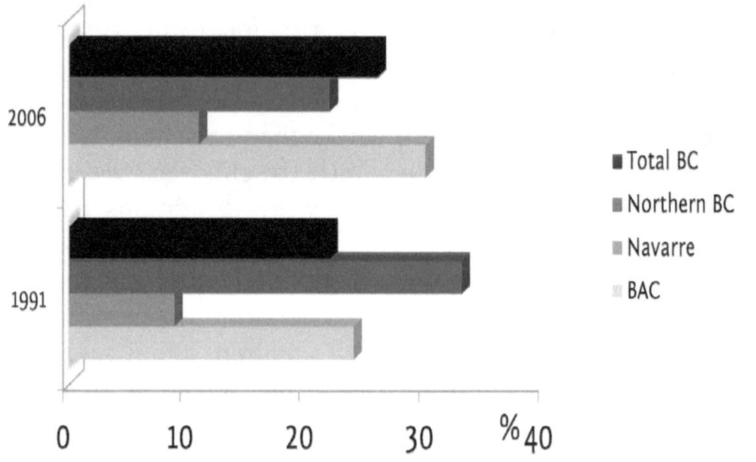

Figure 1.1. Basque language fluency, 1991 and 2006.

What can be noticed however from figure 1.1, is the fact that the increase in fluency is very significant in the BAC, only marginal in Navarre, and that there is a clear decrease in the Northern Basque Country (also known as Iparralde, in the French state).

This difference can be clearly ascribed to the legal protection afforded to the language in the three different territories. While in the BAC the legal status of Basque as co-official language with Spanish at least in the territory of the Basque Country was obtained in 1978, there is no co-officiality afforded in the other two historically Basque territories, Navarre and Iparralde. The co-official status was reinforced by the 1979 Statute of Autonomy of the Basque Country.[43] It should be noticed that in this document, soon after the establishment of territorial jurisdiction, the name of the autonomous region (Euskadi) and legal autonomy (1–4), article 5 addresses the national symbol: the shape and color of the

43. Available at www.lehendakaritza.ejgv.euskadi.net/r48-448/en/contenidos/informacion/estatuto_guernica/en_455/adjuntos/estatu_i.pdf (last accessed July 10, 2012).

national flag, and article 6 addresses language issues: Basque and Spanish are co-official, "All its inhabitants have the right to know and use both languages," (article 6.1), which is in stark contrast to the Spanish constitution of 1978, where citizens have the right to know the languages of their respective autonomous communities (Basque, Catalan, and Galician), but "the right and duty" to know Spanish.

In article 6.2 of the Basque Statute of Autonomy, the public authorities will guarantee access to the languages: "whatever measures necessary to ensure knowledge of them." Article 6.3 sanctions that no one must be discriminated against because of language. With this it is understood that the legislators took the different reality of the various areas of the BAC into account—as in some areas Basque was commonly spoken, whereas in others it had been all but lost.[44] In 1982, the Law on the "Normalization" of Basque Usage (in the sense of recovery, revitalization), established very clear parameters for the public authorities to guarantee a real, equal opportunity access to the knowledge of both languages, and specifically of the less used ancestral Basque.[45]

Specifically, three types of immersion programs where made available, as well as retraining of existing teachers in Basque, and recruiting of Basque speakers for the school system:

> Model A: Spanish is used as the principal medium and Basque is a subject within this program;
>
> Model B: Both Basque and Spanish are used as principal mediums and Basque and Spanish are also subjects within this program.
>
> Model C: Basque is used as the principal medium and Spanish is a subject within this program.

The number of people choosing to send their children to Model C schools has increased steadily throughout the years. As can be seen in table 1.1, data from 2007–2008 show that in preprimary and primary education, as well as secondary, obligatory education (roughly corresponding to middle school in the US educational system), if less significantly, the majority of students attend school in Basque. Upper secondary (corresponding roughly to high school in the US system), on the other hand is split evenly

---

44. Lasagabaster, "The Legal Status of Euskara in the French and Spanish Constitutional Systems," 126.

45. See a detailed description of problems encountered, programs and cultural activities in Aldekoa and Gardner, "Turning Basque Knowledge into Use."

between Basque and Spanish programs.

Article 3.3 of the 1978 Spanish constitution was already an enormous step forward after years of repression during the dictatorship because it foresaw the possibility of languages other than Spanish as being protected by constitutional rights, as well as the recognition of the wealth of these other languages as part

2007–2008	Preprimary	Primary	Secondary	Upper Secondary
Model A	6%	11%	22%	50%
Model B	25%	30%	26%	1%
Model C	69%	59%	51%	49%

Table 1.1. Basque School Enrollment by Educational Model (Percentage)

of Spain's cultural heritage. This is the text of article 3.3 of the Spanish constitution: "The wealth of the different language variations of Spain is a cultural heritage, which shall be the object of special respect and protection."[46] A further advancement, also recognized by the Constitutional Court, is the acceptance of Basic Law 10/1982, whereby it is understood that Basque is co-official in the whole territory of the BAC, and that citizens have the right to expect service in Basque in public offices.[47] The 1982 law also encourages the *social* use of the language, recognizing that for real revitalization, a language must gain not only number of speakers, but also domains of usage and register. This is still currently a hurdle, as pointed out by sociolinguist Begoña Echeverria: "Basques are indeed learning *batua* in schools, but they don't flirt in it."[48] This was a tongue-in-cheek echo of her earlier sociolinguistic research, where she found that despite young people's fluency in the standard taught at school (batua), "Fun, playful, 'hip' uses of Basque are more likely to be found outside school walls—in the public sphere and popular culture—and the variety used in those domains is quite often the vernacular,"[49] that is, in the type of Basque dialect spoken natively by that 22 percent of the population and specifically *not* taught in schools. This state of things is still lamented by the *IV Mapa Sociolingüístico* researchers in 2009, where we find that, as it often happens with recov-

46. Official version available at: www.senado.es/constitu_i/indices/consti_ing.pdf (the translation there is rather deficient compared to the one Lasagabaster uses).
47. Ibid., 129.
48. Question and answer session after lecture/performance, UCSB, May 24th, 2012.
49. Echeverria, "Language Attitudes in San Sebastian," 261.

ering languages, the improvement in territory gained by Basque is mostly due to the education system.[50] This means that there are more and more "new Basque speakers" who learn and speak Spanish at home, but learn Basque in school. However, this has a clear relation with choice of language, since these "new" Basque speakers are more fluent in Spanish than in Basque. Thus, lack of fluency and a social network that speaks mostly Spanish make a "normalized use of Basque very difficult."[51]

Eustat (the Basque statistics institute) data from between 1986 and 2006 shows some interesting trends: the number of original Basque speakers decreased somewhat in this twenty-year period, and the number of original Spanish speakers who commonly use Basque has remained negligible. However, the number of original Spanish speakers has also decreased over the years: overall, but especially in the younger generation, since in 1986 they were about one hundred thousand and in 2006 they are less than twenty thousand—and this is presumably to be ascribed to the school system. What is disturbing in this graph, is that of those people who learned Basque natively, at home, in 1986, only about fifteen thousand commonly chose to speak Spanish, whereas in 2006 that number had increased to about seventy thousand: and again it is the generation between twenty and twenty-four years of age that does this more prominently. As Echeverria concludes, "when it comes to reversing language shift, it is especially important that young people take up the cause as their own."[52] But clearly the legal protection afforded to Basque in the context of the autonomous region, and Basque immersion in the school system together are recruiting more and more speakers for the language. Hopefully, in time, the speakers themselves will choose to add more registers and social domains to their language use, that is, "flirt in Basque."

Navarre and the Northern Basque Country

Looking the data regarding language recovery, where one sees a recovery in number of speakers in the BAC and a clear decline between 1991 and 2006 in Iparralde, Navarre has gained some speakers, but it seems to be merely maintaining the status quo. The status of Basque in Navarre is not co-official over the whole terri-

50. IV Mapa Sociolingüistico 2006, 2009:83
51. Ibid.
52. Echeverria, "Language Attitudes in San Sebastian," 261.

tory, and it is regulated by the so-called 1982 Organic Law for the Reintegration and Improvement of the Charter Law of Navarre,[53] this law guarantees some autonomy to organize internal institutions and Basque is recognized as co-official in those areas where it is spoken, but it is the most restrictive law of any statute of autonomy. As Iñaki Martínez De Luna assessed it, it is a linguistic policy based on "containment and contention."[54] The law states:

> 1. Castilian is the official language of Navarre.
> 2. Basque will also hold official status in the Basque-speaking regions of Navarre.
> 3. A Charter Law will determine these regions, regulate the official use of Euskera and, abiding by the framework of the state's general legislation will also oversee teaching in Basque.

Not only does it not identify Basque as the language of the people of Navarre, but it also does not establish any duties or regulations vis à vis the language. Therefore, it is a much poorer provision in comparison with the status of the language in the BAC.

The Charter Law on Basque 18/1986 is more specific, but equally dissatisfactory: it divides Navarre into three regions: the Bascophone areas, the bilingual areas, and the Spanish-speaking areas. In the mainly Basque speaking areas, full rights are recognized to Basque-speaking people, however, in the other two areas, only some rights are recognized such as the right to have a (nonuniversity level) education in Basque, but only if freely requested by the student, in order to "acquire and adequate level of knowledge of the language."[55] Therefore, if students do not request to learn Basque, they have no obligation to do so, and if they do, the region only has an obligation to provide "adequate knowledge of the language." The vagueness of this statement already makes it very problematic to implement or hold up in a court of law. The regulations needed to implement this law were only passed in 1994, and in general one can say that the Navarrese political institutions, despite social and especially youth interest in Basque, have been very reluctant to support—let alone promote—the study and recovery of Basque, even contradicting provisions and legal rights laid out in the European Chart on Regional and

---

53. Lasagabaster, "The Legal Status of Euskara in the French and Spanish Constitutional Systems," 129.
54. Iñaki Martínez de Luna. Lecture. U.C. Santa Barbara, Santa Barbara, CA. February 23, 2011.
55. Ibid.

Minority Languages.[56] The results can clearly be seen in the status quo maintained with difficulty by the Basque language in Navarre over the last thirty years.

The situation is even worse in Iparralde, where Basque has no official status whatsoever. Neither do any other regional languages, such as Occitan or Breton. Curiously enough, as mentioned above, France signed and ratified the European Charter on Regional and Minority Languages, but before doing so also declared that the provisions included in the Charter did not apply to France, since providing groups of citizens special status in France was against the Constitution, which provides all French citizens with equal status. This is a classic example of the philosophical juxtaposition between cultural rights as rights pertaining to a group, and human rights intended as universal rights of the individual. We saw the consequences of this legal statement, that is, that the UNHCR decided that, because of this, no claims it received about the Breton language would fall under the purview of its jurisdiction.

De facto, in Iparralde, the initiatives to promote Basque are left in private hands, despite the 1951 Loi "Deixonne," which allowed for regional languages to be taught in schools (substituted by other decrees in 1975, Loi Haby and Bas-Lauriol). In 1993, however, the French Constitution was amended stating simply that "The language of the Republic is French," and in 1994, the use of French was made obligatory in public domains to stave off English influence. This was not supposed to affect regional languages, purportedly.[57]

By one vote, a controversial amendment to the French Constitution was passed on July 21, 2008, which stated, "regional languages belong to the heritage of the nation."[58] Such a simple, bare-bones statement had been attacked by the French Academy as threatening "the national identity and the unity of the Republic,"[59] which had requested that it be withdrawn. Despite the recognition of certain rights to regional languages (adapting to European guidelines), and the creation of Office Public de la Langue

56. Lasagabaster," The Legal Status of Euskara in the French and Spanish Constitutional Systems,"131–32.
57. See www.languefrancaise.net/HLF/XX (last accessed on July 20, 2012).
58. Lasagabaster, "The Legal Status of Euskara in the French and Spanish Constitutional Systems," 124.
59. Ibid.

Basque (OPBL) in 2004,[60] whose main tasks are those of making speakers completely fluent, especially the younger generations, and to inform on language policy, create a Basque resource website, and inform the public on existing services in Basque.

One of the recent documents posted on the OPLB website is in fact a sociolinguistic study of proficiency in Basque,[61] where it is observed that while in the BAC and Navarre the status quo has either maintained or improved over the past twenty years (1991–2011), bilingual speakers have decreased and monolingual French speakers have increased in Iparralde. The document also observes that if both parents are bilingual, they will teach Basque to their children in 97 percent of cases in BAC and in 95 percent of cases in Navarre, but only in 87 percent of cases in Iparralde. If the couples are mixed, the situation worsens, but more clearly so in Iparralde: 71 percent BAC, 67 percent in Navarre, and 56 percent in Iparralde.[62] Another disheartening result is that the favorable attitudes toward Basque and the desire to promote the language have increased among the population both in the BAC and Navarre, but not in Iparralde—however, language attitudes have improved among the young people. Clearly education in BAC and in part also in Navarre, and the official status of Basque in the BAC have restored some of the lost prestige to the language, and this is why we notice an improvement in language attitudes and in number of bilinguals. In Iparralde, where Basque has no official status and the implementation of initiatives relies almost fully on volunteering, numbers reveal that Basque is losing ground. Thus, for instance, the *ikastolas* that provide immersion schooling in Basque are private and not available everywhere, which manifests itself in the percentages of how many children are enrolled in Basque immersion schools: where in the BAC we have 63 percent of children in immersion schools, and 27 percent in Navarre, in Iparralde only 9 percent of children are in immersion programs,and language attrition continues.

Italy: Celebrating a Sesquicentennial

The fact that a political philosopher such as Antonio Gramsci, in his *Prison Notebooks*, touches upon the never-ending story of the Italian *questione della lingua* ("the language question" or rather

60. See www.mintzaira.fr/ (last accessed July 20, 2012).
61. OPLB article 2012.
62. Ibid., 6.

the "language conundrum"), should point to the wide-reaching and not exclusively linguistic import of such a topic in Italy both before, and after the unification of 1861/1870.

It is undeniable that in Antiquity and even in the Middle Ages there was a sense of cultural unity that retraced its steps to a first unified Italian peninsula under Roman rule. Rome had imposed her language on other related Italic languages (Oscan, Sabine, Umbrian etc.), which died out as a consequence of Roman territorial expansion. Latin, by the late Middle Ages was a dead language, although the inhabitants of the old Roman provinces who still spoke evolved versions of the language may have thought they were still speaking Latin, that is, the common people's Latin (Vulgar Latin), with a vernacular pronunciation. Virgil speaks of "Italy" in the Aeneid, and the concept is certainly revamped also

Figure 1.2. Broad linguistic areas of modern Italy.

in Dante and Petrarch with a certain nostalgia, although at the time of their writing no such thing as "Italy" existed politically. As Dante points out in his *De vulgari eloquentia*, cultivated and (perhaps at times, forcibly) well-traveled inhabitants of the Italian peninsula in the thirteenth century were well aware of the diversity of languages and varieties spoken on its territory.

Dante divides them up into thirteen varieties and maintains that a national language should accept contributions from all the different varieties (see a contemporary version of these varieties in figure 1.2). In reality, Dante himself used his local Florentine dialect and enriched it with terms and forms from many different varieties—not unlike what he proposed in his *De vulgari eloquentia*.

The idea of a lively, vibrant language enriched by many different varieties, however, clashed with proposals by later purists such as Pietro Bembo (1470-1547), a literary theorist, scholar, poet, and cardinal, who despite his Venetian origins maintained that a national language should be based on fourteenth-century written Tuscan models (excluding Dante, whose vocabulary was at times too low-class and used many words from other dialects).

A quote often attributed to Massimo D'Azeglio, "Now that we have made Italy, we have to make Italians," could be interpreted along the lines of postunification views still maintained in the nineteenth and early twentieth centuries. Language could be a means "to make Italians," no longer an abstract question for intellectual debate, but rather a very pragmatic means to a political end.[63]

Significantly, some of the "fathers of the fatherland," as Italy was referred to during the *Risorgimento*, could hardly speak Italian themselves: Garibaldi, Victor Emmanuel II, Italy's first king, who spoke French at the court and Piedmontese at home, or Camillo Benso, count of Cavour, who was more at ease in French than in "Italian," whatever that concept may have been at the time. Garibaldi, born in Nice, spoke a number of languages, including Franco-Provençal, French (of which he was extremely fond), Ligurian, and English, but in a respected biography we find the following comment about one of Garibaldi's teachers:

> However, he was never able to teach him Italian grammar and

63. It is peculiar that the actual quote could never be found in this formulation in D'Azeglio's writings. He writes something similar in his Ricordi, [1867] 1949: 480, where he seems to refer to the need to make Italian a people of strong and upright moral character. See Malia Hom, "On the Origins of Making Italy."

> syntax: Garibaldi was impervious to them his whole life, and it unfortunately showed on all possible occasions.[64]

Garibaldi had a clear idea that Piedmont was the strong piece of the Italian puzzle and that at least politically, the rest of Italy should defer to it. But whereas his political ideas are to crush the smaller, weaker elements in order to create a unified Italy,[65] he left no linguistic plans for the future of Italy.

Giuseppe Mazzini, born in Genoa, would have also spoken Ligurian and French, but his social and political views stressed the importance of education (as imbued of moral teachings, not as mere "instruction," i.e., aimed at imparting only intellectual notions), as free and accessible to all citizens, in order to enable them to achieve full access and participation to civic and political life. Since he was in favor of free public education for the masses, and conceived of nations as being identified by one language, he would have presumably supported a unified Italian language for the school system.[66] However, it should be remembered that Mazzini saw Italian unification not as an end in itself, and much less as smaller elements having to disintegrate into a union with the strongest ones, but rather as the first step toward the United States of Europe:

> [Nationality] can only be founded by a common effort and a common movement; sympathy and alliance will be its result. In principle, . . . nationality ought only to be . . . the recognized symbol of association; the assertion of the individuality of a human group called by its geographical position, its traditions, and its language, to fulfill a special function in the European work of civilization.[67]

We can perhaps surmise that he would have been lenient toward linguistic minorities, although perhaps not necessarily encour-

---

64. Montanelli and Nozza, *Garibaldi*, 22.

65. This comment in his diary leaves no doubt: "We must create Italy first of all. Italy is nowadays made up of the following elements: Piedmont, republicans, followers of Murat, of the Borbons, of the Pope, Tuscans and other small elements...that detract from national unity. All of these elements must blend with the strongest one or be destroyed; there is no middle ground! The strongest of the Italian elements is Piedmont, I'd advise to blend with it. The power that must lead Italy in freeing itself from the difficult emancipation from the foreign yoke must be strictly dictatorial." www.iltechnologies.net/garibaldi/html/ IT/lingua%20esocieta.htm.

66. See an excerpt from his *The Duties of Man* at www.bassilo.it/area_alunni/mazzini/ lettere.htm.

67. Mazzini, "Europe," 266.

aged bilingualism, although all of these nineteenth-century patriots were at least bilingual (including a local language or dialect), if not multilingual, betraying, of course their usually affluent origins that would have given them access to privileged education.

Among nineteenth-century intellectuals, Manzoni, for one, favored the middle-class Florentine dialect as the national language. Florence, with her 1300s famous poets and writers, and a tradition as an independent, autonomous city, only recently joined to the kingdom of Piedmont and Sardinia (1859), was politically and symbolically an important hub for national feelings. Because of its perceived neutrality and independence from both the Popes and Piedmont, Florence was made the capital of Italy from 1865 to 1871: in exchange Napoleon III would slowly pull out his troop from Rome. Culturally and historically, Florence was the cradle of the Renaissance, a symbol of intellectual and economic power representing a view of "Italy," well known and appreciated outside the peninsula's boundaries. The year 1865 was also marked by the celebrations of the six hundredth anniversary of Dante Alighieri's birth. Statues of Dante were often unveiled in the Austrian-occupied Venetian territories around this time as symbols of Italian cultural unity, thus Manzoni's posture is perhaps not surprising. But while Manzoni suggested the adoption of contemporary Florentine as a national language in a report written for the Minister of Public Education,[68] he was contrasted by a group of Florentine intellectuals supporting yet another version of Bembo's ideas, that is, that the national language should be based on the written language of Florence in the fourteenth century.

The founder of modern Italian philological studies, Graziadio Isaia Ascoli (1829–1907) had a more balanced and modern viewpoint and privileged the importance of spreading literacy,[69] first among the newly minted Italians, and that then dialect leveling would slowly and steadily ensue. A state-sanctioned imposition

68. A summary of the events leading up to Manzoni's report and its consequences are to be found here: www.internetculturale.it/opencms/directories/ ViaggiNelTesto/manzoni/a30.html.

69. A table by ISTAT shows that in the years around the unification of Italy, at least 60 percent of men and 80 percent of women were illiterate (data based on couples that were not able to sign their marriage certificate, from 1867 onward): available at seriestoriche.istat.it/index.php?id=7&user_ 100ind_pi1%5Bid_pagina%5D=9&cHash=b327bf3eae2185defcfbc1066e1756be, literacy summary 1861-2001, available at: www.istat.it/it/files/2011/05/01_analfabetismo.swf.

would not be needed, according to Ascoli, hence his polemics with Manzoni.

Enter Gramsci's viewpoint on the *questione della lingua*:

> Every time the "language question" surfaces somehow, it means in fact that other problems are being raised: building and widening the ruling classes, the need to establish closer relations between the ruling class and the national working classes, i.e. the problem posed by the reorganization of cultural hegemony.[70]

Language is politics, because "it affects the way people think about power"[71] and the concept of hegemony in Gramsci's linguistic thought does rest on the dichotomy between language and dialect.[72] If Manzoni had extolled the spreading of French from the Île de France to the rest of the country, in a way that made other "dialects" obsolete and covering fewer and fewer functions, he could not see this happening in Italy where,

> [The] old and multifarious idioms are in full bloom, and regularly serve all types of people because there is no efficient competition against them by a language that can fight them with the only effective means, which consists in taking over the same functions that they have.[73]

Although in all of these political thinkers there seems to be no consensus as to what the difference between a language, an idiom, or a dialect actually are, there is a rather widespread—and circular—concept that the national language to be considered as such must be spread throughout the nation and, according to Manzoni, supersede all local varieties—which are different only in vocabulary, Manzoni seems to erroneously maintain. Both Ascoli, and even Manzoni to a certain extent see the importance of the local lively expressions in dialect: Manzoni after all wanted to impose one live, local dialect over the others, the middle and higher class Florentine, as the national language. The concept was problematic because at the time of the unification, approximately 3 percent of the Italian population actually spoke Tuscan, and even finding teachers for all the Italian regions would have been problematic. However, the idea (and the vocabulary) of Tuscan/Florentine as national language became more and more popular with

70. My translation of *Quaderni del carcere,* 29, 3, *Questione della lingua:* www.treccani.it/enciclopedia/questione-della-lingua_(Enciclopedia _dell'Italiano)/.

71. Germino, *Antonio Gramsci,* 27.

72. Boothman, "Hegemony," 43–5.

73. Manzoni, "Dell'unità della lingua e dei mezzi per diffonderla."

writers such as De Amicis,[74] who encouraged all Italians to learn the language of the fatherland, directly connecting nationalism and language, and disparaging the use of dialects along the way.

Through De Amicis, despite Benedetto Croce's severe criticism,[75] even educators started to adopt the concept of Tuscan as a national language.

A severe blow to linguistic diversity came with Fascism, unsurprisingly. In Giovanni Gentile's school reform dated 1923, the use of local dialects was still conceived of as a means for pupils throughout the country to learn "proper Italian," and while it relegated dialects as a temporary means to an end—the acquisition of Italian, at least it recognized their existence. Later, however, Mussolini declared a war on dialects in the name of linguistic purism and of an autarchic phobia against anything that was "foreign," whether it be from outside the country or from within. Allegiance to the fatherland meant also allegiance to Italian: one country one language, which gave the fascist regime carte blanche against linguistic minorities (in the recently acquired territories of Trieste, the Upper Etsch valley [South Tyrol], but also in the French speaking areas of the Aosta Valley), for instance through the practice of encouraging movement of state workers from one region to another, or forcibly moving the population of one region to another, or abroad, as in the case of French-speaking Valdotains.[76] The main goals of linguistic policy during the fascist regime were: annihilating the use of foreign languages on the Italian territory (against linguistic minorities), destroying dialects especially through the school system, and expunging all foreign words from the Italian vocabulary.[77] This was set into practice through an intimidating campaign involving the press, the radio, and the school system.[78] The aim was defending the unity of the fatherland symbolized by the use of one language against local usage of minority languages and dialects, the first of which were seen as a threat to Italian integrity from "outside," whereas dia-

74. See for instance his L'idioma gentile (1905), full text available here: www.intratext.com/IXT/ITA2903/_IDX005.HTM#IDIO.1.1 (last accessed July 7, 2012).
75. See Marazzini, *Questione della Lingua*.
76. See Riccarand, *Storia della Valle d'Aosta contemporanea* for forcible movements of Valdotain population to France and Switzerland and of Italian speaking workers to the Val D'Aôte in order to turn the region into an Italian speaking community.
77. Cardia, "Il neopurismo e la politica linguistica del fascism," 44.
78. Ibid.

lects were a threat to Italian unity from the inside, but a threat nonetheless.

The Current Status of the *Questione delle Lingue* (sic)

These campaigns once established in the school system took on a life of their own and did not cease even after the demise of fascism. The school system, coupled with the movement of civil servants from region to region (from teachers to university professors, from museum attendants to office clerks) and compulsory military service,[79] which intentionally brought young men from Sardinia to Milan, and vice versa with the sole purpose of making it impossible for them to use their local dialect and force them to use (some version of) standard Italian. Mass media such as radio and TV gave a final blow to the use of local varieties, relegated to a clearly subordinate position in comparison with the increasing prestige of a standard language that was becoming more and more widespread. The combined pressure on these different fronts produced the steady decline of dialect use that is painfully evident over the last 150 years and continues unabated.[80]

Also clearly indicated in figure 1.3, the main problem is that young people no longer speak dialect, that is, the dialect is not hip, as the standard has encroached on all registers that were

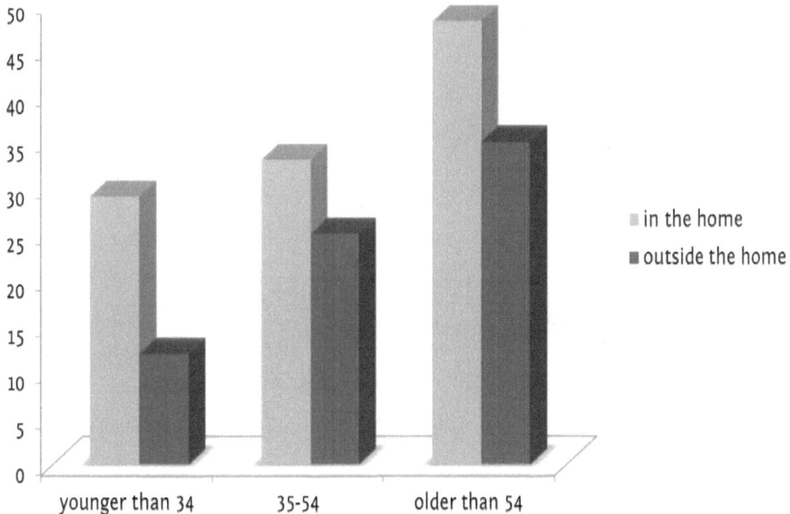

Figure 1.3. Use of dialects according to age group. Source: Grassi et al., 2007.

79.Compulsory military service in Italy was only abolished in 2005.

80. See De Mauro 1970, Grassi et al., *Fondamenti di dialettologia italiana,* and ISTAT 2000.

earlier covered by the local varieties, which are in turn often stigmatized as boorish and uncouth.

While it is true that in some regions such as the northeast, as well as in the south and the islands dialectal usage is still relatively strong, the same decreasing trend can be noticed there (figure 1.4):

Italy signed the *Charter for Regional and Minority Languages*, but did not ratify it, and Italian law recognizes the following minority languages: Albanian, Catalan, Croatian, French, Franco-Provençal, Friulian, German, Greek, Ladin, Occitan, Sardinian, and Slovene.

Regions may have different provisions, for instance:

> Aosta: French co-official in whole region (SSVA, TVle, art. 38); German unofficial but "recognized" in Lystal (art. 40 bis)
>
> Campania: Neapolitan is "promoted" but not recognized (Reg. Gen. nn159/l 198/1, art 1, c 4)
>
> Friuli-Venezia Giulia: Friulian and Slovene are "promoted" but

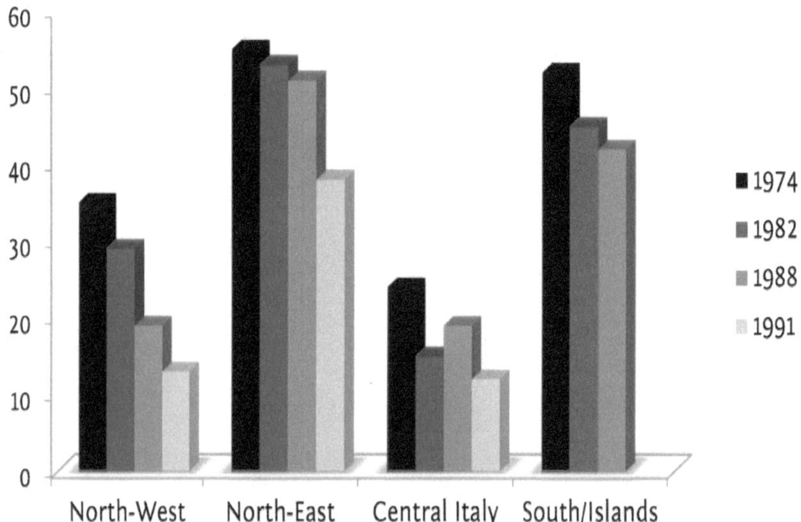

Figure 1.4. Use of dialects according to age group. Source: Grassi et al., 2007.

> not recognized (L r 18 Dec 2007, n. 29, art 1, c. 1)
>
> Piedmont: Piedmontese is unofficial but recognized as the regional language (C Reg Pied, OdG 1118, 30/11/1999). The region promotes Occitan, Franco-Provençal, and Walser (10/4/1990).

Sardinia: Sardinian is co-official in the whole region (LR 15/10/1997, n. 26, art 3, co. 1 bis), Catalan co-official in L'Alguer (art 2, co. 4), Tabarchino, Sassarese, Gallurese are also co-official in their respective territories (ibid.)

TAA-Südtirol: German is co-official in the whole region (SSTAA Titolo XI, art 99), Ladin, Cimbrian, and Mocheno are unofficial but recognized in their respective territories (art. 102).

Veneto: Venetian language is unofficial but recognized (13/4/2007, n.8, art. 2, co. 2). (Tani 2005)

UNESCO, however, recognizes the existence of thirty-one endangered languages in Italy, where Veneto is only vulnerable, definitely endangered are Algherese, Alpine Provençal, Arberesch, Campidanese, Cimbrian, Corsican on Maddalena, Emilian-Romagnol, Faetar, Fracoprovençal, Friulian, Gallo-Sicilian, Gallurese, Ladin, Ligurian, Logudorese, Lombard, Mócheno, Piedmontese, Resian (spoken around Udine), Romani, Sassarese, Yiddish. Töitschu (Lystal), Molise Croatian, Griko, and Gardiol (the alpine Provençal spoken in Calabria) are severely endangered.

At the regional level, there are many differences in the legal provisions and their implementation, but in general, traditionally recognized languages are protected, and their use should be guaranteed in education, public administration, and the mass media. The protection of dialects, however, is seen only as part of preserving cultural heritage. In actual fact, however, regional implementation of the law is often lacking, even where the languages are well-established and recognized—for instance in Friuli and Sardinia (L. Campanotto, p.c.). Theoretically, though, all linguistic minorities have the right to be taught content courses in their language. Nevertheless, the Constitutional Court sentence 159/09 CC complicated matters: because of an official complaint (18/08) against the implementation of the Article 6 of the constitution protecting linguistic minority and giving them rights to education in their language, families have to *request* schooling in the minority language, it is not simply *offered* to them. Moreover, parents of the whole school-class need to agree on using Friulian to teach content courses. This has made it much more difficult for children to obtain schooling in Friulian. It is in fact surprising, and perhaps it denotes a positive trend against all odds that teaching in Friulian has increased even when it is merely based on volunteering.[81]

81.Il Gazzettino di Udine, May 23, 2009.

In practice, despite some legal recognition and protection, funds or the lack thereof decides the level of support of the minority language at hand: as an example, one can consider the law on German-speaking minorities passed by the Friuli region.[82] The German-speaking minority was the only unrecognized minority in the region. The law essentially protects the language as part of the region's cultural and linguistic heritage through schooling and the connection with universities and private companies (mostly promoting tourism). Two hundred thousand euros had originally been earmarked for this purpose, but a year later, the law had not been implemented yet and the money in the budget for 2011 had dropped to one hundred thousand euros.[83]

Lombardy, on the other hand, has adopted the 2003 UNESCO Convention[84] for safeguarding intangible cultural heritage and made it into a regional law, which reads as follows:

> 1. The Lombardy region recognizes and values intangible cultural heritage in its different forms and expressions . . .
>
> 2. Practices, representation, expressions, knowledge, abilities that are part of the cultural heritage, of local communities', social groups or individuals, their history and identity.

Since 2010, the region also offers funds for projects that aim at protecting the intangible cultural heritage of the region.[85] It will be interesting to ascertain whether projects involving the promotion of dialect use are indeed proposed and funded by the region.

What speakers think of their minority language or dialectal variety is fundamental to stave off attrition, but as Gramsci—a speaker of Sardinian himself—observed in his *Prison Notebooks* (see above), establishing a hegemonic dichotomy between (standard or national) language and regional language or dialect already dooms these latter to lack of prestige and attrition. The situation worsens if the minority language has no legal status, protection, and/or funds to promote its active learning. Without these elements, the use of such varieties will be limited and will remain the domain of underprivileged groups because supposedly they cannot be used to deal with academic or scientific topics, lacking the high register for formal communication. Of course,

---

82. Friulian Law20/2009.
83. *Alto Friuli*, article dated 22/11, 2010.
84. UNESCO, Convention for the Safeguarding of the Intangible Cultural Heritage, Paris, October 17, 2003.
85. See www.lombardiacultura.it/uploads/lr-27_2008.pdf.

the relative application of such prejudices depends on cultural tradition: those varieties that have a long literary tradition, preferably a written one, such as De Filippo's Neapolitan and Carlo Goldoni's Venetian will fare considerably better than even the richly expressive Lombard mélange found in Nobel laureate Dario Fo's *Grandmêlo*.

Therefore, factors that cause one variety to dominate the other(s) are the legal protection afforded by official status; the visual reinforcement of a written standard versus purely oral varieties, which lose prestige due to the modern importance of written communication; and the dominant language's extended use of its registers covering all areas that the nonstandard varieties can cover and more. Nonstandard varieties, on the other hand, suffer from their speakers' negative emotional involvement toward them caused by stigmatization through the school system, negative media portrayal, or simply through lack of media presence. The standard offers social and economic improvement, as well as the emotional attachment encouraged by the literary and cultural value of its written artistic production.

Official recognition is key, since without it there can be no funds released to improve the fate of "smaller languages" competing with hegemonic languages: the continued prestige of Venetian is a case in point, since Venetian was the official language of the Serenissima Republic of Venice until the end of the eighteenth century, and has a considerable literary tradition. Just as in Venice until the end of the Serenissima, that official recognition usually comes about with a certain degree of independence of the region where the minority languages or varieties are spoken.

A National Language Spoken by Three Hundred Thousand People: Iceland and Globalization

Iceland is a similar case to Michael Krauss's Faroe Islands:[86] an island nation with a population that numbered historically twenty to fifty thousand people and now has risen to three hundred thousand, the majority of which is composed of ethnic Icelanders, speaking a Germanic language with a very prestigious literary tradition that goes back to the Middle Ages. Language is for Icelanders a pillar of identity. It is surprising perhaps to observe that no official language is ever mentioned in the three separate con-

86. Krauss, "Keynote—Mass Language Extinction and Documentation."

stitutions of 1874, 1920, or 1944; even the last one that sanctioned Iceland's independence from the Danish colonization established in the fourteenth century. Arguably, in a country that is essentially monoethnic and monolingual, the mention of the official language is perhaps superfluous.

Most of the Icelandic population is however now multilingual, and certainly bilingual with English. Many of Iceland's companies have multinational branches and many have offices or factories abroad and employ many foreigners: for many of these companies, English has become a more practical option than issuing documents in Icelandic and then translating them. In fact, a perusal of their statutes and some informal inquiries uncover the following: DeCode Genetics' official language is English, Icelandair writes its official memos in English, the pharmaceutical giant Actavis uses Icelandic only locally, but main documents are in English. Marel's high-tech fishing equipment uses mainly English, and Icelandic only locally. Even the banks, whose main documents are in Icelandic, require English for their job descriptions. Globalization has brought Icelandic products and companies abroad, and foreign workers to Iceland, now at local bakeries people must order in English because the staff does not speak Icelandic.

If Krauss's million number of speakers as a minimum to guarantee the survival of a language is anything to go by, even Icelandic runs the risk of becoming endangered.

Conclusions

Clearly a certain degree of legal representation (officiality or co-officiality) is the only way to avoid further attrition or at least to limit the damages for minority languages. This entails: bilingual administration, and a school system with immersion in the minority language—in other words, to make use of the same legal weapons that have contributed to the emergence of monolingual states and to the attrition of regional and minority languages, which can now reverse their fate, or at least delay the inevitable extinction of a given linguistic variety. Only some degree of political autonomy, as well as cultural and financial commitment by local administrators can revitalize or/and maintain the status of regional languages. The loss of regional languages and varieties constitutes a severe blow to cultural diversity and linguists, educators, local and national administrators should recognize the need for urgent action. The Italian situation, and that of Iparralde, should therefore be considered and assessed in the light of success stories such as the revitalization of Basque in the Basque Autonomous Community.

International law can only help in a marginal way: although there are a series of charters and international covenants that specifically mention the protection of linguistic rights, these are from a juristic point of view, part of cultural rights, rather than fundamental human rights. They are, therefore, "third-generation rights" (after political and social rights) and are less developed than other human rights, and even where there are legal provisions for the protection of cultural and linguistic rights, lack of funds for their implementation often nullifies the goal of the legislation. Thus, reversing the trend of attrition for minority languages is only possible if they acquire some legal status through regional political autonomy (self-determination), and if both grassroots and top-down movements within multinational states encourage the acceptance of cultural diversity and multilingualism as a positive outcome for the whole population, not just for a minority within it.

Bibliography

V° Enquête Sociolinguistique: Communauté Autonome d'Euskadi, Navarre et Pays Basque Nord. 2012. *Vice-ministère de la politique linguistique, Office Public de la Langue Basque.* Donostia-San Sebastián. Available at: www.mintzaira.fr/fileadmin/documents/Aktualitateak/fr_Euskal_Herria_inkesta_soziolg_2011_20120716.pdf.

Aldekoa, J. and N. Gardner. "Turning Basque Knowledge into Use: Normalisation Plans for Schools." *International Journal of Bilingual Education and Bilingualism* (2002): 339–354.

Boothman, D. "Hegemony: Political and Linguistic Sources for Gramsci's Concept of Hegemony," in *Hegemony: Studies in Consensus and Coercion,* edited by Howson, R. and K. Smith. New York: Taylor and Francis, 2008.

Cardia, N. 2008. "Il neopurismo e la politica linguistica del fascismo." *Écho des Études Romanes* 4.1 (2008): 43–54.

Chapman, Audrey R. and S. Russell, eds. *Core Obligations: Building a Framework for Economic, Social and Cultural Rights.* Antwerp: Intersentia, 2002.

Couret Branco, M. *Economics Versus Human Rights*. Routledge: Oxford/New York, 2009.

De Giovanni, Neria. *La lingua italiana e la coscienza dell'unita' d'Italia: Saggi e Studi di Pubblicistica*. Roma: Istituto di Pubblicismo. Available at: www.istitutodipubblicismo.it/Lingua_italiana_e_unita_di_Italia_di_Neria_De_Giovanni.htm. 2010.

De Varennes, Fernand. "Les droits linguistiques en droit international: Une protection méconnue." 11 *R.C.L.F.*, 2009: 187.

Echeverria, B. "Language Attitudes in San Sebastián: The Basque Vernacular as Challenge to Spanish Language Hegemony." *Journal of Multilingual and Multicultural Development*, 26.3 (2005): 249–264

Encrevé, P. "A propos des droits linguistiques de l'homme et du citoyen." Conférence donnée le 16 décembre 2005 à 17 heures dans l'amphithéâtre de l'EHESS, au 105 bd Raspail à Paris. Available at www.dglflf.culture.gouv.fr/lgfrance/LSFconfEncreve.pdf. 2005.

Francioni, Francesco. "Cultural, Heritage, and Human Rights: An Introduction," in *Cultural Human Rights,* edited by Francioni, F. and M. Scheinin. Berlin: Brill. 2008.

Germino, D. *Antonio Gramsci: Architect of a New Politics*. Baton Rouge: Louisiana State U.P., 1990.

Gobierno Vasco, Departamento de Cultura. 2009. IV Mapa Sociolingüístico, 2006. Servicio Central de Publicaciones del Gobierno Vasco.

Gori, E. "Indirizzi di politica linguistica e di politica scolastica ed educativa durante il fascismo (1923–1939)." Available at: www.historied.net/portal/index.php?option=com_content&view=article&id=23. 2009.

Grassi, C., Sobrero, A.A., and T. Telmon. *Fondamenti di dialettologia italiana*. Bari: Laterza, 2007.

Howson, R. and K. Smith, eds. *Hegemony: Studies in Consensus and Coercion*. New York: Taylor and Francis, 2008.

Irujo, X. and I. Urrutia. *A Legal History of the Basque Language*. Donostia-San Sebastián: Eusko Ikaskuntza, 2009.

Krauss, Michael E. "Keynote—Mass Language Extinction and Documentation: The Race Against Time," in *The Vanishing Languages of the Pacific Rim*, edited by Miyaoka, Osahito, Osamu Sakiyama and, Michael E. Krauss. Oxford: Oxford University Press, 2007. pp. 3–24.

Lasagabaster, Iñaki. "The Legal Status of Euskara in the French and Spanish Constitutional Systems," in *The Legal Status of Basque Today: One Language, Three Administrations, Seven Different Geographies and a Diaspora,* edited by Gloria Totoricagüena and I. Urrutia. Bilbao: Eusko Ikaskuntza, 2008.

Mazzini, Giuseppe. "Europe: Its Condition and Prospects," in *Essays: Selected from the Writings, Literary, Political and Religious of Joseph Mazzini,* edited by W. Clark. London: Walter Scott. 1880:. 266, 277–78, 291–92.

Manzoni, Alessandro. "Dell'unità della lingua e dei mezzi per diffonderla." Available at www.classicitaliani.it/manzoni/unita_lingua.htm. 1868.

Marazzini, C. "Questione della Lingua." Available at /www.treccani.it/enciclopedia/questione-della-lingua_(Enciclopedia_dell'Italiano). 2011

Montanelli, I. and M. Nozza. *Garibaldi*. Turin: BUR., 2002.

Pariotti, E. In Bröstl, A. ed. *Human Rights, Minority Rights, Women's Rights: Proceedings of the 19th World*. By International Association for Philosophy of Law and Social Philosophy: World Congress, 1999.

Posner, R. *The Romance Languages*. Cambridge: CUP., 1996.

Riccarand, E. *Storia della Valle d'Aosta contemporanea (1919–1945)*. Aoste: Stylos Aoste, 2002.

Romano, N. "Garibaldi: Lingua, storia e societa." Lecture delivered at UMSA, Buenos Aires, Argentina, May 30, 2007. Available at www.iltechnologies.net/garibaldi/html/IT/lingua%20es-ocieta.htm.

Shelton, Dinah. "The UN Human Rights Committee's Decisions *Human Rights Dialogue*: 'Cultural Rights.'" *Human Rights Dialogue*, 2.12 (2005): Cultural Rights, 2005.

Tani, M. "La legislazione regionale in Italia in Materia di tutela Linguistica dal 1975 ad oggi." Unpublished MA Thesis, 2005.

Totoricagüena, Gloria and I. Urrutia, eds. *The Legal Status of Basque Today: One Language, Three Administrations, Seven Different Geographies and a Diaspora*. Bilbao: Eusko Ikaskuntza, 2008.

UNESCO. *Cultural and Linguistic Diversity in the Information Society*. UNESCO: Paris, 2003.

United Nations—Office of the High Commissioner for Human Rights. *Economic, Social And Cultural Rights: Handbook for National Human Rights Institutions*. UN: New York and Geneva, 2005.

2
Freedom of Language and Language Rights
Promoting Languages as an Overriding Reason in the Public Interest

Iñigo Urruti

Economic (Language) Freedom vis-à-vis Non-State Languages

In an increasingly globalized and interrelated world, regional or minority languages are facing intense challenges. The opening up of markets, freedom of movement and establishment, and the side effects of economic globalization, such as deregulation and privatization have obvious repercussions on all languages. Economic freedoms are not linguistically neutral. They favor some languages and put others under pressure, regardless of their status, producing mutual imbalances. Even though this is a global phenomenon, the mechanisms for coping with their effects are not the same for national languages and for regional or minority languages.

The purpose of creating an internal market as an "area without internal frontiers in which the free movement of goods, persons, services and capital is ensured"[1] requires the removal of any kind of barriers that may obstruct this. From that point of view, any linguistic requirements that might be established at the state or sub-state level could be considered suspicious insofar as they might affect the market freedoms.[2] This effect could have con-

1. Article 26(2) of the Treaty on the Functioning of the European Union (ex art 14 TEC).

2. See Milian, *Globalización y requisitos lingüísticos: Una perspectiva juridical,* 41. See also De Witte "Common Market Freedoms Versus Linguistic Requirements

sequences over the Member States' policies to support and promote languages, to the extent that they may be seen as having restrictive effects not in accordance with European Union law, and particularly not with the fundamental freedoms that it declares: free movement of goods, free movement of workers, right to the establishment, and freedom to provide services.

These same effects can be seen prima facie when language policies in Member States are not set down by means of compulsory language requirements, but rather in conceding aids or advantages for the purpose of promoting the use of the official national languages. To the extent that such aids may affect commercial exchanges between Member States and provide advantages to certain companies, services, or productions, one needs to analyze whether or not this is compatible with EU competition policy, and particularly with regard to the prohibition of state aids established under Article 107(1) of the Treaty on the Functioning of the European Union (ex Article 87 TEC).

On the other hand, instead of the traditional approach of analyzing the influence of the economy on languages (and linguistic diversity), we might take the opposing view: Languages and linguistic diversity also influence the market and the economy. Linguistic knowledge and language learning can be important for economic success.[3] From an economic angle, regional or minority languages should be valued to the extent that they can contribute to economic and social development, injecting life into the language and language communities. From a purely economic point of view, multilingualism is also an opportunity to be sized; this is, definitely, a positive factor. In the final analysis, economic factors can be used to protect and promote regional or minority languages and their social development.

For languages in the process of recovery and normalization, public intervention in the private sector is considered a necessity and a challenge: a first order challenge for those languages that are not state languages, and whose real position in the economy is one of subordination, in addition to being pressured by their relative position vis-à-vis the state language. This is the case of

in the EU States," 119 referring that the EC Treaty guarantees an implied and functionally limited free movement of languages.

3. Until now this perspective has been very little analyzed; see Cristal, *Language Death*, 31. See also Grin, Sfreddo, and Vaillancourt, *The Economics of the Multilingual Workplace*, 250.

Catalan and Euskara (the Basque language), official languages of their respective territories (together with Spanish) that have not been provided the same possibilities as the state languages in order to deal with the pressure exerted on them by economic freedoms. The problem arises when the EU's policy of removing barriers limits the powers of the domestic public authorities to intervene in the market.

Finding a Balance?

European Union law deals with areas that have been transferred, but the European policies are commonly set in operational terms, defining the objective to be attained. This being so, the achievement of an objective in any one given area may equally affect other areas that are managed by means of Member States' public policies. Language matters are a clear example of this expansion effect of the European Union law. Language policy cannot be seen just as an area to be dealt with exclusively under the autonomy of the Member States, but rather as yet another area subject to the discipline of European Union legal order in matters of competition policy and the free market.

This friction area came to the attention of the European Court of Justice in the *Groener* case. The European Court of Justice held that "The EEC Treaty does not prohibit the adoption of a policy for the protection and promotion of a language of a Member State . . . [However], the implementation of such a policy must not encroach upon a fundamental freedom such as that of the free movement of workers."[4] To the extent that language implies the expression of national and cultural identity of Member States, the Court of Justice highlights the full competence of them in order to regulate the national languages. The position of cultural values with regard to European integration was confirmed.[5] This is

4. Case C-379/87, Groener v. Minister for Education and the Dublin Vocational Education Committee [1989] ECR 3967, paragraph 19.

5. The European Court considered that "[t]he policy followed by Irish governments for many years has been designed not only to maintain but also to promote the use of Irish as a means of expressing national identity and culture. It is for that reason that Irish courses are compulsory for children receiving primary education and optional for those receiving secondary education. The obligation imposed on lecturers in public vocational education schools to have a certain knowledge of the Irish language is one of the measures adopted by the Irish Government in furtherance of that policy." (Case C-379/87, *Groener* para 17).

important, especially given that at the time of the ruling, the European Community had not yet taken on competences of cultural matters. Some years later, the Maastricht Treaty of 1992 recognized cultural competences to the European Union.[6]

Nevertheless, at this point, one must also acknowledge thoughts to the contrary, given that the ruling confirmed that the European Court has full jurisdiction to evaluate the extent to which Member States' language policies are or are not compatible with European Community law. Linguistic diversity was considered in the pre-Maastricht period as a value the European Community should protect, although this does not imply that Member States have absolute freedom to define the scope of the promotion of linguistic diversity. It has effectively become an area for conditioned national autonomy.[7]

This area of friction, which can be identified as the level to which cultural and linguistic promotion can justify restrictions on European Community freedoms, has not been directly addressed in European Union primary law. Preservation of European linguistic diversity is the main goal of Article 22 of the Charter for Fundamental Rights of the European Union, which states, "The Union shall respect cultural, religious and linguistic diversity."[8] The enforcement of the Treaty of Lisbon has modified the legal value of the Charter for Fundamental Rights, reaching the same legal value as the Treaties since December 1, 2009.[9] Furthermore, Article 3 of the Treaty of the European Union, as amended by the Lisbon Treaty has introduced new strategic or foundational goals for the Union, such as the commitment to respect its rich cultural and linguistic diversity and to ensure that Europe's cultural heritage

6. Regarding the cultural competencies of the EU in both pre Maastricht era and post Maastricht, see Psychogiopoulou *The Integration of Cultural Considerations in EU Law and Policies*, 393 pages. See also Smith, "Community Intervention in the Cultural Field: Continuity or Change" in *Culture and European Union Law* ed. R. Smith, 49-53; Niamh Nic Shuibhne, *EC Law and Minority Language Policy: Culture, Citizenship and Fundamental Rights*, at 107–114; Littoz-Monnet, *The European Union and Culture: Between Economic Regulation and European Cultural Policy*, 32–45.

7. See De Witte, "Common Market Freedoms" cit., 117.

8. This article is considered the "most flexible element of Equality Chapter" of the Charter of Fundamental Rights of the European Union. See Bell "The Right to Equality and Non-Discrimination," 107.

9. By virtue of the first subparagraph of Article 6(1) of the Treaty on European Union (as amended by the Lisbon Treaty), the Charter proclaimed in 2007 has the same legal value as the Treaties.

is safeguarded and enhanced. These Articles provide safeguards against homogenization of national or regional cultural and linguistic characteristics, but their role appears to be more about setting boundaries than driving positive actions. To date, the EU has not followed any clearly defined language policy guidelines when dealing with national or regional languages. When it has had to regulate market respects that in some way affect regional languages, developing linguistic diversity has not been one of its reference points. Indeed, its approach seems to focus on overcoming language barriers that stand in the way of the exercise of essentially economic rights.[10] An analysis of the judicial approach to this issue follows with an emphasis on considering language measures as "overriding reasons in the public interest."[11]

Restrictions to Economic Fundamental Freedoms on Grounds of Language?

According to the jurisprudence of the Court of Justice, national measures liable to hinder or make less attractive the exercise of fundamental freedoms guaranteed by the Treaty must fulfill four conditions: these measures must be applied in a nondiscriminatory manner, they must be justified by imperative requirements in the general interest, they must be suitable for securing the attainment of the objective that they pursue, and they must not go beyond what is necessary in order to attain it (proportionate).[12] Restrictions to economic fundamental freedoms can be allowed in exceptional situations, if indistinctly applied, in areas where the harmonization of European Community regulations is not yet complete, based on grounds of "overriding reasons relating to the public interest."[13] Obstacles to circulation within the Union resulting from national laws must be accepted in so far these national measures may be "recognized as being necessary in order to satisfy mandatory requirements relating in particular to the effectiveness of fiscal supervision, the protection of public health, the fairness of commercial transactions and the defense of the

10. See Urrutia and Lasagabaster "Language Rights and Community Law," 6–8.
11. Ibid.
12. Inter alia Case C-55/94 Reinhard Gebhard v. Consiglio dell'Ordine degli Avvocati e Procuratori di Milano [1996] ECR I-4165 (Gebhard).
13. This method has been developed in the field of services, but is now being applied to all the fundamental freedoms. See Hatzopoulos "Exigences essentielles, impératives ou impérieuses: Une théorie, des théories ou pas de théorie du tout?," 236.

consumer."[14]

The concept of "overriding reason in the public interest" was introduced by the European Court of Justice in order to balance the expansive force of the market freedoms, and may be argued when analyzing limitations to the freedom to provide services (Articles 56 TFEU and 57 TFEU), to the freedom of establishment (Article 49 TFEU), to the freedom of movement of capital (Article 63 TFEU, Section 1) and to the freedom of movement for workers (Article 45 TFEU). This concept offers the Court a flexible tool to balance the sometimes, competing interests of market integration and market national regulations.[15] The concept of "overriding reasons relating to the public interest" has been developed by the Court of Justice in its case law and may continue to evolve.

Overriding reasons may be looked at from two points of view: on the one hand they may be considered as an acknowledgment of residual competences of the Member States in areas that affect freedom of movement and the free market;[16] whereas, on the other hand, they imply a sort of spreading of European community action into fields in which it has no competences, by the analysis of the grounds of the member State intervention based on an European Community viewpoint. The overriding reasons would be a sort of compensation to counterbalance the sweeping extension of the scope of the Treaty prohibitions. Those national interests should be appropriate to protect from a European community perspective. A sort of "*communiterization*" of national language policies arise based on European community principles.[17] The Eu-

14. Case 120/78 *Rewe_Zentral AG v Bundesmonopolverwaltung für Branntwein* ("Cassis de Dijon") [1979] ECR 649, para 8. This judgment, known as the 'Cassis de Dijon judgment', is a keystone of the development of case-law relative to the prohibition of quantitative restrictions on imports and of measures having equivalent effect on the free movement of goods.

15. See Scott "Mandatory or Imperative Requirements in the EU and the WTO," 269.

16. This view can explain the apparent laxity of the Court in accepting any reason put forward by Member States as being "overriding" should not be overstated. It is true that the Court may not, without aggrieving Member States, openly reject a legitimate objective invoked by a State as not being "overriding." Nevertheless, the Court retains some control over the reasons which are qualified as "overriding" under EC law, by rejecting reasons of a purely administrative nature and reasons pursuing an openly economic objective.

17. It should be pointed out that the legal competences of the European Court of Justice have expanded to the point that they now cover a multitude of Member State policies, including some that are language related. On this regard see Boch "Language Protection and Free Trade" cit. at 40 "the ECJ checks on the

ropean Court of Justice has effectively become the institution that analyzes the objectives and resources for language policies that Member States have chosen from the perspective of European Community interests.

In order to rely on mandatory requirements, the measures must not be discriminatory[18] and they must be applied without distinction to national and imported products.[19] The second criterion to be fulfilled is that of the absence of complete harmonization on the subject. In the event of total harmonization, the harmonizing legislation itself has to take into consideration any possible reasons of general interest and establish exceptions. If there is a complete harmonization, any measures adopted by Member States would have to be analyzed on the basis of the harmonizing legislation itself, and not even Article 36 of the TFEU would therefore apply.[20] The *Wilson* case shows us a clear example of this. The European Court of Justice stated that "[A]rticle 3 of Directive 98/5 must be interpreted as meaning that the registration of a lawyer with the competent authority of a Member State other than the State where he obtained his qualification in order to practice there under his home-country professional title cannot be made subject to a prior examination of his proficiency in the languages of the host Member."[21] The scope of this

---

adequacy of the methods designed to ensure such protection. According to this model, it is not for the French to decide how to protect the French language." See also Craufurd Smith "The Evolution of Cultural Policy in the European Union," 877.

18. Article 18 TFEU (ex 12 TEC) applies independently only to situations governed by Community law for which the TFEU lays down no specific rules of non-discrimination. *Vid.* Case C-100/01 *Oteiza Olazabal* [2002] ECR I-10981, paragraph 25; Case C-289/02 *AMOK* [2003] ECR I-15059, paragraph 25; Case C-222/04 *Cassa di Risparmio di Firenze and others* [2006] ECR I-289, paragraph 99; and Case C-40/05 *Lyyski* [2007] ECR I-99, paragraph 33.

19. See Case C-110/05, *Commission/Italy*, [2009] paragraph 61; Case C-282/04 and C-283/04, *Commission/Netherlands* [2006] ECR I-9141, paragraph 32; Case C-112/05 *Commission/Germany* [2007] ECR I-8995, paragraph 72; and Case C-274/06, *Commission/Spain* [2008] ECR I-0000, paragraph 35; Case C-207/07, *Commission/Spain* [2008] paragraph 41.

20. Case C-37/92, *Vanaker,* [1993] ECR I-4948 paragraph 16; Case C-47/90 *Delhaize* [1992] ECR I-3669, paragraph 26; Joined Cases C-427/93, C-429/93 y C-436/93, *Bristol Mayres* [1996] ECR I-3457, paragraph 27.

21. Directive 98/5/EC of the European Parliament and of the Council of 16 February 1998 to facilitate practice of the profession of lawyer on a permanent basis in a Member State other than that in which the qualification was obtained (OJ 1998 L 77, p. 36). See alo Case C-506/04 *Wilson,* [2006] ECR I-8613 paragraph 77 and Case C-193/05 *Commission/ Luxembourg* [2006] ECR I-8676, paragraph 35;

statement is clarified by taking into account the following assertion by the Court of Justice, "[i]n Article 3 of that directive[,] the Community legislature carried out a complete harmonisation of the prior conditions for the exercise of the right it confers."[22] The Court highlights the fact that the Community legislature, with a view to making it easier for a particular class of migrant lawyers to exercise the fundamental freedom of establishment, did not opt for a system of prior testing of the knowledge of the persons concerned.[23]

The underlying idea is that, whereas the Community freedoms do not exclude the possibility of establishing reasonable language requirements for professionals,[24] the *Wilson* case shows that said possibility disappears if the European Union legislator regulates, in a totally harmonized way, the conditions for establishment of professionals and fails to include linguistic requirements.[25] It may, however, be rather excessive to consider the European Court has either closed the door on language requirements or that it is simply not aware of them. To the contrary, it appears more likely that the Court found enough opportunities within the harmonizing legislation itself to allow the Member States to establish these requirements themselves.[26] The European Court did consider the possibility of including language guarantees through the Lawyers Association code of practice, specifically linked to exercising that particular profession, but not as a condition for establishment.[27] What remains up in the air is whether or not the European Court would have reached the same conclusion had such possibilities not existed.

Another example of an area in which total harmonization of legislation renders it impossible to apply overriding reasons in the

---

on these judgments, see Jan Vanhamme "L'équivalence des langues Dans le marché intérieur; l'apport de la Cour de Justice" in *Cahiers de droit européen* no 359, 2007, at 373-378.

22. Case C-506/04 *Wilson,* [2006] ECR I-8613 paragraph 66.

23. Case C-168/98 *Luxembourg / Parliament and Council* [2000] ECR I-9131, paragraph 43

24. See Case C-424/97 *Salomone Haim* [2000] ECR I-5123 paragraph 59

25. See the reflections of De Witte, "Common Market Freedoms," 123.

26. See Case C-506/04 *Wilson*, [2006] ECR I-8613 paragraph 71: "[t]he exclusion of a system of prior testing of the knowledge, particularly of languages, for European lawyers is, however, accompanied in Directive 98/5 by a set of rules intended to ensure, to a level acceptable in the Community, the protection of consumers and the proper administration of justice."

27. See Case C-506/04 *Wilson*, [2006] ECR I-8613 paragraph 74.

general interest to justify restrictions to the freedoms of movement could be the labeling of food products. Article 16.2 of the Directive 2000/13/EC of the European Parliament and of the Council of March 20, 2000, on the approximation of the laws of the Member States relating to the labeling, presentation, and advertising of foodstuffs states, "Within its own territory, the Member State in which the product is marketed may, in accordance with the rules of the Treaty, stipulate that those labeling particulars shall be given in one or more languages which it shall determine from among the official languages of the Community." The Member States are allowed to require the compulsory use of languages in labeling but only the compulsory use of the official languages of the EU. Keeping in mind that not all the official languages *in* Europe (inside the Member States) are official languages *of* the European Union, the mentioned article renders it impossible to require the compulsory use of the official languages in Member States that are not official languages of the European Union.[28] The question that remains unanswered is whether or not, as a result of the most recent stance taken in case law in this regard, which is analyzed below, it might be adequate to amend the European Union labeling legislation that limits the possibility to set down language requirements to the official languages of the European Union, extending this to the official languages *in* Member States.[29]

Language Promotion as an Overriding Reason Related to the Public Interest.

European Court of Justice case law relating to the encouragement of language diversity as being an overriding reason in the public interest has been quite limited; however, the most recent rulings show us an increasingly solid stance by the European Court of Justice in favor of this.

The Groener Case

The origin of the dispute in this caser was the Minister's refus-

28. See Case C-33/97 *Colim* [1999], ECR I-3175, paragraph 34/35 stablishing the following doctrine: "[W]hen those directives fully harmonise the language requirements applicable for a given product, the Member States cannot impose additional language requirements. By contrast, where there is only partial Community harmonisation or none at all, the Member States in principle retain the power to impose additional language requirements."
29. See Milian, Globalización y requisitos lingüísticos, 64.

al to appoint Mrs. Groener, a Netherlands national, to a permanent full-time post as an art teacher, employed by the Education Committee after she had failed a test intended to assess her knowledge of the Irish language. It's important to note that the particular teaching post in this case did not require the use of *Irish Gaelic* for teaching.[30] This fact did not prevent the Court from concluding that the restriction of freedom of movement via a language requirement pursued a legitimate aim. It was indeed considered reasonable on the basis of the regulatory powers of Member States to promote a national (joint official) language at a disadvantage in comparison to the other official language of the Member State. The Court stated:

> The EEC Treaty does not prohibit the adoption of a policy for the protection and promotion of a language of a Member State which [sic] is both the national language and the first official language. However, the implementation of such a policy must not encroach upon a fundamental freedom such as that of the free movement of workers. Therefore, the requirements deriving from measures intended to implement such a policy must not in any circumstances be disproportionate in relation to the aim pursued and the manner in which they are applied must not bring about discrimination against nationals of other Member States."[31]

The Court upheld that the policy to defend and promote a national language was deemed to be a legitimate aim, justifying some degree of restrictions on European community freedoms, as long as this adheres to the principle of proportionality and is applied without discrimination. Nevertheless, emphasis was placed on two points: on the one hand, on the transcendence of the education for implementation of such a language policy,[32] and on the

---

30. The Regulation (EEC) No 1612/68 of the Council of October 15, 1968 on freedom of movement for workers within the Community does not completely harmonize the rules relating to the areas which it covers (see the 5th recital of the Preamble). The second indent of Article 3(1) of Regulation No 1612/68 provides that national provisions or administrative practices of a Member State are not to apply where, "though applicable irrespective of nationality, their exclusive or principal aim or effect is to keep nationals of other Member States away from the employment offered." The last subparagraph of Article 3(1) provides that that provision is not to "apply to conditions relating to linguistic knowledge required by reason of the nature of the post to be filled."
31. Case C-379/87, Groener v. Minister for Education and the Dublin Vocational Education Committee [1989] ECR 3967, paragraph 19.
32. See Case C-379/87, *Groener* paragraph 20: "[T]he importance of education for the implementation of such a policy must be recognized. Teachers have an essential role to play, not only through the teaching which they provide

other hand, the European Court stressed the legal qualification of the language in question, "the national language which is, at the same time, the first official language."[33] This raised doubts as to whether the broad interpretation of the European Court might be limited to a certain type of posts or to languages depending on their internal legal status. Nevertheless, *Irish Gaelic* was not an official language of the European Union at that point in time.

The Haim Case

In this case, the Court was asked about the legality of making the appointment of a national of another Member State as a dental practitioner under a social security arrangement conditional upon his having sufficient knowledge of the language of the Member State of establishment.[34] The Court stated:

> The reliability of a dental practitioner's communication with his patient and with administrative authorities and professional bodies constitutes an overriding reason of general interest such as to justify making the appointment as a dental practitioner under a social security scheme subject to language requirements. Dialogue with patients, compliance with rules of professional conduct and law specific to dentistry in the Member State of establishment and performance of administrative tasks require an appropriate knowledge of the language of that State.[35]

The Court had never previously been quite so clear on the point that limitation to freedoms arising out of language requirements may be justified as being "overriding reasons in the public interest." Nevertheless, one should say that the grounds highlighted by the Court were intended to guarantee the communication between patients and the professional. This being so, one doubt that remains unresolved is to know whether or not the overriding reason is the States' language policy of promoting the

---

but also by their participation in the daily life of the school and the privileged relationship which they have with their pupils. In those circumstances, it is not unreasonable to require them to have some knowledge of the first national language."

33. Case C-379/87, *Groener* paragraph 24.

34. The applicant did not hold one of the qualifications specified in Council Directive 78/686 (repealed and replaced by Directive 2005/36 -amended several times), but had been authorized to practice as a dentist in German. He applied to work on a social security scheme in Germany, but was told that he would have to complete a further two-year training period.

35. Case C-424/97 Salomone Haim v Kassenzahnärztliche Vereinigung Nordrhein [2000] ECR I-05123, paragraph 59.

national language or the communicative function inherent to all languages, expressed as guaranteeing reliable communication. If it is the latter, then this falls under the scope of consumer rights, which are deemed to be an overriding reason in the public interest, although strictly from the point of view of communication.[36] However, the Court emphasizes that such language requirement may not go beyond what is necessary to attain that objective.

In the end, after having resolved the questions posed, the Judgment of the European Court made an *obiter dicta* interesting here. The Court stated that "it is in the interest of patients whose mother tongue is not the national language that there exist a certain number of dental practitioners who are also capable of communicating with such persons in their own language."[37] This "Turkish clause" represents an interesting approach to the legal recognition of the European linguistic diversity by means of an advanced level of consumer protection, and also, perhaps, as a mean of social integration of new European minorities. In line with the transformation of other linguistic minorities' rights, the right to integration is already being transformed into a right to language diversity.[38] The recognition of European language diversity as a tool for safeguarding the European regional languages has been applied also to the languages of "new immigrant" communities. The question arises as to whether the same approach should be consistent in both cases, and especially when language rights of the speakers of regional European languages have not been fully recognized by internal, national legislation.[39] All in all, the free movement of persons does not per se reduce linguistic diversity. Free movement of persons can instead be used for securing linguistic diversity.[40]

The Bickel and Franz Case

An Austrian citizen, Mr. Bickel, and a German national, Mr. Franz,

36. See also Case C-85/94 *"Piageme II"* [1995] paragraph 24.
37. Case C-424/97 *Salomone Haim* paragraph 60 (*in fine*).
38. See the reflections in Burch "Regional Minorities, Immigrants, and Migrants: The Reframing of Minority Language Rights in Europe," 140.
39. Some scholars argue that newcomers/immigrants cannot demand the same linguistic rights as the members of old and established minority linguistic groups. Kymlicka, *Multicultural Citizenship: A Liberal Theory of Minority Rights,* 34.
40. See the reflections by Toggenburg "The EU's Linguistic Diversity: Fuel or Brake to the Mobility of Workers," 675–721.

visiting the Trentino-Alto Adige region of Italy were charged with minor criminal offences in separate incidents. Criminal proceedings in this region can be conducted in either German or Italian, but this linguistic right under the Italian law was limited to German-speaking citizens of the province.[41] Bickel and Franz both requested that judicial proceedings be held in German, even though they were not citizens of Italy. The plaintiffs claimed that to deny them the right to a trial in German was discrimination on the basis of nationality in relationship to the freedom to provide services and freedom of movement.[42] The Court held that,

> The Italian Government's contention that the aim of those rules is to protect the ethno-cultural minority residing in the province in question does not constitute a valid justification in this context. Of course, the protection of such a minority may constitute a legitimate aim. It does not appear, however, from the documents before the Court that that aim would be undermined if the rules in issue were extended to cover German-speaking nationals of other Member States exercising their right to freedom of movement.[43]

The Court relied on the argument that it had already put forward in the case of *Mutsch,*[44] while introducing a significant new aspect. The Court would never have gone so far in evaluating a national law on an issue that, like minority protection, is outside of the realm of EC law.[45] In spite of the absence of human rights

41. Under article 100 of the Presidential Decree No 670 of 30 August 1972 concerning the special arrangements for the Trentino-Alto Adige Region (GURI No 301 of 20 November 1972) the German-speaking citizens of the Province of Bolzano (the area where most of the German-speaking minority live) are entitled to use their own language in relations with the judicial and administrative authorities based in that province or entrusted with responsibility at regional level.

42. The national court asked to the European Court of Justice whether the right conferred by national rules to have criminal proceedings conducted in a language other than the principal language of the State concerned falls within the scope of the Treaty and must accordingly comply with Article 6 thereof (non-discrimination on grounds of nationality; art 18 TFEU). If so, the national court also asked whether Article 6 of the Treaty (Article 18 TFEU) precludes national rules, such as those in issue, which, in respect of a particular language other than the principal language of the Member State concerned, confer on citizens whose language is that particular language and who are resident in a defined area the right to require that criminal proceedings be conducted in that language, without conferring the same right on nationals of other Member States travelling or staying in that area, whose language is the same.

43. Case 274/96 *Bickel and Franz* [1998] ECR 7637, paragraph 26.

44. Case 137/84 *Mutsch* [1985] ECR 268.

45. On this regard see Palermo "The Use of Minority Languages: Recent Devel-

or minority rights considerations in the Judgment, the legitimate aim referred to by the Court seems to confirm that the essential aspects of those regimes are, or may be, justified in the EU legal order.[46] It effectively confirmed, for the first time, that protection of a (language) minority could be deemed a legitimate objective. A legitimate objective within which it would be possible to justify restrictions to the European community freedoms, but which is nevertheless not negatively affected by whether or not all European citizens that share such a minority language might be able to benefit from the scheme applied to it. In other words, despite the fact that the Court does not specifically say so, one may deduce from the wording that if freedom of movement might affect the objective being sought by the collective measure protecting the language minority group, then the Court would have come to the opposite conclusion.[47] The general idea being that the principle of equality (Article 18 TFEU *ex* 12 TEU) is opposed to any national legislation granting citizens of a language, other than the main language of the Member State concerned, the right to have criminal proceedings held in their own language, without granting citizens with the same language but of other Member States, the same right. Protecting a local linguistic minority is perfectly in harmony with the Treaty, but denying visitors the right to use German was neither necessary nor appropriate to achieve that goal.

It is a matter of extending the language rights recognized under national legislation to all European Union citizens when applying European Union Law. One should bear in mind that such extension of language rights does not arise by extending the language diversity clause in each and every Member State, but rather guaranteeing an equal (linguistic) treatment to all European nationals in each State when applying the EU Law.[48] In view of this, one cannot then say that the recognition of language diversity predetermines a specific linguistic model that Member States are

---

opment in EC Law and Judgments of the ECJ," 311.

46. See Pentassuglia, Minorities in International Law: An Introductory Study, 145.

47. Nevertheless *Bickel and Franz* suggests that the ECJ is ready to intervene when Member State rules designed to protect minority groups are in conflict with the exercise of individual Community rights. See Weber "Individual Rights and Group Rights in the European Community's Approach to Minority Languages," 403.

48. See Urrutia, "The Legal Regime of Languages in European Union Law," 720.

under an obligation to adopt, not even when applying European Union Law.

The United Pan-Europe Communications Belgium and Others Case

This ruling dealt with the compatibility of Belgium's "must carry" regulation with the Treaties. The reference has been made in the course of proceedings brought by some cable operators against the Belgian State, relating to the obligation imposed on them by the latter to broadcast in the bilingual region of Brussels-Capital, television programs transmitted by certain private broadcasters designated by the authorities of that State. The cable operators in question argued that the contested measures grant private broadcasters with "must-carry status" a special right that was liable to distort competition between broadcasters, and to disadvantage broadcasters established in Member States other than the Kingdom of Belgium.

The Belgian Government argued that the aim of the measure was to preserve the pluralist and cultural range of programs available on television distribution networks and to ensure that all television viewers had access to pluralism and to a wide range of programs, particularly by guaranteeing to Belgian citizens of the bilingual region of Brussels-Capital that they would not be deprived of access to local and national news and to their culture. In this regard, the European Court stated that,

> It must be accepted that the national legislation at issue in the main proceedings pursues an aim in the general interest, since it seeks to preserve the pluralist nature of the range of television programs available in the bilingual region of Brussels-Capital and thus forms part of a cultural policy the aim of which is to safeguard, in the audiovisual sector, the freedom of expression of the different social, cultural, religious, philosophical or linguistic components which exist in that region.[49]

The Court ruled that the purpose of this was indeed in the public interest and that it formed part of a general cultural policy.[50] However, the case-law show us that the principle of media

49. Case C-250/06, *United Pan-Europe Communications* (cit supra), paragraph 42.
50. The ECJ has elaborated a consistent set of judgements regarding the application of the freedom of movement rules where the presence of national regulations that could result in impediments to trade can be justified, and thus upheld, because they aim to safeguard media pluralism. This approach stems from the reasoning that media pluralism forms part of cultural policy which

pluralism that forms part of cultural policy is not interpreted in an expansive manner by the Court of Justice, but by a case-by-case basis, in light of a strict proportionality and necessity test. In this way, one could say that the ECJ interferes with Member States' regulation, despite clearly recognizing that media pluralism is part of a policy domain reserved to Member States.[51] Regarding the proportionality of the language restrictions to the freedom to provide services, the European Court stated the following in this ruling:

> Having regard to the bilingual nature of the Brussels-Capital region national legislation, such as that at issue in the main proceedings constitutes an appropriate means of achieving the cultural objective pursued, since it is capable of permitting, in that region, Dutch-speaking television viewers to have access, via the network of cable operators broadcasting in that area, to television programs having a cultural and linguistic connection with the Flemish Community and French-speaking television viewers to have similar access to television programs having a cultural and linguistic connection with the French Community. Such legislation thus guarantees to television viewers in that region that they will not be deprived of access, in their own language, to local and national news as well as to programs which are representative of their culture.[52]

What is remarkable in this ruling is that guaranteeing language diversity in the TV programming in a given bilingual region and in accordance with its cultural policy was considered an objective in the public interest. In contrast to some antecedents,[53] one may therefore assert that it is not merely guaranteeing the cultural pluralism in TV programming that constitutes an

---

may constitute an overriding requirement relating to the general interest thus justifying a restriction on the freedom to provide services. See Case 352/85, *Bond van Adverteerders and others / The Netherlands State*, [1988] ECR 2085; Case C-211/91, *Commission of the European Communities / Kingdom of Belgium*, [1992] ECR I-6757; Case C-288/89, *Stichting Collectieve Antennevoorziening Gouda and others / Commissariaat voor de Media ("Mediawet I")*, [1991] ECR I-04007; Case C-353/89, *Commission of the European Communities / Kingdom of the Netherlands*, [1991] ECR I-4069; Case C-148/91, *Vereniging Veronica Omroep Organisatie / Commissariaat voor de Media*, [1993] ECR I-00487.

51. See Craufurd Smith, *Broadcasting Law and Fundamental Rights*, 186; De Witte, "Non-market Values in Internal Market Regulation," 61.

52. Case C-250/06, *United Pan-Europe Communications* (cit supra), paragraph 43.

53. See Case C-288/89 *Stichting Collectieve Antennevoorziening Gouda* [1991], ECR I-4007, paragraph 23; Case C-148/91 *Veronica Omroep Organisatie* [1993] ECR I-487, paragraphs 9 and 10; and Case C-23/93 *TV10* [1994] ECR I-4795, paragraphs 18 and 19.

overriding reason in the public interest, but rather, particularly, guaranteeing to television viewers access in their own language (being the official languages of the Region) to local and national news. In any event, the legal (linguistic) requirement that limits the freedom to provide TV services must be subject to a transparent procedure based on objective and non-discriminatory criteria known in advance.

The UTECA Case

The leading case regarding the consideration of language requirements as overriding reasons relating to the public interest of the EU is the UTECA case,[54] which settled a question for a preliminary ruling brought before the Spanish Supreme Court. The issue came about as a result of a challenge lodged against Royal Decree 1652/2004, of July 9, 2004, approving the Regulation governing compulsory investment for the pre-funding of European and Spanish cinematographic feature-length and short films and films made for television. In effect, the Union of the Associated Commercial Televisions (UTECA) filed an appeal against this Royal Decree that requires television operators to earmark five percent of their operating revenue for the pre-funding of European cinematographic films and films made for television and, more specifically, to reserve sixty percent of that five percent for the production of works of which the original language is one of the official languages of that Member State. The Supreme Court set down several preliminary issues in the framework of those proceedings to be dealt with by the European Court of Justice and which basically required a pronouncement with regard to the compatibility of Articles 12 EC and 87 EC with the requirement to reserve sixty percent of the obligatory funding for the production of films of which the original language is one of the official languages of the Kingdom of Spain.

The European Court of Justice, upholding the Opinion of the Advocate General,[55] considered that the language arrangements included under the system of advanced financing of films amounts to a restriction of several fundamental freedoms, that is to say of the freedom to provide services, the freedom of establishment, the free movement of capital and the freedom of movement for

54. Case C-222/07 Unión de Televisiones Comerciales Asociadas (UTECA) [2009] ECR I-0000.

55. See Case C-222/07, *UTECA* paragraph 24.

workers.[56] Considered in this way, such a restriction may be justified only where it serves overriding reasons relating to the general interest, is suitable for securing the attainment of the objective that it pursues, and does not go beyond what is necessary in order to attain it. For example, the restriction on a fundamental freedom must have a legitimate objective and must pass the test of proportionality.

The first issue the Court had to deal with was to what extent a linguistic measure (deemed to be restrictive from the point of view of the market freedoms) could be considered suitable for ensuring the achievement of a legitimate objective pursued by the Treaty. In this regard, the European Court contextualized the language measure within the cultural field, namely, "the defense of Spanish multilingualism."[57] It should be said here that the Court, in this regard, does go further than the approach proposed by the Advocate General in her Opinion, where she refers exclusively to promotion of multilingualism in European audiovisual productions.[58] This issue is important in that the European Court does not circumscribe its ruling to the audiovisual industry, but rather takes it further to what might be termed the defense of multilingualism *in genere*.

Having thus acknowledged that language promotion is a common objective of the Union and of its member States, the European Court of Justice does confirm in no uncertain terms that "the objective, pursued by a Member State, of defending and promoting one or several of its official languages constitutes an overriding reason in the public interest."[59] The Court had never, prior to this point, quite so clearly expressed that the policy of defending and promoting one or several of the official languages within the Member State is deemed to be an overriding reason in the public interest that does to some extent legitimize a certain degree of limitation to European Community freedoms.

The second aspect taken into consideration by the Court, in order to analyze the compatibility of the Decree with the Treaty of the measure refers to its nature. The Commission adopted the view that the scheme for advanced financing of films was too

---

56. See the Opinion of the Advocate General at the sitting on September 4, 2008, case C-222/07, paragraphs, 78–87.
57. Case C-222/07, *UTECA*, paragraph 26.
58. Opinion of the Advocate General (case C-222/07), paragraph 90.
59. Case C-222/07, *UTECA*, paragraph 27.

general and non-specific. In other words, the scheme did not refer exclusively to "cultural products" and this was what, in the Commission's opinion, rendered it disproportionate. The Court found the scheme lacking in objective and verifiable criteria that might render it possible to ensure that the advanced financing scheme would only be applied to cinema and television products deemed to be "cultural products."[60] The European Court of Justice, however, did not agree with the opinion of the Commission and stated:

> Since language and culture are intrinsically linked, as pointed out by, inter alia, the Convention on the Protection and Promotion of the Diversity of Cultural Expressions, adopted at the General Conference of UNESCO in Paris on October 20, 2005 and approved on behalf of the Community by Council Decision 2006/515/EC of May 18, 2006 (OJ 2006 L 201, p. 15), which states in paragraph 14 of its preamble that "linguistic diversity is a fundamental element of cultural diversity," the view cannot be taken that the objective pursued by a Member State of defending and promoting one or several of its official languages must of necessity be accompanied by other cultural criteria in order for it to justify a restriction on one of the fundamental freedoms guaranteed by the Treaty. Indeed, in the present proceedings, the Commission has been unable to state precisely what those criteria should actually be.[61]

The European Court effectively sets down that measures for promoting languages, in order to be justified, need not refer strictly to cultural aspects (such as, for example, culture related companies or films that might be categorized as being "cultural products"). The criterion for qualifying is not the (cultural) nature of the object that the measure affects, but rather the linguistic instrument used to carry it out. The Court thus confirmed the autonomous nature of language criteria as an overriding reason in the public interest.

That statement by the Court has great importance and reach, especially for non-standardized regional official languages. Bearing in mind the fact that any language policies on non-normalized language have effects on all social (public and private) roles of language, it can be gleaned from the Ruling in the *UTECA* case that any language requirements established on the basis of the language standardization process will have to be analyzed by taking the process of language standardization itself into consideration,

60. The Commission was guided on this point, by the Case C-17/92 *Distribuidores Cinematográficos* [1993] ECR I-2239, paragraph 20.

61. Case C-222/07, *UTECA*, paragraph 33.

and not limiting the analysis to areas that can be defined as being strictly cultural. The open approach of the Court, confirming the substantive nature of linguistic criteria as cultural justification was issued in a matter having to do with fundamental freedoms. The question that should be asked is whether this same approach might be applied in other areas, such as the prohibition of State aids for example.[62]

The fact is that it can be extremely difficult to establish any objective and, above all, fair criteria for determining what may be deemed to be culture and, even harder still, which "cultural products" are worthy of promotion. It can likewise not be denied that promoting languages in all areas, including the audiovisual industry, does appear cultural in nature, keeping in mind the importance of languages in defending and promoting cultural expression and linguistic diversity itself.[63] The Court was not dealing with nuances when it stated that "the view cannot be taken that the objective pursued by a Member State of defending and promoting one or several of its official languages must of necessity be accompanied by other cultural criteria in order for it to justify a restriction on one of the fundamental freedoms."[64] Following the *UTECA* ruling, there is nothing to stop Member States from disregarding additional content or quality related criteria in order to promote culture in the widest possible sense.

Conclusions

As a consequence of the process of European integration, European languages take on an economic and a political dimension that influence their development. The free market does not remain neutral from a language perspective. It benefits certain languages and places the rest under pressure, as a result of the loss of position that this implies. Economic freedoms are not linguistically neutral, thus negatively affecting European linguistic diversity. Bearing in mind the impact on languages of the EU building process, it is paradoxical to note what little progress has been made for counteracting this effect.

The main focus of the EU action has been on overcoming any language barriers in the exercise of essentially economic rights.

62. See art 107 TFEU (ex 87 TCE).

63. See Urrutia "Libre competencia, prohibición de ayudas de Estado y fiscalidad lingüística," 67–80.

64. Case C-222/07, *UTECA*, paragraph 33.

Language requirements are considered in general as an obstacle to the common market, instead of taking into account the positive effects of multilingualism in the economic arena. Facing the creeping expansion of the competence of the Union in order to remove internal barriers, linguistic matters have been considered domestic issues that each State must assess individually. The problem arises when the policy of removing barriers limits the powers of the domestic public authorities to intervene in the market. An additional problem that occurs is the lack of sensitivity and respect for their internal language diversity among certain Member States. The deregulatory approach of the EU has not been balanced with a comprehensive EU policy fostering language diversity.

Till now, the level to which cultural and linguistic promotion can justify restrictions on market freedoms has not been directly addressed in European Union law. However, it should be stressed that the recent Treaty of Lisbon has given centrality and new impetus to the cultural values and to the wealth of European linguistic heritage. The treaties recognize the respect for European linguistic diversity as a principle for action. This principle must gain centrality and substance.

The balance between common market freedoms and internal language policies has been defined progressivity by the Court of Justice of the EU. It has been left up to this court to find a position of equilibrium between market freedoms and guaranteeing European linguistic diversity. If we can speak today about linguistic delimitation of the EU freedoms, it is only due to the case-law of the Court of Justice.

The most recent rulings clearly express that the objective of defending and promoting one or several of the official languages within the Member States is considered an overriding reason in the public interest that may legitimize limitations to European Community freedoms to some extent. The Court has also confirmed the autonomous nature of language itself as an overriding reason in the public interest. The key element is not the (cultural) nature of the area or the production to which the measure applies, but rather the language resource used itself. Bearing in mind the fact that the language normalization policies cover all social and economic areas, any language requirements established on the basis of the language normalization process will have to be analyzed taking the process itself into consideration and not limiting the analysis to areas that can be defined as being strictly cultural.

The main problem that still remains to be solved relates to the analysis of the proportionality of the measure of language policy. The case law has introduced certain guidelines, but the proportionality of each provision has to be analyzed taking into consideration each individual measure.

In any case, the possibility of resorting to the overriding reasons in the public interest depends on two factors: first, it depends on the existence of an internal language policy fostering the regional language. That is to say it depends initially on the power of the regional authorities and also on their political will and commitment to defend and promote their regional language. Second, it depends on the absence of a complete harmonization by the European legislation. If there is a complete harmonization, any measures adopted by Member States would have to be analyzed on the basis of the harmonizing legislation itself.

European language diversity comprises both EU's official languages and non-official languages, widely spoken languages and less widely spoken languages, regional languages, national languages and state languages, minority languages and majority languages, all of them enrich the European linguistic heritage. The commitment of the European Union in favor of linguistic diversity should move forward by means of a resolute action fostering and promoting all languages as an overriding reason in the European public interest. It is in Europe's best interest to move toward a European Union language policy that develops and implements the recognition of European linguistic diversity and places it on the same footing with its economic freedoms.

Bibliography

Bell, Mark. *Anti-Discrimination Law and the European Union*. Oxford: Oxford University Press, 2004.

———. "The Right to Equality and Non-Discrimination," in *Economic and Social Rights Under the EU Charter of Fundamental Rights: A Legal Perspective*, edited by Tamara K. Hervey, Jeff Kenner. Portland: Hart Publishing, 2003: 91–110.

Benoît Rohmer, Florence. "Article 22: Diversité culturelle, religieuse et linguistique," in *EU Network of Independent Experts on Fundamental Rights: The Commentary of the Charter of Fundamental Rights of the European Union*. Brussels:

European Commission, 2006.

Boch, Christine. "Language Protection and Free Trade: The Triumph of the Homo McDonaldus?" *European Public Law* 4, no 3 (1998): 379–402.

Burch, Stella J. "Regional Minorities, Immigrants, and Migrants: The Reframing of Minority Language Rights in Europe," *Yale Law School Student Scholarship Papers*. Paper 79.

Candela Soriano, Mercedes. "Les exigences linguistiques: Une entrave légitime à la libre circulation," *Cahiers de droit Européen* 1, no 2 (2002): 9–44.

Craig, Paul. *The Lisbon Treaty: Law, Politics and Treaty Reform*. Oxford: Oxford University Press, 2010.

Craufurd Smith, Rachael. "Community Intervention in the Cultural Field: Continuity or Change," in *Culture and European Union Law*, edited by Rachael Craufurd Smith. Oxford: Oxford University Press, 2004: 19–78.

———. "The Evolution of Cultural Policy in the European Union," in *The Evolution of EU Law*, edited by Paul Craig and Gráinne de Búrca. Oxford: Oxford University Press, 2011: 869–894.

———. *Broadcasting Law and Fundamental Rights*. Oxford: Oxford University Press, 1997.

Cristal, David. *Language Death*. Cambridge: Cambridge University Press, 2000.

Daniel, Andrea. *Is Economic Integration the Motor of All European Integration?: The Debate Surrounding the Services Directive*. San Francisco: Grin Publishing, 2009.

De Varennes, Fernand. *Language, Minorities and Human Rights*. The Hague: Martinus Nijhoff, 1996.

De Witte, Bruno. "Common Market Freedoms Versus Linguistic Requirements in the EU States," in *Mundialització, lliure circulació i immigració, i l'exigència d'una llengua com a requisit*, edited by Antoni Milian. Barcelona: Institut d'estudis autònomics, 2008: 109–132.

De Witte, Bruno. "Non-Market Values in Internal Market Regulation," in *Regulating the Internal Market*, edited by N. Nic Shuibhne. Cheltenham: Edward Elgar Publishing, 2006: 61–86.

———. "Surviving in Babel? Language Rights and European Integration," in *The Protection of Minorities and Human Rights*, edited by Yoram Distein and Mala Tabory. Dordrecht, Boston-London: Martinus Nijhoff, 1992: 277–300.

Edward, David And Niham Nic Shuibhne. "Continuity and Change in the Law Relating to Services," in *Continuity and Change in EU Law: Essays in Honour of Sir Francis Jacobs*, edited by Anthony Arnull, Piet Eeckhout, and Takis Tridimas. Oxford: Oxford University Press, 2009: 243–259.

Grin, François; Claudio Sfreddo, and François Vaillancourt. *The Economics of the Multilingual Workplace*. New York: Routledge, 2010.

Hatzopoulos, Vasilis. "Recent Developments of the Case Law of the ECJ in the Field of Services," *Common Market Law Review* 37, (2000): 43–82.

Hatzopoulos, Vassilis. "Exigences essentielles, impératives ou impérieuses: Une théorie, des théories ou pas de théorie du tout?" *Revue Trimestrielle de Droit Européen* 34, no 2 (1998): 191–236.

Jarvis, Malcom A. *The Application of EC Law by National Courts: The Free Movement of Goods*. Oxford: Clarendon Press, 1998.

Kymlicka, Will. *Multicultural Citizenship: A Liberal Theory of Minority Rights*. Oxford: Oxford University Press, 1996.

Littoz-Monnet, Annabelle. *The European Union and Culture: Between Economic Regulation and European Cultural Policy*. Manchester: Manchester University Press, 2007.

McGonagle, Tarlach. "The Quota Quandary," in *The European Union and the Culture Industries*, edited by David Ward. Aldershot: Ashgate Publishing, 2008: 187–212.

Milian, Antoni. *Globalización y requisitos lingüísticos: Una perspectiva juridical*. Barcelona: Atelier, 2008.

Mortelmans, Kamiel J.M. "The Functioning of the Internal Market," in *The Law of the European Union and the European Communities*, edited by Paul Joan George Kapteyn et al. Dordrecht: Kluwer Law International, 2008: 575–784.

Nic Shuibhne, Niamh. "Labels, Locals and the Free Movement of Goods," in *Culture and European Union Law* edited by

Rachael Craufurd Smith. Oxford: Oxford University Press, 2004: 81–112.

———. *EC Law and Minority Language Policy: Culture, Citizenship and Fundamental Rights*. The Hage, London, NY: Kluwer Law International, 2002.

Palermo, Francesco. "The Use of Minority Languages: Recent Development in EC Law and Judgments of the ECJ," *Maastricht Journal of European and Comparative Law* 8, no 3 (2001): 299–318.

Pentassuglia, Gaetano. *Minorities in International Law: An Introductory Study*. Strasbourg: Council of Europe Publishing, 2007.

Plender, Richard. "Equality and Non-Discrimination in the Law of European Union" *Pace Int'l L. Rev.* Vol 7, no 57 (1995): 57–80.

Prat, Carles. "La llengua a Catalunya en el context del mercat interior: Una revisió del concepte de 'mesura d'efecte equivalent'" *Revista de Llengua i Dret* 32 (1999): 65–114.

Psychogiopoulou, Evangelia. *The Integration of Cultural Considerations in EU Law and Policies*. Leiden: Martinus Nijhoff Publishers, 2004.

Scott, Joanne. "Mandatory or Imperative Requirements in the EU and the WTO," in *The Law of the Single European Market: Unpacking the Premises*, edited by Catherine Bernard and Joane Scott. Oxford/ Portland: Hart Publishing, 2002: 269–294.

Toggenburg, Gabriel N. "The EU's Linguistic Diversity: Fuel or Brake to the Mobility of Workers," in *Cross-Border Human Resources, Labor and Employment Issues: Proceedings of the New York University 54th Annual Conference on Labor Law*, edited by Andrew P. Morriss and Samuel Estreicher. New York: Kluwer International, 2004: 675–721.

Urrutia, Iñigo and Lasagabaster, Iñaki. "Language Rights and Community Law" *European Integration online Papers* 12, no 4 (2008): 1–34.

Urrutia, Iñigo. "Libre competencia, prohibición de ayudas de Estado y fiscalidad lingüística," in *Estudios Jurídicos sobre Fiscalidad Lingüística: Incentivos Fiscales como instrumento de Política Lingüística*, edited by I. Urrutia et al. Cizur Menor: Aranzadi/Thomson/Reuters, 2010: 43–197.

———. "The Legal Regime of Languages in European Union Law," *Revue Juridique Themis* 3, no 40 (2006): 707–743.

Vanhamme, Jan. "L'équivalence des langues Dans le marché intérieur; l'apport de la Cour de Justice," *Cahiers de droit européen* no 359 (2007): 359–380.

Weber, Robert F. "Individual Rights and Group Rights in the European Community's Approach to Minority Languages," *Duke Journal of Comparative & International Law* 17 (2007): 361–413.

3
The Language Rights of Minorities in Europe
A Critical Look at the Law and Practice

Fernand de Varennes

"To have another language is to possess a second soul."
—Quote attributed to Charlemagne (Carolus Magnus), eighth century

Though frequently invoked with some abandon, the expression "language rights" or "linguistic rights" is one that may involve very different or even contradictory meanings, depending on whether a sociolinguist, a philosopher or an educator is using the term. Even within the same discipline such as law, there is widespread diversity, even disagreement, as to what the expression means, from a legal point of view. What is undeniable on the one hand, is that internationally there have been in the last few decades some very significant developments in relation to the language rights of minorities from a legal point of view, particularly, but not exclusively in Europe. On the other hand, these advances have not come as far as one may assume or has been suggested: the actual rights or protections that may be recognized are often much more restricted in legal terms than seems initially to be the case, these also usually suffer from extremely weak enforcement mechanisms and unfortunately, there remains resistance in a number of states that are uneasy with the very concept of language rights or any kind of "identity" claims.

Development and Continued Unease over Language Rights: What Is It All About?

There remains a great deal of uncertainty and even unease both in terms of state practices and academic writing over language and minority rights.[1] Minorities, such as the Basque and the Catalans in Spain, the Malay of south Thailand, the Irish in Northern Ireland, indigenous peoples around the world and many other vulnerable groups are likely to continue experiencing resistance in the field of language rights due to a backlash that seems to be occurring, and a growing, not to say surprising, refusal from governments to comply with their international, legal obligations in the area of language preferences.

For some, language rights are a category of new cultural rights that are collective, or at the very least not traditional human rights, and therefore, probably less worthy of recognition and respect.[2] For others, there is no such thing as language rights in international law, except for a few specialized treaties that recognize such rights.[3] This second view tends to be the position of those who believe that a state's sovereignty—and a country's official language—is beyond the reach of human rights and international law.[4]

---

1. More generally, many object to the concept of minority rights in the sense that these might involve collective rights—perceived as a completely unacceptable category of rights—since these go against the individualistic nature of human rights as emerged after the Second World War and underscored in the *Charter of the United Nations*. For others, only individuals can be the holders of rights; see Rand, *The Virtue of Selfishness*, 101: 'Any group or "collective," large or small, is only a number of individuals. A group can have no rights other than the rights of its individual members.'
2. While there are a few scattered rights that relate to culture in various international treaties, there is no treaty on cultural rights as such. One attempt to bring together cultural rights in a non-binding declaration gave rise to the 2007 *Fribourg Declaration on Cultural Rights*. Language rights do not figure prominently in this document. Though this 20-year initiative did have the support of UNESCO, it has still not become an official UN or UNESCO text, and remains therefore simply a 'private' initiative. See the English text of the *Declaration* at www.unifr.ch/iiedh/assets/files/eng-declaration3.pdf, last accessed on April 7, 2011.
3. These include in particular the Council of Europe's *Framework Convention for the Protection of National Minorities*, text available at conventions.coe.int/Treaty/en/Treaties/html/157.htm (last accessed on April 7, 2011) and *European Charter on Regional or Minority Languages*, available at conventions.coe.int/Treaty/EN/Treaties/Html/148.htm (last accessed April 7, 2011).
4. See the dissenting opinion of a few members of the United Nations Human Rights Committee in *Diergaardt v. Namibia*, Communication No. 760/1997,

Nevertheless, there have been in recent decades a number of legal and political developments internationally and regionally that have, if at times timidly, given the nod to some form of rights or obligations relating to language. Indeed, one can actually identify three different types of language rights that have been taking shape since the Second World War: while the expression "language rights" and "linguistic rights" may have a certain convenience to it, what is often not appreciated is that these actually refer to three quite different forms of rights or protections from a legal point of view in international law.

Legal protection for endangered languages.

1. Legal recognition of obligations for the protection and promotion of linguistic diversity.
2. Legal protection of human rights (especially, but not exclusively of minorities, national minorities or indigenous peoples) that have a linguistic impact.

Part of the unease, or at very least the widespread disagreements and confusion, partially lie in the fact that different parties may be referring to very different types of rights or obligations and not acknowledging that language rights—and this is at least true in a legal sense—probably should most accurately be thought of as containing different strands of measures, each following very different paths and objectives. These different legal strands or approaches are due in no small part to the very nature of international law. It is, after all, law created by states mainly through treaties adopted for different reasons over time, and because of this, language issues have also appeared for different reasons and pursuant to different objectives in different treaties.

The Different "Language Rights" Approaches in International Law

According to Ahmed Djoghlaf in his *Biological Diversity and Culture Diversity or the Compents of Life on* Earth,

> A language is not only a technical means of communication between human beings. It is also a vehicle for expressing

U.N. Doc. CCPR/C/69/D/760/1997 (2000), where they stated amongst others that: 'Once a State party has adopted any particular language or languages as its official language or languages, it would be legitimate for the State party to prohibit the use of any other language for official purposes and if the State party does so, its action cannot be branded being in violation [of international human rights obligations].'

> emotions and transferring cultural, social, ethical and spiritual values. Uniting communities, it is an integral part of their identity heritage and their distinctive integrity. A language is also and above all a treasure of ancestral knowledge and a real living encyclopaedia of traditional knowledge, passed down, orally in the majority of cases, from one generation to another. Through the centuries, the peoples of the world, the indigenous populations in particular, have accumulated traditional knowledge of irreplaceable value that is disappearing as ancient tongues become extinct.[5]

A better understanding of the different meanings of "language rights," at least from a legal perspective, can therefore be reached by describing what each of these approaches actually involves and what kind of protection rights are legally recognized, if any.

There is a first category of international legal instruments that has emerged in response to this phenomenon of the rapid, and even accelerating disappearance of languages globally. The six thousand or so languages in the world are extremely diverse, some only spoken by a few individuals, others spoken of course by hundreds of millions. Often quoted data from UNESCO suggests that more than 50 percent of the world's languages are in grave danger and could disappear within one to four generations, and that at least one language disappears every two weeks. If that were not bad enough, it is clear that the rate of language extinction has increased dramatically in the last few hundred years, especially following the colonization of various parts of the globe by European powers after the fifteenth century.

As a result of what many feel is an unfortunate and even cataclysmic phenomenon,[6] a very small number of treaties have been adopted by the international community to provide a timid global law response to the extinction of so many languages and the treaties are intended to provide some protection, more or less directly, for endangered languages. The first such treaty that is sometimes mentioned as arguably being useful in protecting endangered languages—if somewhat tangentially—is the 1992 *Convention on Biological Diversity*.[7] The link between biological and

5. Ahmed Djoghlaf, *Biological Diversity and Cultural Diversity or the Components of Life on Earth*.
6. See generally for example Nettle and Romaine, Vanishing Voices: The Extinction of the World's Languages; The Tragedy of Dying Languages, BBC News, February 5, 2010, news.bbc.co.uk/2/hi/8500108.stm, last accessed April 8, 2011.
7. Opened for signature in Rio de Janeiro on June 5, 1992, entered into force on December 29, 1993.

linguistic diversity is often described in quite eloquent terms:

> There is an inherent link between linguistic and cultural diversity and biological diversity. . . . Linguistic erosion is . . . a corrosive element of collective memory and of the identity and integrity of human communities; it is also a manifestation of the loss of biological diversity. Languages, such as we know them today, are the result of an age-old evolution. They first appeared in Africa more than 150,000 years ago and spread around the world. Language is an integral part of the cultural and civilization heritage of the peoples of the world. Biological diversity is also the result of millions of years of evolution of life on earth. . . . Ecosystems provide the essential needs of life, protection from natural disasters and diseases and constitute the very foundation of human culture. Ecosystems and life on earth, including its cultural, spiritual and ethical dimension, are therefore co-substantial.[8]

As inspiring as the above speech is, the *Convention on Biological Diversity* doesn't actually refer to the need to protect endangered languages: at most, language could be said to fall under the purview of provisions dealing with culture, traditions or knowledge—and even this is quite a stretch since the most relevant section, Article 8(j), only requires state:

> To preserve and maintain knowledge, innovations and practices of indigenous and local communities embodying traditional lifestyles relevant for the conservation and sustainable use of biological diversity and promote the involvement of the holders of such knowledge, innovations and practices and encourage the equitable sharing of the benefits arising from the utilization of such knowledge, innovations and practices.

The absence of any reference to language diversity itself, or the desirability of protecting endangered languages anywhere in the treaty is suggestive that this legal instrument's usefulness might be quite limited. In addition, the document does not create any rights for either individuals or indigenous communities to enforce any kind of obligations under the *Convention*. At most, it creates legal obligations for the governments of those states that have ratified the treaty, mainly to elaborate National Biodiversity Strategies and Action Plans, (NBSAP) and submit a periodic national report on the status of implementation of the treaty—but

8. *Biological Diversity and Cultural Diversity or the Components of Life on Earth*, Address by Dr Ahmed Djoghlaf, Executive Secretary of the Convention on Biological Diversity to the 47th Annual General Meeting of the Canadian Commission for UNESCO, Ottawa, March 16, 2007, available at www.cbd.int/doc/speech/2007/sp-2007-03-16-unesco-en.pdf. Accessed April 10, 2011.

not much else. Without diminishing the value of this agreement and its potential impact in addressing issues of biological diversity, it is amply clear that the document has no real impact and cannot play a role of any significance in saving languages from extinction, though as indicated earlier it is sometimes referred to as potentially one such tool.

More convincingly and accurately however, the UNESCO 2003 *Convention for the safeguard of intangible cultural heritage*[9] appears to be a treaty that does address language disappearance in its provisions, though it is still a weak legal instrument. The treaty aims at developing safeguarding measures to ensure the survival of various forms of intangible culture, including language, as explained in Article 2, as intangible cultural heritage "is manifested inter alia in the following domains: (a) oral traditions and expressions, including language as a vehicle of the intangible cultural heritage."

This treaty also only creates legal obligations on state governments and does not provide for any rights that could be exercised by individuals or communities. In addition, the types of possible measures envisioned are mainly in support of short-term projects and specific aspects of heritage of international interest, and only those proposed by governments occasionally. In other words, it does not create any direct entitlement to use or for the protection of indigenous or endangered languages as such. In reality it is left to the discretion of national governments to occasionally submit some kind of proposal for specific action that can then be supported—usually financially—by the UNESCO Fund for this purpose. While it is a legal instrument that does show an acceptance of the desirability of preserving some aspects of intangible heritage—including languages—and a willingness to take a small legal step in creating some kind of obligations, its potential impact remains vaporous to say the least, since it imposes no actual demands on governments to take concrete and tangible steps to address the massive difficulties and threats currently faced by thousands of languages around the world. It also means that in most cases, for most languages, this treaty has absolutely no significance—it will not affect or help the vast majority of endangered languages. At the risk of sounding too harsh, this *Convention* is mainly about folklore with no coercive effect on governments themselves, though as indicated earlier it nevertheless is a positive develop-

9. Adopted in Paris on October 17, 2003, entered into force on April 20, 2006.

ment in attitude, if not so much in actions in relation to the exponential disappearance of languages globally.

The second category of treaties that offer a quite distinct type of "language rights" from the first are those that aim to protect and promote linguistic diversity as such, and not only the languages that are endangered. As with the first category, this kind of instrument does not create any right that individuals or communities can exercise directly, rather they create obligations for ratifying states to take steps in favor of the maintenance of languages in general—and not only those on the verge of extinction. There are at least two treaties that fall clearly within this category: the first and most developed being the 1992 *European Charter for Regional or Minority Languages*,[10] and the other much weaker instrument at the international level being the 2005 UNESCO *Convention on the Protection and Promotion of the Diversity of Cultural Expressions*.[11]

In many respects a ground-setting legal document, the type of linguistic diversity that the *European Charter for Regional or Minority Languages* seeks to protect—or as it is stated in its Article 7 because of "the need for resolute action to promote regional or minority languages in order to safeguard them"—remains however limited, since in theory its provisions only apply to languages traditionally used in a country, thus excluding languages used by recent immigrants, though theoretically it might be possible for a state to extend the treaty to non-traditional languages. In addition, the treaty excludes the protection of dialects (without clarifying what distinguishes a dialect from a language) and of a state's official language(s) (such as Irish in Ireland). In addition, a government may limit the application of the treaty upon ratification to only a number of prescribed languages—thus making it possible for a state to ratify and exclude a significant language—or even perhaps all minority languages—from the purview of the instrument's application.

Despite these limitations, the *European Charter for Regional or Minority Languages* represents a major breakthrough in international law, as it contains very detailed provisions for each lan-

10. Adopted on November 5, 1992, entered into force on March 1, 1998. Text of the treaty is available at conventions.coe.int/Treaty/EN/Treaties/Html/148.htm (last accessed April 7, 2011).

11. Adopted on October 20, 2005, entered into force on March 18, 2007. Available at www.unesco.org/new/en/unesco/themes/2005-convention/the-convention/ Last accessed April 10, 2011.

guage falling under this treaty for how and to what degree it must be used by state authorities, once again in theory, supposedly reflecting the situation of each language. According to one of the main fundamental principles of the treaty under Article 7, in other words, essentially following the principle of proportionality: the larger and more concentrated are those who use a regional or minority language, the greater the extent authorities should use that particular language. This is exemplified by part of Article 10 that shows that not all languages can—or should—be treated identically in relation to the use of minority or regional languages by administrative authorities:

> *Article 10—Administrative authorities and public services*
>
> 1. Within the administrative districts of the state in which the number of residents who are users of regional or minority languages justifies the measures specified below and according to the situation of each language, the Parties undertake, as far as this is reasonably possible:
>
>   a. . . .
>
>   i. To ensure that the administrative authorities use the regional or minority languages; or
>   ii. To ensure that such of their officers as are in contact with the public use the regional or minority languages in their relations with persons applying to them in these languages; or
>   iii. To ensure that users of regional or minority languages may submit oral or written applications and receive a reply in these languages; or
>   iv. To ensure that users of regional or minority languages may submit oral or written applications in these languages; or
>   v. To ensure that users of regional or minority languages may validly submit a document in these languages;
>
>   b. To make available widely used administrative texts and forms for the population in

the regional or minority languages or in bilingual versions;

c. To allow the administrative authorities to draft documents in a regional or minority language.

At the global level, linguistic diversity has gained recognition as a legal concern under the UNESCO *Convention on the Protection and Promotion of the Diversity of Cultural Expressions*. The UNESCO treaty, however, is very different from, and in many respects weaker than the *European Charter for Regional or Minority Languages*: whereas the *European Charter* can be used to impose legal obligations on governments to guarantee some degree of education in minority languages, for example, the UNESCO *Convention* simply cannot impose any such legal obligation. While it does create some legal obligations on states to protect and promote linguistic diversity, it is for the most part limited to a number of "promotional" actions, such as to encourage translations, and permits UNESCO to be involved in activities to promote linguistic diversity, such as the International Mother Language Day. Article 8 of this *Convention* shows the very limited obligations this treaty actually creates:

1. Without prejudice to the provisions of Articles 5 and 6, a Party may determine the existence of special situations where cultural expressions on its territory are at risk of extinction, under serious threat, or otherwise in need of urgent safeguarding.
2. Parties may take all appropriate measures to protect and preserve cultural expressions in situations referred to in paragraph 1 in a manner consistent with the provisions of this Convention.
3. Parties shall report to the Intergovernmental Committee referred to in Article 23 all measures taken to meet the exigencies of the situation, and the Committee may make appropriate recommendations.

Even if languages, as forms of cultural expression, were clearly endangered, Article 8 would not force a national government to take any steps to protect the linguistic diversity within its borders—Article 8 (1) and (2) above are only permissive, indicating that a state may take measures if it freely decides to do so—or conversely a government could also decide to do absolutely nothing. The only actual obligation is that states that have ratified this treaty must make a report to the Intergovernmental Committee set up under the treaty. Overall, and unlike what are set out as legal obligations under the *European Charter for Regional or Minority Languages*, nowhere is there in this treaty any obligation on states to use or protect any language. In practical terms then, the UNESCO *Convention* deals in a very minimal way with the need to protect or promote linguistic diversity, though it does signal a not so insignificant acknowledgement of the relevance of cultural and linguistic diversity issues to the international community.

There is finally a third category involving treaties that indirectly recognize a limited number of "language rights" as a consequence of protecting individuals as rights holders. This category involves a fairly large number of treaties protecting human rights, including those of specific groups such as indigenous peoples, minorities or even children. Individuals, through basic standards, such as freedom of expression, the right to private life, non-discrimination and other human rights, can in some situations obtain in a number of areas some form of protection or recognition of their language preferences in the following illustrative treaties: the International Covenant on Civil and Political Rights,[12] the International Covenant on Economic, Social or Cultural Rights,[13] ILO Convention 169 on Indigenous and Tribal Peoples,[14] the UNESCO Convention against Discrimination in Education, [15] the European Convention on Human Rights,[16] and the Framework Convention for the Protection of National Minorities.[17]

It is important to understand how exactly the legal obligations these instruments create are fundamentally different from the other categories of "language rights" previously mentioned.

12. Adopted by the United Nations General Assembly on December 16, 1966, entered in force March 23, 1976.

13. Adopted by the United Nations General Assembly on December 16, 1966, entered in force January 3, 1976.

14. Adopted by the General Conference of the International Labour Organisation on June 27, 1989, entered into force on September 5, 1991.

15. Adopted by the UNESCO General Conference on December 14, 1960, entered into force on May 22, 1962.

16. Formally known as the *Convention for the Protection of Human Rights and Fundamental Freedoms*, adopted on November 4, 1950, entered into force September 3, 1953.

17. Adopted by Council of Europe's Committee of Ministers on November 10, 1994, entered into force February 1, 1998.

Essentially, languages are not actually objects of protection in this third category as they were in the first two: these treaties give rights to individuals as subjects of international law, including in some cases individuals who are members of minorities or indigenous peoples. Languages, therefore, are not in themselves of any direct concern in this last category. What occurs, however, is that indirectly, the implementation of a particular human right may in effect have some kind of linguistic dimension.

While at first glance one might be forgiven in assuming that such indirect protection might not have much impact, in reality it can cover quite extensive areas of language use. The following list summarizes some of the more significant "language rights" in this category, which international jurisprudence has in recent years demonstrated can emanate indirectly from individual human rights standards:

- The right to use one's language of choice in private activities, including social, artistic, economic and any other private realm, based on the exercise of freedom of expression.[18]
- The right to a person's name or surname in his/her own language, through the application of the right to private life.[19]
- The right to secondary education in public schools in one's own language after receiving primary education in the same, in compliance with the right to private life and right to education.[20]
- For large concentrations of minority or indigenous language speakers, it is possible they also have a right to government services, such as public education, public health and social services, even government departments using minority or indigenous languages where this is reasonable and justified, in application of the prohibition of discrimination on the ground of language.[21] In addition, this is specifically provided for in the *Framework Convention for the Protection of National Minorities* as a distinct right (as

18. *Ballantyne, Davidson, McIntyre v. Canada*, Communications Nos. 359/1989 and 385/1989, U.N. Doc. CCPR/C/47/D/359/1989 and 385/1989/Rev.1 (1993).
19. *Raihman v. Latvia*, UN Doc. CCPR/C/100/D/1621/2007, October 29, 2010.
20. *Cyprus v. Turkey*, May 10, 2001 judgment of the European Court of Human Rights.
21. *Diergaardt v. Namibia*, Communication No. 760/1997, U.N. Doc. CCPR/C/69/D/760/1997 (2000).

are the other language rights only listed here).

One point that needs to be emphasized is that this category of language rights emanating as they do from human rights treaties is part of a relatively recent phenomenon—largely the result of decisions handed down in the last twenty years—and as a consequence not an area of international law that is well understood, even amongst jurists. These language rights are thus still very much a part of a developing field as to the potential of human rights in protecting particularly vulnerable segments of society, such as minorities and indigenous peoples—and indirectly sometimes their language(s).

Language Rights: Recognition and Resistance

While the above three categories of language rights certainly represent a positive change of attitude, even if at times the legal measures actually undertaken are far more timid than may be initially assumed: old habits die hard and the common practice by certain states may not be as strong or as clear as many would like and hope for.

For a long time there has been a tradition of language diversity in many parts of Europe and elsewhere—or at least of the desirability of recognizing any kind of language rights that would limit a state's sovereignty in language preferences[22]—which has had a great deal of influence and impact in many countries, and this has been linked to both left and right ideologies. Diversity of language and culture has sometimes been deemed to be dangerous and a threat to national unity because it has been perceived to discourage assimilation or integration, even to be backward. Under this logic, it is better not to recognize or support minority languages in order not to encourage segregation and separation. It is in a sense the view that one should not have divided or distinct identities within a state. At its worst, it is racist and intolerant: a kind of *Ein Reich, ein Volk, eine Sprache* that is not unique to any particular political ideology, or to put it differently, it can be found in any. Intolerance of the other is thus, not uniquely a trait of the right or left, as the following examples of John Stuart Mill and Friedrich Engels show. While it may be argued that such examples are selective and therefore not necessarily representa-

22. See the well-written presentation of the case for imposing only one language in a state in Patten, *The Justification of Minority Language Rights*, 102–128.

tive of the current political ideologies in the modern world, it could still nevertheless be maintained that the influence of these traditional "fathers" of the right and left has far from completely disappeared either politically and legally since clearly Western liberalism, as well as Marxism both continue to show ambivalent behavior toward linguistic and ethnic diversity and how the state show relate to it.

John Stuart Mill refers, for example, to the "half-savage" relics of past times like the Irish or Basques, and other inferior and more backward portions of the human race and that the world could only benefit from their being absorbed into the majority of a country:

> Experience proves it is possible for one nationality to merge and be absorbed in another: and when it was originally an inferior and more backward portion of the human race the absorption is greatly to its advantage. Nobody can suppose that it is not beneficial to a Breton, or a Basque of French Navarre, to be brought into the current of the ideas and feelings of a highly civilized and cultivated people—to be a member of the French nationality . . . than to sulk on his own rocks, the half-savage relic of past times.[23]

Friedrich Engels advances something quite similar, calling minorities "ethnic trash" that must lose their character—in the sense of identity including their own language—in the name of progress:

> There is no country in Europe which does not have in some corner or other one or more fragments of peoples, the remnants of a former population that was suppressed and held in bondage by the nation which later became the main vehicle for historical development. These relics of nations . . . this ethnic trash always became the fanatical bearers of counterrevolution and remain so until their complete extirpation or loss of national character, just as their whole existence in general is itself a protest against a great historical revolution.[24]

Left and right: they may both be in opposite ideological camps, but the similarity between the views held by Engels and Mills is striking: these nationalities or minorities were doomed to be absorbed, even eliminated, as far as their languages and cultures were concerned, all in the name of progress, development or uni-

---

23. Mill, *Considerations on Representative Government*. Available at oll.libertyfund.org/?option=com_staticxt&staticfile=show.php%3Ftitle=234&chapter=16569&layout=html&Itemid=27. Last accessed April 10, 2011.
24. Engels, *The Magyar Struggle*. Translation available at www.marxists.org/archive/marx/works/1849/01/13.htm. Last accessed April 10, 2011.

ty. Minority languages for many liberals and Marxists alike have for a long time traditionally been seen as obstacles to progress and development—and to some degree still do today.[25] For both Marxists and liberals, the "great nations" were the carriers of historical development. The smaller nationalities and their languages and identities were regarded as backward and stagnant. They were expected to abandon their identity and assimilate into the majority nation, *period*. At least, that was according to the *air du temps*, the Zeitgeist of the nineteenth and most of the twentieth centuries: progress and civilization demanded the assimilation of minorities. That was modernization and scientific progress.

That seems to have changed following the end of the Second World War and the acknowledgment that all this talk of national unity, scientific progress, modernization and "great nations" in the end also gave rise to state-endorsed policies of racial superiority and even policies of physical extermination of the *Untermenschen*—the "inferior peoples" that often seemed to include most ethnic minorities according to Engels and Mill. From the mid-twentieth century, the international community and many of the world's governments had accepted the need to have human rights integrated for the first time in international law and thus, restrict the sovereignty of the state to allow for the protection of all individuals, including minorities. This eventually led to an acknowledgment that part of what constitutes an individual is his or her identity, and that an individual's religious, linguistic and cultural characteristics also needed at times to be protected, especially against the harm of discrimination that had reared its head so fiercely in the days of the Nazi regime in Germany.

This eventually led also to the adoption of a number of documents or the recognition of events that acknowledged in a sense that diversity—and in particular linguistic diversity—is part and parcel of the human condition, and therefore, needs to be embraced rather than feared or despised, as can be seen in the following very brief list: the UNESCO *Universal Declaration on Cultural Diversity*,[26] the UN *Declaration on the Rights of Indigenous Peoples*,[27] the UN *Declaration on the Rights of National or Ethnic Religious or*

25. See generally on this point Leuprecht, 'Minority Rights Revisited: New Glimpses of an Old Issue.'"

26. Adopted unanimously by the 31st session of the UNESCO General Conference on November 2, 2001.

27. Adopted by the UN General Assembly on September 13, 2007.

Linguistic Minorities, [28] *The Hague Recommendations Regarding the Education Rights of National Minorities,*[29] the *Oslo Recommendations Regarding the Linguistic Rights of National Minorities,*[30] the *International Mother Tongue Day,*[31] and the *European Language Day.*[32]

While the above, and many others emanating from, for example, the United Nations, UNESCO, the European Union and the Council of Europe, certainly demonstrate a positive attitude toward language and diversity, as well as include an acceptance of the broad concept of language rights, they are not part of international law and have no real impact in relation to imposing legal obligations on states that would ensure the protection or promotion of minority or indigenous languages. Even the two legal instruments from the Council of Europe that do recognize some rights or obligations relating to language use and preferences from a legal point of view, the *Framework Convention for the Protection of National Minorities* and the *European Charter for Regional or Minority Languages*, must be acknowledged with a degree of disappointment or at least realistic caution in practice for the reasons outlined earlier.[33] The practice and enforcement of these two treaties is in addition nowhere close to what people may believe, and much weaker than is the case, for example, of the *European Convention on Human Rights*. While the *Framework Convention for the Protection of National Minorities* and the *European Charter for Regional or Minority Languages* are both treaties in international law, neither directly creates any language right that can be claimed by individuals in any court of law. Some of the other limitations that make these two treaties very pale legal documents can be summarized as follows:

---

28. Adopted by the UN General Assembly on December 18, 1992.
29. Organization for Security and Co-operation in Europe, *The Hague Recommendations Regarding the Education Rights of National Minorities*, High Commissioner on National Minorities, October 1996, available at: www.unhcr.org/refworld/docid/3dde52563.html (last accessed on April 10, 2011).
30. Organization for Security and Co-operation in Europe, *Oslo Recommendations Regarding the Linguistic Rights of National Minorities*, High Commissioner on National Minorities, February 1998, available at: www.osce.org/hcnm/67531 (last accessed on April 10, 2011).
31. Adopted by the UN General Assembly on May 16, 2009.
32. Proclaimed by the Council of Europe on December 6, 2001.
33. As a reminder, the reason the Council of Europe has two treaties with a degree of overlapping content in language matters is because the *Charter* is premised on the protection of language diversity itself, while the *Framework Convention* deals with language more indirectly as a result of protecting the human rights of individuals who belong to national minorities.

- Most language rights or obligations are not automatic in either the *Framework Convention* or the *European Charter,* since in relation to the use of any of the covered languages by public authorities they are usually limited to situations where justified, reasonable, or where the numbers of speakers of a language in part of a territory is substantial or sufficient;
- Neither treaty is directly enforceable in a court of law by individuals or groups unless there is legislation allowing direct enforcement in a country's judicial system;
- The *European Charter for Regional or Minority Languages* specifically indicates that it does not create any "right" at all for either individuals or communities–it only creates obligations on states.

On this last point, the reason the *European Charter* explicitly declares that it creates no right for any individual or group is that the object of the treaty is languages themselves, while the only subjects intended to have rights or obligations under the treaty are governments. As for the *Framework Convention*, its very title as a framework treaty has a very specific meaning in international law: it only contains provisions setting out objectives that governments undertake to pursue. In other words, the content of the treaty cannot be applied directly by individuals in a court of law, unless a national government were to decide to transform the treaties rights and obligations into the domestic legal system through some form of enabling legislation.

Finally, not only can neither treaty be invoked before the European Court of Human Rights or any other court of law, the only enforcement mechanism both provide for is an advisory committee. The main function of both committees is to consider every few years the periodic report of a state and the information provided by other interested parties, after which they can issue a report on how well or not a government is complying with its legal obligations and provide recommendations as to what should be done to improve the situation. While there is a political oversight role for the Council of Europe's powerful Committee of Ministers, it remains that there is no mechanism allowing individual cases to be dealt with, and that these two advisory committees can only make general recommendations and cannot rule on specific breaches involving individuals and either treaty. While there can be no doubt that this can be a useful "carrot" approach to bring governments into compliance with their international legal obligations, there is in truth, little in terms of a "stick" that can be used to attempt to enforce this compliance.

Is There a Backlash against Minorities and Their Rights—and a Reassertion of State Sovereignty and the "Tyranny of the Majority"?

More recently and worryingly, the rejection of international legal obligations involving minorities appears to be increasing in Europe, with a few countries starting to simply ignore these treaties altogether in rather surprising ways if it involves language, religious rights or minorities that are deemed by the majority "inconsistent with European values" or "troublesome."[34] Perhaps the most surprising—and to some embarrassing—example is the recent behavior of the United Kingdom in relation to the Irish minority in Northern Ireland.

The British government has since 2007 essentially refused to provide any response or to comply with its legal obligations under the *Framework Convention* in relation to the Irish language, religion or culture and the Irish Catholic minority. To the astonishment of many observers, the Irish of Northern Ireland have largely "disappeared" from the UK's last report in 2010[35]—clearly in breach of the government's legal obligations under the treaty. In what may be an interesting case example of overcompensation, the British government's official report often refers to how its census and various programs cover the situations of immigrants, the Roma and other groups of more recent arrivals to the country, although it remains obstinate about not dealing with the language and other rights of the Irish minority, except for one brief mention.

---

34. Although focusing on linguistic minorities, religious minorities in many European countries have increasingly been targeted by laws that reflect Western/Christian values, or as is sometimes stated, the rights of others, and even sometimes the rights of animals. Muslim minorities are increasingly subject to restrictions, particularly in the case of what Muslim women can wear in public. In the Netherlands, a law is being considered that would ban Jewish and Muslim traditions on the ritual slaughter of animals. Also in the Netherlands, individuals—both EU and non-EU citizens—who cannot speak Dutch will no longer be eligible for basic benefit payments.

35. Third Report Submitted by the United Kingdom Pursuant to Article 25, Paragraph 1 of the Framework Convention for the Protection of National Minorities, March 23, 2010, www.coe.int/t/dghl/monitoring/minorities/3_FCNMdocs/PDF_3rd_SR_UK_en.pdf (last accessed on April 10, 2011).

Thus, despite the British government often being considered to be a "good citizen and model" and the requests of the Advisory Committee, since 2007 British authorities have by and large ignored their obligations under what is commonly assumed to be one of Europe's strongest legal instruments for the protection of minorities. Since the treaty is only a framework document, individuals such as the Irish have no other legal recourse: on the one hand, the treaty appears to grant them certain rights, yet on the other the same treaty was intentionally crafted to deny to individuals any direct legal recourse in the case of any violation of these same rights.

Similarly to what the Northern Irish have encountered, the Basque and Catalan minorities in Spain have in recent years seen increasing restrictions on the use of their language: some private radio stations in Navarra are unable to obtain licenses to broadcast in Basque.[36] In addition, Spain's constitutional court in 2010 issued a ruling that may mean that Catalan—and presumably Basque—cannot be favored over Castilian/Spanish by regional governments, even in areas falling clearly within the regional government's jurisdictions.[37]

Even Europe's main protector of the human rights of all individuals, the European Court of Human Rights, has more recently seemed to be moving in a similar direction in relation to minority, and particularly language claims, concluding that governments could force on individuals a name and surname in the official language against their will in Lithuania and Latvia.[38]

Despite many aspects of language rights in Europe being well developed, particularly to the standard-setting impact of the two Council of Europe treaties, as well as most governments complying with their legal obligations in relation to language rights in these documents, not to mention the hopefully growing influence and impact from these treaties in the years to come, it re-

36. Irujo and Urrutia, "Basque in the Foral Community of Navarre (CFN)," 212–213; 216.

37. Milian-Massana, "Brief Discussion of the Language Regulations in the 2006 Statute of Autonomy of Catalonia and Spanish Constitutional Court Decision 31/2010 of 28 June." available at www.linguapax.org/fitxer/384/Language%20regulations_%202006%20Statute%20of%20Autonomy%20of%20Cataloni....pdf (last accessed on April 10, 2011).

38. See *Mentzen alias Mencena v. Latvia*, Decision on admissibility of 7 December 2004, European Court of Human Rights, and *Tadeuš Klečkovski v. Lithuania*, Decision on admissibility of May 31, 2001, European Court of Human Rights.

mains that both treaties were intentionally very seriously limited by European governments and there appears to be a less tolerant attitude toward minorities, and even multiculturalism emerging in parts of Europe.[39]

Conclusion

In relation to language rights, while in more recent years there have been some negative developments, the overall situation should not be seen as too gloomy in Europe and elsewhere. Standards have emerged in the last few decades that fairly clearly set out the nature of state conduct in relation to language that should be respected and implemented, although it is a process still in its developmental stages, with many aspects that are not yet settled. This is particularly true in the case of the interaction between language rights and international human rights law. On the one hand, it is clear that the choice of an official language is not affected in any way by international human rights law. As in the case of an official religion, international law simply does not impose any preference. The European Court of Human Rights, in recent years, has on a number of judgments made this quite clear: "subject to the rights protected by the Convention, each Member State is free to impose and regulate the use of its official language(s)"[40] On the other hand, despite states being free to choose their own official language in international law, they must still comply with human rights standards. In other words, whatever a government's official language policies or preferences are, they cannot result, for example, in your freedom of expression being breached, or in policies that are discriminatory. It is this point where there are at times tensions between official language practices and some human rights that have an impact in the area of language:

39. See 'David Cameron's muddled speech on multiculturalism', *The Economist*, February 11, 2011, at www.economist.com/blogs/bagehot/2011/02/britain_and_multiculturalism (last accessed on April 10, 2011); 'Sarkozy: le multiculturalisme, "un échec"', *Le Figaro*, February 10, 2011, at www.lefigaro.fr/flash-actu/2011/02/10/97001-20110210FILWWW00731-sarkozy-le-multiculturalisme-un-echec.php (last accessed April 10, 2011); and 'Angela Merkel declares death of German multiculturalism', *The Guardian*, October 17, 2010, at www.guardian.co.uk/world/2010/oct/17/angela-merkel-germany-multiculturalism-failures (last accessed April 10, 2011).
40. *Mentzen alias Mencena v. Latvia*, Decision on admissibility of December 7, 2004, European Court of Human Rights.

- 1993 *Ballantyne v. Canada*:[41] the UN Human Rights concluded that the right to use a language in private activities was covered by freedom of expression. The official language policies of the government of Québec that banned non-French commercial signs were therefore in violation of this "language right" under freedom of expression. Nevertheless, because protecting and promoting the French language were deemed legitimate, steps to require French—in addition to your own language of choice—would be possible.

- 2000 *Diergaardt v. Namibia*:[42] the UN Human Rights Committee was of the opinion that a minority language, Afrikaans in Namibia, had to be used to some degree by administrative authorities in addition to English, the country's only official language, in order to comply with non-discrimination issues on the grounds of language, since there was no explanation why only using English was reasonable and justified in the circumstances in exclusion of any use of Afrikaans.

- 2001 *Cyprus v. Turkey*:[43] the European Court of Human Rights concluded that the official language policies in Northern Cyprus breached the rights to education and private life, which in that particular context included the right to be instructed in Greek in a secondary level state school rather than in Turkish, the official language, or English.

Language rights such as the freedom to use one's own language in private activities, to have one's name in one's own language, to be educated in state schools using a minority language as language of instruction in some still unclear situations where you have substantial enough numbers and where it is reasonable and justified, following broadly what could be described as the principle of proportionality, and even to have government officials respond in a non-official, minority language, all of these situ-

41. *Ballantyne, Davidson, McIntyre v. Canada*, Communications Nos. 359/1989 and 385/1989, U.N. Doc. CCPR/C/47/D/359/1989 and 385/1989/Rev.1.
42. *Diergaardt v. Namibia*, Communication No. 760/1997, U.N. Doc. CCPR/C/69/D/760/1997 (2000).
43. *Cyprus v. Turkey*, May 10, 2001 judgment of the European Court of Human Rights.

ations have been recognized, at least in some situations, as being protected under international human rights standards, and that these human rights must, from a legal point of view prevail over a state's official language policies, even in a case such as *Diergaardt v. Namibia* where the country's constitution mandates an exclusive official language.

The third category of language rights which show the potential of a small number of human rights to cover matters of language use and preferences is, however, from an international legal point of view, not yet well understood or appreciated. This will be part of a continuing evolution that will take many more years to coalesce and be clarified.

The evolution of these three broad categories of language rights in international law—while all positive developments—will not be able to dam the flood of languages that are likely to disappear this century, especially when one keeps in mind the very limited and timid obligations these treaties impose on states in most cases. At the same time though, the prevailing Zeitgeist is at least much more sympathetic to language rights and diversity than in the past. To a large degree—despite some holdouts—the notion that we should all be identical ethnically, religiously or linguistically seems to have been rejected—though not entirely or everywhere as strongly as might be hoped for.

The future of language rights in Europe and elsewhere, looking at these continuing legal developments, should probably be one of cautious optimism, even if there has been some significant progress, especially with the Council of Europe, and it seems that there has been some dramatic changes in terms of the legal treatment as well as the political and perhaps also public perception of the importance and place of languages in society. One could suggest that many today would agree that language diversity is an asset, a richness that needs to be embraced, protected and promoted. At the same time, not all is what it seems, and the legal measures approved in Europe are not necessarily as dramatic in their influence and impact as one might initially think, this being due to their timid content and their weak obligations on governments.

Unfortunately, while there has been undeniable progress from a legal point of view, there continues to be resistance, and some degree of backsliding in terms of enforcement and commitment in practice, which means that minorities and indigenous peoples in Europe and elsewhere must be doubly vigilant and proactive in demanding what is increasingly acknowledged in human rights law and other treaties as a fundamental aspect of everyone's identity: their own language.

Bibliography

"Angela Merkel declares death of German multiculturalism." *The Guardian*. October 17, 2010. January 20, 2014. www.guardian.co.uk/world/2010/oct/17/angela-merkel-germany-multiculturalism-failures.

Ballantyne, Davidson, McIntyre v. Canada, Communications Nos. 359/1989 and 385/1989, U.N. Doc. CCPR/C/47/D/359/1989 and 385/1989/Rev.1 (1993).

BBC News. "The Tragedy of Dying Languages." February 5, 2010. January 20, 2014. news.bbc.co.uk/2/hi/8500108.stm.

Council of Europe. *European Convention on Human Rights*. Rome, November 4, 1950.

———. *European Charter for Regional or Minority Languages*. Strasbourg: November 5, 1992. January 20, 2014. https://conventions.coe.int/Treaty/EN/Treaties/Html/148.htm.

———. *Framework Convention for the Protection of National Minorities*. Strasbourg: February 1, 1995. January 20, 2014. http://conventions.coe.int/Treaty/en/Treaties/html/157.htm.

———. *Fribourg Declaration on Cultural Rights*. January 20, 2014. http://www.unifr.ch/iiedh/assets/files/Declarations/declaration-eng4.pdf.

———. Third Report Submitted by the United Kingdom Pursuant to Article 25, Paragraph 1 of the Framework Convention for the Protection of National Minorities. Strasbourg: March 23, 2010. January 20, 2014. www.coe.int/t/dghl/monitoring/minorities/3_FCNMdocs/PDF_3rd_SR_UK_en.pdf.

"David Cameron's muddled speech on multiculturalism." *The Economist*, February 11, 2011. January 20, 2014. www.economist.com/blogs/bagehot/2011/02/britain_and_multiculturalism.

Djoghlaf, Ahmed. *Biological Diversity and Cultural Diversity or the Components of Life on Earth*. 47th Annual General Meeting of the Canadian Commission for UNESCO. Ottawa, March

16, 2007. April 10, 2011. www.cbd.int/doc/speech/2007/sp-2007-03-16-unesco-en.pdf.

Engels, Friedrich. *The Magyar Struggle*. April 10, 2011. www.marxists.org/archive/marx/works/1849/01/13.htm.

European Court of Human Rights. *Cyprus v. Turkey*. May 10, 2001.

———. *Mentzen alias Mencena v. Latvia*, Decision on admissibility. December 7, 2004. Case number 710740/01.

———. *Tadeuš Klečkovski v. Lithuania*, Decision on admissibility. May 31, 2001.

International Labor Organization. *Indigenous and Tribal Peoples Convention, 1989*. Geneva, 76th ILC session (June 27, 1989).

Irujo, Xabier and Iñigo Urrutia, "Basque in the Foral Community of Navarre (CFN)." In *The legal status of the Basque language today: one language, three administrations, seven different geographies and a diaspora*, edited by Gloria Totoricagüena, Iñigo Urrutia, 197-220. Donostia / San Sebastian: Eusko Ikaskuntza - Sociedad de Estudios Vascos - Society for Basque Studies.

Leuprecht, Peter. "Minority Rights Revisited: New Glimpses of an Old Issue." In *Peoples Rights. Collected courses of the Academy of European Law* 12, no 2, edited by Philip Alston, 111-26. 2001.

Mandela, Nelson. *Address to the People of Cape Town, Grand Parade, on the Occasion of his Inauguration as State President*, Cape Town, May 9, 1994. January 20, 2014. www.polity.org.za/article/sa-mandela-address-to-the-people-of-cape-town-on-the-occasion-of-his-inaguaration-09101994-2007-11-16.

Milian-Massana, Antoni. *Brief Discussion of the Language Regulations in the 2006 Statute of Autonomy of Catalonia and Spanish Constitutional Court Decision 31/2010. June 28*, 2010. April 10, 2011. www.linguapax.org/fitxer/384/Language%20regulations_%202006%20Statute%20of%20Autonomy%20of%20Catalonia.pdf.

Mill, John Stewart. *Considerations on Representative Government*. April 10, 2011. oll.libertyfund.org/?option=com_staticxt&staticfile=show.php%3Ftitle=234&chapter=16569&layout=html&Itemid=27.

Nettle, Daniel and Suzanne Romaine. *Vanishing Voices: The Extinc-*

tion of the World's Languages. USA: Oxford UP, 2002.

Organization for Security and Co-operation in Europe. *Oslo Recommendations Regarding the Linguistic Rights of National Minorities*. High Commissioner on National Minorities. February 1998. April 10, 2011. www.osce.org/hcnm/67531.

———. *The Hague Recommendations Regarding the Education Rights of National Minorities*, High Commissioner on National Minorities, October 1996. April 10, 2011. www.unhcr.org/refworld/docid/3dde52563.html.

Patten, Alan. "Survey Article: The Justification of Minority Language Rights." *Journal of Political Philosophy*, 17 no. 1 (March 2009): 102-28.

Rand, Ayn. *The Virtue of Selfishness: A New Concept of Egoism*. New York: Signet, 1964.

"Sarkozy: le multiculturalisme, 'un échec.'" *Le Figaro*, February 10, 2011. January 20, 2014. www.lefigaro.fr/flash-actu/2011/02/10/97001-20110210FILWWW00731-sarkozy-le-multiculturalisme-un-echec.php.

Third Report Submitted by the United Kingdom Pursuant to Article 25, Paragraph 2 of the Framework Convention for the Protection of National Minorities, March 23, 2010. January 20, 2014. www.coe.int/t/dghl/monitoring/minorities/3_FCNMdocs/PDF_3rd_SR_UK_en.pdf.

UNESCO. *Convention against Discrimination in Education*. Paris, December 14, 1960.

———. *Convention for the safeguard of intangible cultural heritage*. Paris, September 29-October 17, 2003.

———. *Convention on the Protection and Promotion of the Diversity of Cultural Expressions*. Paris, October 20, 2005. April 10, 2011. www.unesco.org/new/en/unesco/themes/2005-convention/the-convention/.

———. *Universal Declaration on Cultural Diversity*. November 2, 2001.

United Nations. *Convention on Biological Diversity*. Rio de Janiero, Brazil, 1992.

———. *Declaration on the Rights of Indigenous Peoples*. September 13, 2007. February 3, 2014. http://www.un.org/esa/socdev/

unpfii/documents/DRIPS_en.pdf.

———. *Declaration on the Rights of Persons Belonging to National or Ethnic, Religious and Linguistic Minorities*. December 18, 1992. February 3, 2014. http://www.ohchr.org/Documents/Publications/GuideMinoritiesDeclarationen.pdf. Accessed February 3, 2014.

———. *Diergaardt v. Namibia*, Communication No. 760/1997, U.N. Doc. CCPR/C/69/D/760/1997. (2000). January 20, 2014. http://www1.umn.edu/humanrts/undocs/session69/view760.htm.

———. *International Covenant on Civil and Political Rights*. New York. December 19, 1966.

———. *International Covenant on Economic, Social or Cultural Rights*. New York, December 19, 1966.

———. *Raihman v. Latvia*, UN Doc. CCPR/C/100/D/1621/2007. October 29, 2010.

4
Challenges for Minority Languages in Gaining More Top Level Domains on the Internet

Peter Gerrand

Minority language activists in Western Europe, especially in Spain, have taken significant initiative to exploit the potential of the Internet as a source of visibility and prestige for their languages, as well as extending their use in all aspects of daily life.[1] For a minority language, gaining visibility is the most minimal requirement to achieve formal recognition within the dominant cultures, but gaining prestige is vital to ensure continued use by the next generation of native speakers.[2]

For example, the first Basque online forum, EuskaraZ, appeared in 1992. The following year, the newly founded Open University of Catalonia (UOC) made the far-sighted decision to deliver all its courses—in Catalan—via the Internet. By the late 1990s, the Basque, Catalan and Galician regional governments were using websites to promote their regional languages and cultures. And in March 2001, Catalan became the second language to be used in Wikipedia, one month after the English version was initiated, and one month before any other language.[3] Many more examples of

---

1. Gerrand, *Minority Languages on the Internet*.
2. To quote Amadeu Abril i Abril, the strategist of the .cat campaign: "Prestige and glamour are important for sustaining a living language. You don't like being in the second league. It is important to demonstrate that Catalan, with its ten million speakers, is a top-division language."
3. Gerrand, *Minority Languages*, 237.

online initiatives by Basque, Catalan and Galician language activists are described elsewhere,[4] but the most impressive and historic initiative taken by any of the world's regional language activists has been persuading the custodians of the Internet's domain name system, the ICANN Board, to support a single, non-sovereign, language and culture with as a top level domain (TLD).

Creation of the .cat Top Level Domain

On September 15, 2005 .cat, the first Internet generic top level domain (gTLD) dedicated to a single language and culture, Catalan, was approved by ICANN. Five months later, the .cat registry was implemented and launched.[5]

In the following five years, .cat has met its proponents' key goals: to raise the visibility and prestige of the Catalan language and culture, to provide a major focus for Catalan ethnic identity, and to be an aggregator of global Catalan culture on the Internet.[6] For example, the more than a hundred Catalan community and cultural centers (*casals*) scattered around the world, as well as virtually all Catalan-language-using cultural, educational and other public organizations in Catalonia, use .cat domain names for their websites. Statistics from the .cat registry quantify how well the goals have been realized: by January 2011 more than 46,000 second-level domain names (e.g., fcbarcelona.cat for the Barcelona Football Club) were registered under .cat; and with more than 30 million webpages implemented, .cat now has the highest average figure (approximately 660) of webpages per registered domain name of all the TLDs—including .com, .net, and .org![7]

Despite this resounding success, it remains the sole TLD devoted to a minority or regional language, despite the best efforts of Basques, Bretons, Galicians, Scots, the Welsh, and others to achieve similar status. Why is this so?

ICANN's Governance Mechanisms

To understand the reasons, one must explore the politics controlling the governance and decision-making processes of ICANN,

---

4. Ibid., 202–238; "Promoting the Regional Languages of Spain Online."
5. Fundació puntcat, "A short history of .cat," at www.fundacio.cat/historia/en_index.html.
6. Gerrand, "Cultural Diversity in Cyberspace."
7. Gerrand, "Estadístiques del domini .cat" [Statistics of the .cat domain], at www.puntcat.cat/estadistiques/index.html

the body governing the Internet's domain name system.

The Clinton Administration created ICANN in 1998, following a period of international agitation for the reform of the governance of the Internet's domain name system, including the introduction of competition to the lucrative monopoly acting as both registry and registrar for the sole commercial TLDs: .com, .net and .org, during a period of exponential growth of the Internet (the "dot com boom").[8]

On July 1, 1997, as part of that administration's Framework for Global Electronic Commerce, the US president directed the secretary of Commerce to "privatize the management of the domain name system (DNS) in a manner that increases competition and facilitates international participation in its management."[9] Note the two driving principles were "competition" and "facilitating international participation"; the extent to which these driving principles lead to cultural diversity on the Internet depends crucially of course upon the actual processes which ICANN uses for implementing them.

ICANN was set up in November 1998 via a Memorandum of Understanding (MoU) with the US Department of Commerce (DOC).[10] The choice of the DOC as the governance agency for the Internet—rather than, say, the internationally focused US Department of State—confirms the prism through which the administration—and more chauvinistically, the US Congress—views the Internet. Because the Internet was created and nurtured with funding from successive US governments over its first thirty years, many US politicians tend to see it as being primarily a commercial asset of the United States. To be acceptable to the DOC, ICANN was set up as a not-for-profit US corporation, and was based in Marina del Rey, California.[11]

The MoU makes it clear that ICANN's role is to coordinate and manage the Internet's addressing system as the Internet evolves, and in doing so, to abide by four guiding principles: (1) stability (of the Internet); (2) competition; (3) private, bottom-up coordina-

8. Lindsay, "History of DNS Governance," 32–40.

9. National Telecommunications and Information Administration (NTIA), "Memorandum of Understanding between the U.S. Department of Commerce and the Internet Corporation for Assigned Names and Numbers," at www.ntia.doc.gov/ntiahome/domainname/icann-memorandum.htm.

10. Ibid.

11. So as to be close to the staff of the Internet Assigned Numbers Authority which provides the technical management of the Internet's root servers.

tion; and (4) representation: reflecting "the global and functional diversity of Internet users and their needs."[12]

The words "competition" and "private" clearly reflected the US government's view of ICANN's commercial role in the marketplace. On the other hand, the phrases "bottom-up co-ordination" and "global and functional diversity of Internet users" provided recognition of the strong grassroots, collectivist culture that had formed amongst the international participants within the Internet Engineering Task Force and the Internet's other technical support forums, who were responsible for the Internet's technical co-ordination and growth during (and beyond) its first thirty years. The phrase "global and functional diversity of Internet users" clearly recognized the desirability of involving the international user community in making decisions on changes to the Internet's global addressing system.

ICANN's mechanism for achieving "bottom-up co-ordination" is to delegate most—in theory, all—of its policy development to its constituent organizations, each of which is represented by elected members on the ICANN Board—see figure 4.1. In the case of policies on new generic top-level domains (gTLDs), the relevant constituency is the Generic Names Supporting Organization (GNSO). But the GNSO is itself formally composed of six different stakeholder groups: domain name registries, registrars, intellectual property interests, Internet Service Providers, business users and the noncommercial user constituency (NCUC). The NCUC would logically be a support base for minority languages and cultures, but these have not yet appeared on its agenda.

In the rest of this paper, it will be demonstrated that the Government Advisory Group (GAC) is the most powerful stakeholder in ICANN's organization, and provides the greatest challenges to minority language communities seeking new "linguistic and cultural community" TLDs (lcTLDs).

ICANN's Decision Making Processes Relevant to New gTLDs

ICANN's first major achievement, during 1999, in opening up international competition between domain name registrars for the lucrative .com, .net, and .org domains, satisfied its goal of

12. The MoU was superseded in 2006 by a Joint Project Agreement (JPA), which re-affirmed ICANN's role and its four guiding principles (NTIA 2006), and by an Affirmation of Commitments (ICANN 2009), which did likewise.

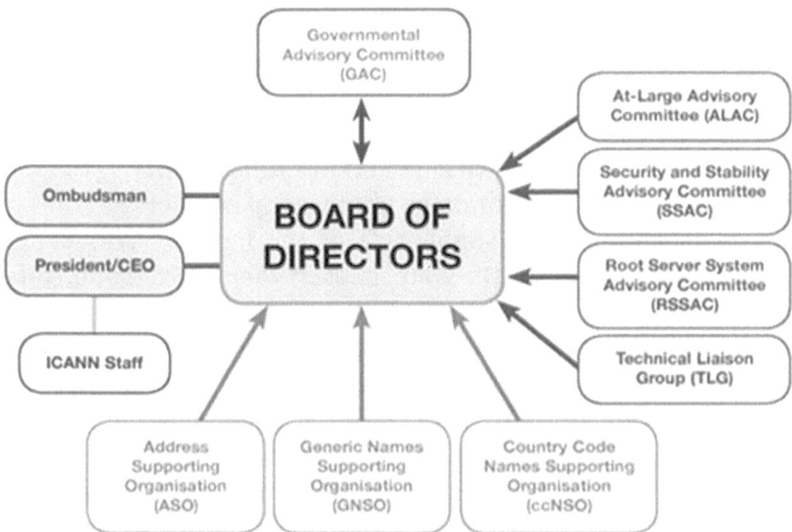

Figure 4.1. ICANN's "multi-stakeholder model" organization chart. The key influencers of policy on new gTLDS are the GNSO, GAC and ICANN Board members and staff. ICANN's positioning of the GAC at the top may have been unintentional, but is telling. A more detailed organizational chart can be found at www.icann.org/en/about/, in which the GAC is positioned less dominantly. Source: ICANN website, 2007.

competition without causing friction with its other three guiding principles (once a three-month registrar-testing phase in 1999 had demonstrated no harm to the Internet's stability). Indeed the additional revenues available to domain name registrars after 1999 enabled some of the strongest proponents of new lcTLDs, such as the CORE group of registrars, to gain additional cash flow to support their campaign for new lcTLDs (as well as promoting new gTLDs for "world cities" such as .bcn [Barcelona], .berlin, .paris and .nyc [New York City]).

But since 2005, tensions between stakeholders in ICANN's decision making on opening up the market to new gTLD registries have been acute, and have caused continuing postponements of ICANN's timetable for selecting new gTLDs[13]—to the frustration of several minority language communities.

Under ICANN's modus operandus of "private, bottom up coordination" and global "representation," new policies on domain

13. National sovereignty generally remains pre-eminent in the allocation of, and autonomous governance granted to, country code TLDs: the ccTLDs. The exception is where ICANN allows for supranational regional codes such as .eu (for the European Union) and .asia.

names should be developed through ICANN's General Names Support Organization (GNSO), while the ICANN Board makes the ultimate decisions on both the selection process and the granting of contracts to new gTLD registries.

The First Selection Round

The timeliness of the first selection round for new gTLDs, in year 2000, satisfied the concerns of most stakeholders.

The procompetition supply-side of the industry was happy, because seven new gTLDs were chosen (aero, biz, coop, info, museum, name, and pro), including direct competition to .com through new TLDs .biz and .info; and they would have noted that of the seven new TLDs selected by ICANN in 2000, all but one (.museum) were primarily intended for large-scale commercial use. The prostability stakeholders were content, because only seven new gTLDs had been added to the existing eight (let alone to the more than 250 country codes, the ccTLDs, that are also supported by the Internet's root servers). And most of the Intellectual Property constituents were satisfied, because a "sunrise" period of early registration at new TLDs provided an advantage to holders of trademarks and global brands. The noncommercial user constituency would have been pleased at the selection of a cultural TLD, .museum.

But to some insiders, the hidden role of the GAC in vetoing candidate TLDs had already become evident.

Since its inception, the ICANN Board has made public commitments toward achieving a high level of transparency and accountability of its decision making processes, including the holding of public Board meetings, and the posting of all its Board Minutes on its website. However, its Minutes prior to 2007 do not reveal two secret agreements between the GAC and the Board, both crucial to the allocation of new TLDs to minority languages.

The first secret agreement was exposed at the October 2000 meeting of ICANN in Marina del Rey, California, where the main business of the Board was to decide on the successful applications for new gTLDs in ICANN's first selection round. An application for the .per domain by Melbourne IT was excluded from the final short-listing by the Board; the reason provided privately by ICANN staff was that it was excluded because it was the three-letter ISO 3166 code for Peru, and that ICANN had made an agreement with the GAC that no ISO three-letter country codes would be allocated for any TLD unless it was specific to that country.[14]

The convenor of the campaign for .cym for the Welsh language [cymraeg], Hedd Gwynfor, was also informed of this agreement at an early stage in his inquiries with ICANN, as constituting a major impediment to the Welsh proposal for .cym, on the grounds that "cym" is the ISO 3166 three-letter country code for the Cayman Islands.[15]

Initially the Welsh persevered,[16] noting that ICANN has never issued a formal policy to exclude ISO 3166 three-letter codes from use for new gTLDs. And none of the ISO 3166 three-letter codes, such as .cym, have ever been implemented in the Internet domain name system.[17] Four years later, the Welsh proponents of .cym admitted defeat.[18]

However a second secret agreement between the GAC and the ICANN Board, having additional potential to scupper candidate lcTLDs, was exposed following the second selection round for new gTLDs.

The Influence of the GAC in the Second Selection Round

The second selection round, from 2003 to 2005, created six new gTLDs: asia, cat, jobs, mobi, tel, and travel. The .xxx proposal (for sexually explicit online material) was initially approved in principle by the ICANN Board in 2005, despite having been passed by ICANN's independent selection panels of experts. The ICANN Board then reversed its decision in May 2006 following lobbying by the GAC and the US DOC. But in a much later demonstration of independence, the ICANN Board reapproved the .xxx proposal on June 25, 2010.[19]

The nine-year, politically fraught campaign to win the .cat domain has been described elsewhere.[20]

Subsequently Richard Thwaites, the ITU's Liasion Officer on the ICANN Board during this period, wrote to me on July 2, 2007

---

14. Gerrand, *Minority Languages on the Internet*, 251.
15. Gwynfor, Hedd. E-mail to the author. January 24, 2006.
16. dotcym, "Should New Generic Top Level Names be Introduced?," ICANN ; Madoc-Jones, "The Case for a TLD for Wales," at www.bentham.org/open/tocommj/articles/V002/136TOCOMMJ.pdf.
17. Only the ISO 3166 two-letter codes are used for ccTLDs.
18. BBC News. "Wales Loses to Cayman Islands in Battle for .cym Domain."
19. Levine, "The .XXX Fiasco is Almost Over," *CircleID*, June 26, 2010 at www.circleid.com/posts/the_xxx_fiasco_is_almost_over/.
20. Gerrand, "Cultural Diversity in Cyberspace"; Gordillo, *Nació.cat*.

with these recollections:

> Thanks for drawing my attention to your published account [Gerrand 2006] of the establishment of the .cat TLD.
>
> The paper refers to Paul Twomey [ICANN's CEO and President] seeking support from the Spanish govt. As I recall, there were two levels to this. One (which you record) is the concerns held by several members of the ICANN Board faced with accepting or rejecting the establishment of .cat.
>
> The other level to this question is the more complex issue regarding the position of the Government Advisory Committee. The GAC had advised the Board on several occasions about the concerns of governments that registration of .cat would give comfort to regional secessionists in many parts of the world.
>
> ICANN's procedures do not require "approval" of any government for any decision (except, implicitly, the approval of the US Dept of Commerce for any action to be taken by the operators of the root registry). However, the Board and Executive (Paul Twomey) had responded to strong representations from the Government Advisory Committee that they would not approve any geographic name TLD if it was opposed by the national government of the region concerned. [...]
>
> Because .cat could be seen as referring to Catalonia (geographic) as much as to Catalan (linguistic), the Board in this case required that Paul Twomey have written assurance from the government of Spain that they did not object to .cat.
>
> The letter from the Spanish Minister was couched precisely in terms of "having no objection to" the .cat TLD, rather than positively supporting it. Prior to the change of government in Spain,[21] the ICANN Board had been informed that the Spanish central government would definitely oppose .cat. But in the light of the letter from the new Minister, several Board members, for whom the issue was essentially about government sovereignty issues, decided to support .cat.
>
> Those Board members with broader objections continued to oppose it, concerned about the ambiguous precedent that could be seen to blur the line between geographic and quasi-geographic TLDs that departed from the ISO 2-letter country code rule. The numbers at the end of the discussion were with supporters of .cat. [...] "
>
> In my view, the relationship between the GAC and the Board remains one of the thorniest and therefore most interesting issues for ICANN. ICANN's constitution does not allow it to recognize any national governments' claims of ownership over any geographical names, including ccTLDs. But the ICANN Board did not, in my experience, want to risk alienat-

21. in March 2004.

ing national governments to the point that ICANN's authority itself might be challenged. Geographic names as TLDs remain a very live issue on the Board agenda, as I understand.[22]

The Role of the GAC Post-2006

The GAC, reacting in part to proposals for "world city" gTLDs being floated during 2006, and perhaps also to the concerns expressed in ICANN circles about the GAC's lack of transparency, published the "GAC Principles regarding new gTLDs" on the ICANN website on 28 March 2007.[23] These GAC principles remain unchanged today.

The most important GAC principles, as far as regional and minority language proponents are concerned, are its paragraphs 2.1, 2.2, and 2.7:

> 2.1 New gTLDs should respect:
> a) . . .
> b) The sensitivities regarding terms with national, cultural, geographic and religious significance.
> 2.2 ICANN should avoid country, territory or place names, and country, territory or regional language or people descriptions, unless in agreement with the relevant governments or public authorities."
> 2.7 Applicant registries for new gTLDs should pledge to:
> a) Adopt, before the new gTLD is introduced, appropriate procedures for blocking, at no cost and upon demand of governments, public officials or IGOs, names with national or geographical significance at the second level of any new gTLD.

Minority languages with names having "no geographical significance,"[24] such as Romany or Yiddish, have only to deal with perceived cultural or religious sensitivities, if any, in the eyes of GAC members.

Paragraph 2.2 of the GAC Principles makes it clear that regional languages such as Welsh, Basque or Galician—even if they have

22. Thwaites, "ICANN 2005 and .cat," Canberra: email July 2, 2007 to author; quoted in full in Gerrand, *Promoting Minority Languages on the Internet*, 249–50.
23. ICANN Government Advisory Committee (GAC), "GAC Principles Regarding New gTLDs," at gac.icann.org/system/files/gTLD_principles_0.pdf.
24. i.e. the misfortune to no longer be the majority language in any city or region.

become global languages, through emigration—need to obtain the agreement of the relevant sovereign national governments to proceed as candidate gTLDs, if they are to avoid being vetoed by the GAC. However they do not need to obtain the agreement of other governments.

This is consistent with the GAC's role during the second selection round, where ICANN, in considering the candidature of .cat during 2004, requested that its proponent punt.Cat obtain formal letters in support from the governments of Spain (mentioned above) and Andorra, being the only sovereign states that give official status to the Catalan language.[25]

Formation of the lcTLD Community

Following the well-publicized allocation of the .cat domain, Amadeu Abril from the .cat registry (punt.Cat) was generous in meeting and giving advice to Galician, Basque, Welsh, Breton, Scots, and other would-be applicants for linguistic and cultural domains, from 2006 onward.[26] The various activists set up websites[27] to promote their causes, and began the process of enlisting support from regional and local governments, as well as relevant cultural organizations worldwide so as to demonstrate the existence of a significant global linguistic and cultural community.

The Current (Third) Selection Round

The preparation for a third round of applications for "generic" TLDs, gTLDs, has already taken more than four years,[28] and the detailed rules for the selection process, planned in 2010 to be finalized in the month of this conference (March 2011) have now been postponed again, for the third or fourth time.

Because of the longevity and uncertainty of the process, most regional language groups supporting new TLDs for their languages

25. Gerrand, *Promoting Minority Languages on the Internet*, 247.
26. See for example, Consello da Avogacía Galega [The Galician Law Society], "Reunión da Asociación PuntoGal" [Meeting of the PuntoGal Association], November 20, 2006, at www.avogacia.org/w3/article.php3?id_article=1562.
27. See for example, the Basques (www.puntueus.org), Bretons (www.pointbzh.com), Galicians (www.puntogal.org), Welsh (www.dotcym.org), and Scots (www.dotscot.com).
28. The ICANN Board formally launched its preparation of selection processes for its third (current) round of new gTLDs in June 2008, but its relevant policy-making constituent organization, the GNSO, had been working on the relevant policies since late 2005.

and cultures ceased to attend ICANN's international policy-making meetings, for a lack of funds, after 2008.

What are the reasons for the excessive gestation period in finalizing rules for the third selection process and inviting new applications?

The Competing Influences of ICANN's Major Stakeholders

The procompetition lobby, led by the domain name registrars, no doubt frustrated at the slowness of ICANN's second round, was successful from 2006 onward in the development of gLTD policy via the GNSO to promote the idea of ICANN releasing a virtually unlimited number of new gTLDs in its third selection round. Of course—as in the first round—new gTLDs would be required to meet predetermined, objective technical and business criteria, to be sufficiently differentiated to avoid confusion, and to collectively avoid threatening the stability of the Internet domain name system.

This proposal immediately set off alarm bells for the intellectual property (IP) constituency, led by members of the World Intellectual Property Organization, concerned about the increased potential for IP infractions. It also alarmed ICANN's business constituency (usually represented at ICANN meetings by their IP lawyers), who foresaw increased costs in having to defensively register their corporate brands over a huge number of new gTLDs. The US business constituency started to lobby members of the US Congress against any large-scale expansion of commercial gTLDs, while the IP constituency lobbied the ICANN Board directly to withhold approval until their concerns had been adequately addressed.

As mentioned above, the GAC was also troubled by the floating of "world city" names as gTLDs, with the possibility of such iconic brands being allocated by ICANN to commercial registries without any control by the relevant national governments. The prospect of an open-ended number of new gTLDs, selected purely on technical and financial criteria and ignoring issues of national sovereignty, was also a factor in causing the GAC to publish, for the first time in March of 2007, its own set of concerns and its broad criteria for potentially objecting to new gTLDs.[29]

The result of continuing objections from such powerful com-

29. ICANN Government Advisory Committee (GAC).

mercial and governmental lobby groups was to cause a several years delay as the most powerful stakeholders tried to resolve—or in some cases, abort—the policy development process. The GNSO, led by the registrars, went through several iterations of its proposed guidelines for gTLD applicants,[30] expanding the selection process to allow greater scope for objection filing, public comment and dispute resolution.[31] The ICANN Board has from June 2008 to March 2011 announced three successive intended launch dates for the gTLD Applicant Guidebook, only to have to postpone each in turn.[32]

In the meantime, the "linguistic and cultural community" activists representing regional language communities with hopes for cultural gTLDs were sidelined by the process. These groups found they did not have the financial resources to keep attending the GNSO policy development meetings, had no influence whatsoever through the GAC, and no longer had direct contacts on the ICANN Board through sympathetic GNSO representatives (such as Amadeu Abril in 1999-2003). The unequal power of ICANN's stakeholders had become starkly apparent.

The Critical Role of the Government Advisory Committee

ICANN's authority and legitimacy, since its creation in 1998, has been critically dependent on international support at two levels. First, from the global Internet user community (in ICANN's terms, its constituencies), whom it depends upon to contribute to its policy forums and, where relevant, to pay license fees to ICANN. Second, ICANN depends upon support from major national governments, whom ICANN hopes can collaborate within the GAC to resolve their internal disagreements before channeling their unanimous, or at least majority, views in communiqués to ICANN on policy issues. ICANN's successive Presidents have all understood this second political imperative well, which explains the ICANN Board's preparedness to allow the GAC to veto gTLD proposals such as .per, .cym and .xxx in advance of ICANN developing open policy principles that would have supported those decisions.

ICANN's accommodation of GAC's concerns paid off hand-

30. ICANN Generic Names Support Organization (GNSO), "GNSO policy work on new gTLDs," at gnso.icann.org/issues/new-gtlds/

31. ICANN, *gTLD Applicant Guidebook,* at www.icann.org/en/topics/new-gtlds/draft-rfp-clean-12nov10-en.pdf.

32. Gasser, Burkert, Palfrey, "Accountability and Transparency at ICANN."

somely in the lead-up to, and during, the two meetings of the World Summit Information Society in 2003 and 2005. The major powers supported ICANN when it was explicitly under attack from several third world countries, some of who proposed transferring governance of the Internet from ICANN to the International Telecommunications Union.[33]

However, the concerns within some ICANN constituencies on lack of transparency in the Board's decision-making processes continued. ICANN's new (and current) agreement with DOC requires ICANN to "maintain and improve robust mechanisms for public input, accountability, and transparency," and to appoint independent review teams to assess ICANN's performance in respect to this commitment.[34]

The first review of ICANN's accountability and transparency was conducted in 2010 by Harvard's Berkman Center for Internet and Society.[35] The Berkman Center has had a continuous, collaborative relationship with ICANN since its inception, often donating expert secretarial services for ICANN's public meetings during ICANN's early, under-funded years. The contribution of so many Harvard academics to the 2010 review has instilled greater confidence in its objectivity, while perhaps not in its insights. Significantly, the Berkman review concentrated on ICANN's formal communications with the GAC and its other constituencies, augmented by interviews largely restricted to ICANN staff and supporters. As a result, the conclusions are as a result rather bland and largely uncontroversial.

The Berkman report includes three detailed case studies, one being on the introduction of new gTLDs. It makes no specific adverse findings on failures of governance or transparency. It praises ICANN's "significant progress in improving its public participation mechanisms," but nevertheless, reports that "ICANN's greatest challenge ahead, despite significant recent efforts, remains corporate and board governance." Concerning solutions, however, "there is no straightforward way to address the various challenges that ICANN faces."[36]

---

33. Twomey, private discussion with the author, March 18, 2010, in Sydney.
34. ICANN, "Affirmation of Commitments by the United States Department of Commerce and the Internet Corporation for Assigned Names and Numbers," at icann.org/en/announcements/announcement-30sep09-en.htm#announcement.
35. Gasser, et al, "Accountability and Transparency at ICANN."
36. Ibid.

Recent Developments

In November of 2010, the ICANN Board held a special off-site meeting in Norway to resolve "four over-arching issues" that needed resolution before the Board could finalize the gTLD Applicant Guidelines, which inter alia define the detailed ICANN selection process for new gTLDs. The Board thought that it had achieved sufficient progress with all its key stakeholders to be able to announce the likely launch of the gTLD Applicant Guidelines in March 2011.[37]

However, the GAC made an unexpected intervention on February 23. It issued a "GAC indicative scorecard on new gTLD outstanding issues,"[38] which made it clear that it had several "overarching issues" of its own that required resolution. Of particular interest to the lcTLD community, the GAC advises ICANN,

> To reconsider its objection to an "early warning" opportunity for governments to review potential new gTLD strings[39] and to advise applicants whether their proposed strings would be considered controversial or to raise national sensitivities.

As this article is being written, ICANN is holding a consultation meeting with the GAC in Brussels, from February 28 to March 1, no doubt hoping to improve its scorecard sufficiently to get the GAC's blessing to proceed with the launch.

It is reasonable to conclude from ICANN's twelve-year history that ICANN cannot proceed with its current large-scale expansion of the domain name system, without first ensuring it has strong support for this initiative from both the DOC and the dominant members of the GAC.

Conclusions

While some influential futurists have predicted that national boundaries would not survive the transition to a global digital society,[40] the reality is that national sovereignty is still a powerful force in the Internet, not just in controlling local infrastructure, but also within the decision-making processes of ICANN, the cus-

---

37. The third launch date announced to date; now superseded.
38. ICANN Government Advisory Committee, "GAC Indicative Scorecard on New gTLD Outstanding Issues Listed in the GAC Cartagena Communiqué," at www.icann.org/en/topics/new-gtlds/gac-scorecard-23feb11-en.pdf.
39. Strings: the characters used in domain names, since a domain name is not necessarily a 'word'.
40. Negroponte, *Being Digital*, 7.

todian of the Internet's addressing systems.

Successive ICANN Presidents have recognized that ICANN needs broad support from national governments to ensure its ongoing legitimacy, and have therefore taken GAC advice very seriously. The consequent support from GAC members for ICANN, especially when it was under attack during the World Summit on the Information Society in 2003 and 2005, has been crucial for ICANN's continuing governance of the Internet's addressing systems. This lesson will not have been lost on ICANN's new President and Board members, who at the time of writing this article are still in negotiations with the GAC so as to avoid an embarrassing fourth postponement of the launch of the third selection round for new gTLDs. The continuing "governance deadlock" on new gTLDs does not reduce support for ICANN amongst the world's sovereign governments, but may reduce its authority amongst its grassroots constituencies.

Meanwhile, the "linguistic and cultural communities" have some consolation: the publishing of the GAC Principles in 2007 has provided transparency concerning the GAC's areas of sensitivity that can lead to the rejection of candidate TLDs, compared with its former behind-the-scenes veto process. Furthermore, the GAC's key principle 2.2 says,

> ICANN should avoid country, territory or place names, and country, territory or regional language or people descriptions, unless in agreement with the relevant governments or public authorities.

This can be logically interpreted in the following positive way, as indeed was the case for .cat: Country, territory or place names, and country, territory or regional language or people descriptions, are potentially acceptable as new gTLDs if agreement is reached with the relevant governments or public authorities.

Post Script

On June 20, 2011 in Singapore, the ICANN Board finally announced approval of the third selection round for new gTLDs based upon an eighth and final version of the gTLD Application Guidebook, published on May 30, 2011.[41] Applications for new gTLDs will be accepted from January 12 to April 12, 2012.

The conclusions of this paper remain unchanged concerning

41. ICANN, *New gTLD Applicant Guidebook*, at www.icann.org/en/topics/new-gtlds/comments-7-en.htm.

the challenges for linguistic and cultural communities in getting their candidate gTLD names approved. In particular, ICANN has "accepted that governments can raise objections to proposed new gTLD strings through the GAC," in other words, in confidential discussions, as an alternative to ICANN's original proposal that the open and transparent "Limited Public Objections" procedures, the only avenue for non-governmental objections, should also apply to governments.[42]

Nevertheless, ICANN's new Guidebook makes it clear that the ICANN Board is unlikely to accept objections from the GAC to a new gTLD application unless advised that it is the consensus of the GAC that a particular application should not proceed.[43] This seems designed to limit the vetoing of a particular gTLD application by a particular sovereign state, without the support of its peers.

Bibliography

"Affirmation of Commitments by the United States Department of Commerce and the Internet Corporation for Assigned Names and Numbers." *ICANN*. Accessed September 30, 2009. icann.org/en/announcements/announcement-30sep09-en.htm#announcement.

"A Short History of .cat." *Fundació puntcat*. Accessed 2010. www.fundacio.cat/historia/en_index.html (accessed 2010).

"Estadístiques del domini .cat: Statistics of the .cat domain." *Fundació puntcat*. Accessed February 2011. www.puntcat.cat/estadistiques/index.html.

Gasser, Urs, Herbert Burkert, John Palfrey, and Jonathan Zittrain. "Accountability and Transparency at ICANN: An Independent Review," in *Berkman Report*. The Berkman Centre for Internet and Society: Harvard University. nrs.harvard.edu/urn-3:HUL.InstRepos:4555854 (accessed October 20, 2010).

Gerrand, Peter. "Cultural Diversity in Cyberspace: The Catalan Campaign to Win the New .cat Top Level Domain," *First*

42. Government Advisory Committee, "GAC comments on the Applicant Guidebook (April 15th, 2011 edition)." at www.icann.org/en/topics/new-gtlds/gac-comments-new-gtlds-26may11-en.pdf.
43. ICANN. *New gTLD Applicant Guidebook*. Section 3.1, "GAC Advice on New gTLDs."

Monday, 11, no. 1 (January, 2006). firstmonday.org/htbin/cgiwrap/bin/ojs/index.php/fm/article/view/1305/1225.

———. *Minority Languages on the Internet: Promoting the Regional Languages of Spain*. Saarbrücken: VDM-Verlag:, 2009.

———. "Promoting the Regional Languages of Spain Online," *EuskoNews*, June 11, 2010. www.euskonews.com/0536zbk/gaia53603en.html.

Generic Names Support Organization. "GNSO Policy Work on New gTLDs." Accessed 2011. gnso.icann.org/issues/new-gtlds/.

Gordillo, Saül. *Nació.cat*. Barcelona: Mina, 2007.

Government Advisory Committee. "GAC Principles Regarding new gTLDs." Accessed March 28, 2007. gac.icann.org/system/files/gTLD_principles_0.pdf.

———. "GAC Indicative Scorecard on New gTLD Outstanding Issues Listed in the GAC Cartagena Communiqué." Accessed February 23, 2011. www.icann.org/en/topics/new-gtlds/gac-scorecard-23feb11-en.pdf.

———. "GAC Comments on the Applicant Guidebook (April 15th, 2011 edition)." Accessed May 26, 2011. www.icann.org/en/topics/new-gtlds/gac-comments-new-gtlds-26may11-en.pdf.

Gwynfor, Hedd. E-mail message to author, January 24, 2006.

"gTLD Applicant Guidebook: Proposed Final Version." *ICANN*. Accessed November 12, 2010. www.icann.org/en/topics/new-gtlds/draft-rfp-clean-12nov10-en.pdf.

"Joint Project Agreement between the U.S. Department of Commerce and the Internet Corporation for Assigned Names and Numbers." *National Telecommunications and Information Administration (NTIA)*. Accessed September 29, 2006. www.ntia.doc.gov/ntiahome/domainname/agreements/jpa/ICANNJPA_09292006.htm.

Levine, John. "The .XXX Fiasco is Almost Over," *CircleID*. Last modified June 26, 2010. www.circleid.com/posts/the_xxx_fiasco_is_almost_over/.

Lindsay, David. "History of DNS Governance." *International Domain Name Law: ICANN and the UDRP*. Portland: Hart, 32–40, 2007.

Madoc-Jones, Iolo. "The Case for a TLD for Wales." *The Open Communications Journal,* No. 2 (2008): 136–142.

"Memorandum of Understanding Between the U.S. Department of Commerce and the Internet Corporation for Assigned Names and Numbers." *National Telecommunications and Information Administration (NTIA)*. Accessed November 25, 1998. www.ntia.doc.gov/ntiahome/domainname/icann-memorandum.htm.

Negroponte, Nicholas. *Being Digital*. Knopf: New York, 1995.

"New gTLD Applicant Guidebook: Final Version." *ICANN*. Accessed May 30, 2011. www.icann.org/en/topics/new-gtlds/comments-7-en.htm.

"Reunión da Asociación PuntoGal" [Meeting of the PuntoGal Association]. *Consello da Avogacía Galega* [The Galician Law Council]. Accessed November 20, 2006. www.avogacia.org/w3/article.php3?id_article=1562

"Should New Generic Top Level Names be Introduced?" *dotcym.org*. Accessed February 1, 2006. gnso.icann.org/issues/new-gtlds/dotcym-01feb06.pdf.

"The Munich Conference on new TLDs." *Newdomains.org*. Accessed 2010. www.newdomains.org.

Thwaites, Richard. "ICANN 2005 and .cat." E-mail to author. July 2, 2007, in *Minority Languages on the Internet,* by Paul Gerrand. VDM-Verlag: Saarbrücken, 2009: 249–50.

Twomey, Paul, interview by Peter Gerrand. Sydney, Australia, March 18, 2010.

"Wales Loses to Cayman Islands in Battle for .cym Domain." *BBC News*. Accessed November 4, 2010. www.bbc.co.uk/news/uk-wales-mid-wales-11683239.

5
Language and Culture in Canadian Jurisprudence

Pierre Foucher

There seems to be a large consensus to the effect that language is intimately related to culture and represents one of its main avenues of expression. Language performs two main functions: an instrumental one, by which it serves as a means of communication; and one related to individual and collective identity and thus, linked intimately to culture. The instrumental value of language is important in itself because it enhances democratic participation and debate, as well as territorial and social mobility. This value of language is individually centered—the more a person knows many languages, the more she can communicate with the world. Language can also be understood as the expression of a "worldview," a manifestation of the culture of a people who speak a particular language, a reservoir of traditions, as well as a gateway to modernity. Language is then associated with culture, the way a people sees and interprets the world, the way it creates art, the way it takes place among nations.

But it is one thing to express doctrinal opinions and quite another to have them translated into a legal rule. Canadian courts have been making this link and using extensively the paradigm, "language-as-culture" as a tool for interpreting constitutional language rights when dealing with French language minorities across Canada, outside of Quebec. The present text intends to retrace the Courts' jurisprudence to this effect and to show how this link has become a primary rule of interpretation in Canadian jurisprudence around language rights and language legislation.

I have intentionally left out aboriginal language rights in Canada,[1] as well as jurisprudence dealing with the French majority and Anglophone minority in Quebec.[2] My aim here is more modest: I wish to illustrate how the jurisprudence surrounding the Francophone and Acadian communities in Canada relies heavily on the link between language and culture, and uses this link as a tool to give constitutional language rights a purposive, liberal and generous interpretation, based on their collective object, distinguishing them from the linguistic aspects of "basic" Human Rights.

The Legal Framework of Language Rights in Canada

Demographically, Canada is comprised of 24 percent of Francophones, about 20 percent who don't have French or English as their mother tongue, and 56 percent of English descent; the rest being of neither French nor English as a mother tongue.[3] Francophones are in a majority within Quebec, but there are also 1 million Francophones outside that province, half of them living in Ontario.[4] In New Brunswick, French-speaking Acadians are a majority in the north and east of the Province and represent one third of the total population. There are also Acadians in the other maritime provinces. Elsewhere in Canada, outside Quebec, Francophones are either the descendants of French Quebeckers or immigrants for whom French is a normal language of use.

The federal structure of Canada is partly due to the insistence

1. I do think that they are protected under s. 35 of the *Constitution Act*, 1982 (*infra*), but no case law so far has made this connection. A federal territory, Nunavut, has declared Inuktitut the official language alongside with French and English, and is taking steps to make it a practical reality: see *Official Languages Act (Nun)*, SN 2008 ch. 10, and *Inuit Language Protection Act* (Nun.), SN 2008 ch. 17.

2. When interpreting the rights of the English minority in Quebec, the courts have had a tendency to revert to a "language-as-communication tool" approach, singling out the individual aspects of language rights. See for instance *Ford v. Quebec* [1988] 2 SCR 712; *Solski v. Quebec*, [2005] 1 SCR 201; *N'Guyen v. Quebec* [2009] 1 SCR 826. This double-edged approach to the same language rights would need a much longer development that this paper allows.

3. These figures and the following ones are issued from the 2006 census, available online at: www.40.statcan.ca/l01/cst01/demo15-eng.htm (last accessed June 9, 2011).

4. See www40.statcan.ca/l01/ind01/l3_50000_50003-eng.htm?hili_demo11 (last accessed June 9, 2011).

of the French majority in Quebec. In the *Secession reference*, the Supreme Court said: "Federalism was the political mechanism by which diversity could be reconciled with unity."[5] The Court then acknowledged the fact that Quebec, being a minority within Canada, took advantage of the federal structure co-constituting itself as a majority within its own territory:

> The principle of federalism facilitates the pursuit of collective goals by cultural and linguistic minorities which form the majority within a particular province. This is the case in Quebec, where the majority of the population is French-speaking, and which possesses a distinct culture. This is not merely the result of chance. The social and demographic reality of Quebec explains the existence of the province of Quebec as a political unit and indeed, was one of the essential reasons for establishing a federal structure for the Canadian union in 1867. . . . The federal structure adopted at Confederation enabled French-speaking Canadians to form a numerical majority in the province of Quebec, and so exercise the considerable provincial powers conferred by the *Constitution Act, 1867 in such a way as to promote their language and culture.*[6]

A federation implies a division of legislative and executive powers between a central government and federated states; language has to be addressed as a legislative field. In Canada, no choice was made in 1867, so it was left to the courts to decide who, between the federal Parliament and the provinces, had legislative authority over language matters. And when presented with the question, the Supreme Court of Canada decided that language was not an exclusive jurisdiction, but a shared one, an accessory to a legislative power already granted by the Constitution; therefore, there could coexist a federal law and provincial laws over language of whatever subject-matter the legislation was about.[7] This is why in Canada there is the potential for 14 different language regimes: the federal one and one for each of the 10 provinces and 3 northern territories. There is therefore an element of cultural protection within the very division of legislative powers in a federation. But this is a double-edged sword: a legislative majority might want, for its own reasons, to stifle the rights of its minorities. When a language is in a minority position within the whole state, but in a majority within a federated unit, to what extent may that minority promote its language and culture? A

5. *Secession of Quebec*, [1998] 2 SCR 217 at [43].
6. Ibid. at 59. Italics added.
7. Jones v. Attorney General for New Brunswick [1975] 2 SCR 182.

compromise must be worked out and put into the Constitution in the form of language rights.

In 1867, constitutional rights in general were not as widely acknowledged as they are today. The original *Constitution act, 1867*,[8] is somehow scarce with regard to minority language rights. There is only one section directly devoted to the matter: s. 133, and its ambit is limited to the federal institutions and Quebec. It provides for the printing and publishing of legislation in both French and English—which has been interpreted as including the adoption of the acts, and therefore, their presentation in both languages throughout the legislative process[9]—and the right to use either one in Parliament, before courts of law and in judicial proceedings, which has been interpreted as granting the right to use one's language in court proceedings and orally, but not the right to be understood directly without an interpreter.[10] It is supplemented by s. 23 of the Manitoba Act, 1870, which provides the same for that province.[11]

With regard to education, the framers of the original constitution were more preoccupied with religion than language, so the only provision related to minority status is s. 93 of the Constitution Act, 1867, and it preserves the vested rights of Catholics and Protestants with regard to denominational schools.[12] There were also no guarantees for the language of public service, and language rights were not extended to the other founding provinces.[13]

The federal government appointed a Royal Commission of Inquiry on bilingualism and biculturalism in 1963. In the first book of its final report,[14] it concluded that French and English should become the official languages of Canada, considering that a successful language planning model involves giving status to a minority language by declaring it official and using it as the govern-

8. *Constitution Act, 1867*, 30 & 31 Vict. c. 3 (U.K.).

9. Blaikie v Attorney general for Quebec [1979] 1 SCR 1012.

10. MacDonald v. Montreal (city), [1986] 1 SCR 460; Société des Acadiens du Nouveau-Brunswick v. Association of Parents for Fairness in Education, [1986] 1 SCR 549.

11. *Manitoba Act, 1870*, 33 Vict. (Can) c. 4, confirmed by *Constitution Act, 1871*, 34 & 35 Vict. c. 28 (U.K.).

12. Constitution Act, 1867.

13. Ontario, Nova Scotia or (more surprisingly) New Brunswick who hosted at the time a fairly important Acadian population; see Migneault, *Les Acadiens du Nouveau-Brunswick et la Constitution canadienne*, Ch. 3.

14. Royal Commission on Bilingualism and Biculturalism, *Final Report: Book 1—The Official Languages*.

ment's language. And so it came about that French and English were declared the official languages of Canada,[15] and as the provinces could also act on this front, New Brunswick followed suit,[16] whereas Quebec, a few years later, declared French the official language of the province.[17]

After much constitutional debate and one Quebec referendum on sovereignty in 1980, the *Canadian Charter of Rights and Freedoms* was finally adopted.[18] It includes some constitutional language rights. Although Quebec refused politically to adhere to the document, it is legally binding on all provinces and territories.[19]

So there are now six language rights enshrined in the *Canadian Charter of Rights and Freedoms*, added to the earlier language guarantees that were alluded to above. They impose obligations on the federal jurisdiction and New Brunswick only. They are:

- A declaration that French and English are the official languages and that they have equality of status, rights and privileges with regard to their use within public institutions (s. 16);
- The right to use either one in Parliament and the legislative assembly (s.17);
- The obligation to adopt acts and to publish parliamentary proceedings in both languages (s. 18);
- The right to use either official language in judicial proceedings (s. 19);
- The right to government services in the official language of choice (there are some conditions for the federal jurisdiction) (s.20);
- The right to primary and secondary instruction in the minority language of the province for qualified right holders (s. 23).

Furthermore, the protection of minorities has been styled by the Supreme Court of Canada as an unwritten constitutional principle, along with democracy, the Rule of law, federalism and constitutionalism. The Court, expressly referring to s. 16 t 23 of

15. *Official Languages Act*, RSC 1970, c. O-2, s. 2.
16. *Official Languages Act*, RSNB 1973 c. O-1 , s. 2.
17. *Official Language Act*, LQ 1974 c. 22 , s.2 ; *Charter of French Language*, LRQ 1977 c. C-11, s. 1.
18. Constitution Act, 1982, Annex B of the Canada Act, 1982 (U.K.) c. 11.
19. Objection by Quebec to a Resolution to Amend the Constitution, [1982] 2 SCR 793.

the *Charter,* wrote:

> However, we highlight that even though those provisions were the product of negotiation and political compromise, that does not render them unprincipled. Rather, such a concern reflects a broader principle related to the protection of minority rights.[20]

And the Court signals:

> The protection of minority rights had a long history before the enactment of the *Charter*...the protection of minority rights was clearly an essential consideration in the design of our constitutional structure even at the time of Confederation: *Senate Reference, supra*, at p. 71.[21]

It is not our purpose to analyze here the content of each constitutional language right, each provincial or federal legislation on language, or the unwritten principle of protection of minorities in great detail. We will rather focus on how the cultural aspect of language has influenced the courts in interpreting them. It will be shown that when they consider the role of language as a marker of identity and culture, they breathe life into these rights. We will also see that this stands true not only for constitutional rights alone, but also for language legislation as well. We will proceed by analyzing the cases according to the rights involved.

Language of Statutes and of Judicial Proceedings

There are several jurisdictions in Canada that are under a constitutional obligation to legislate in both English and French.[22] Manitoba had ceased to conform to its obligation since 1890,[23] meanwhile in 1977, Quebec intended to legislate in French only.[24] In the very first case involving this obligation, the Supreme Court issued a quite formal decision stating that outside the constitutional obligations, parliaments were free to regulate the use of language as they pleased, saying that s. 133 is limited: "The words of s. 133 themselves point to its limited concern with language rights." [25] One will note the literal approach to the constitutional guarantee; in the context of expanding on language rights, the position taken

20. Secession reference, at [80].

21. Ibid.

22. The Federal Parliament; Quebec; Manitoba; New Brunswick.

23. An Act to Provide that the English Language Shall be the Official Language of the Province of Manitoba, 1890 (Man.), c.14.

24. Charter of French Language, part III.

25. *Jones*, 193.

by the court is explainable as it wanted to allow the Federal parliament and the New Brunswick legislature to expand on official bilingualism. A few years later, the Court sanctioned both Quebec and Manitoba for having attempted to modify unilaterally their constitutional obligation, again in a very formal legal reasoning,[26] although in Quebec's case, it adopted the first judge's reasoning to the effect that s. 133 had to be characterized as a pact from which neither Quebec nor the federal government could opt out by way of legislation without going through the process of a constitutional amendment:

> s. 133 is not part of the Constitution of the Province within s. 92(1) but is rather part of the Constitution of Canada and of Quebec *in an indivisible sense*, giving official status to French and English in the Parliament and in the Courts of Canada as well as in the Legislature and Courts of Quebec.[27]

But when faced with the situation where Manitoba was in violation of a constitutional obligation for over the last hundred years, the Court chose to analyze more deeply the meaning of the constitutional requirement to legislate in two languages. Chief Justice Dickson wrote for a unanimous court:

> If more evidence of Parliament's intent is needed, it is necessary only to have regard to the purpose of both s. 23 of the *Manitoba Act, 1870* and s. 133 of the *Constitution Act, 1867*, which was to ensure full and equal access to the legislatures, the laws and the courts for Francophones and Anglophones alike.[28]

And further more: "This duty protects the substantive rights of all Manitobans to equal access to the law in either the French or the English language."[29] But it is in the next paragraph that a link between language and some deeper meaning is presented:

> Section 23 of the *Manitoba Act, 1870* is a specific manifestation of the general right of FrancoManitobans to use their own language. The importance of language rights is grounded in the essential role that language plays in human existence, development and dignity. It is through language that we are able to form concepts; to structure and order the world around us. Language bridges the gap between isolation and community, allowing humans to delineate the rights and duties they hold

26. Blaikie v Attorney General for Quebec, supra; Forest v. Attorney General for Manitoba [1979] 2 SCR 1032.
27. *Blaikie*, 1025. Italics added.
28. Reference re Manitoba Language Rights [1985] 1 SCR 721 at [31].
29. Ibid., at [45].

> in respect of one another, and thus to live in society.[30]

The "essential role" of language is twofold: cultural ("form concepts, structure and order the world . . . live in society") and instrumental as a tool for communication ("bridges the gap between isolation and community"). Both aspects are underlined as equally important. The Court goes on to conclude that not only is the constitutional obligation mandatory, but that the consequence for not having complied with it invalidates all Manitoba laws on the subject.[31] So the object and purpose of this seemingly benign measure—to legislate in both languages—is to strengthen the possibility for the French minority in Manitoba to interact with the majority, as well as among its members, and to have equal access to legislation for that purpose. This decision by the Court led to the dramatic conclusion that unilingual laws were invalid. There could have been other ways to skirt the problem, but that would have been detrimental to the rights of the French minority. It was the cultural role of language that led the Court to such a decision.

Nevertheless, in a strange turn of opinion, only one year later the Court reverted to a literal approach to constitutionally entrenched language rights and to the fact that they are the result of a political compromise (which is generally true), as if that special nature would command a "black letter law" approach to their interpretation. In question was the right to use English or French in judicial proceedings before the courts of New Brunswick.[32] Specifically, the issue was to determine if that right created a corresponding obligation for the Judge to hear the case without interpreters. Justice Beetz, for the majority, stated that this right was individual and had nothing to do either with one's identity or culture, but only as a power to use one's language—a power given to all participants in a judicial proceeding, including the judge:

> They vest in the speaker or in the writer or issuer of court processes and give the speaker or the writer the constitutionally protected power to speak or to write in the official language of his choice. And there is no language guarantee, either under s. 133 of the *Constitution Act, 1867*, or s. 19 of the *Charter*, any more than under s. 17 of the *Charter*, that the speaker will be heard or understood, or that he has the right to be heard

30. Ibid., at [46].
31. To protect the Rule of Law, the Court suspended its declaration of invalidity for the time required to translate and readopt all faulty legislation.
32. S. 19 of the Canadian Charter of Rights and Freedoms, supra.

> or understood in the language of his choice.[33]

Justice Beetz then contrasted s. 19 and s. 20 of the *Charter*, noting that when the drafters had wanted to grant a right to *communicate* in one's language of choice, it had said so:

> I am reinforced in this view by the contrasting wording of s. 20 of the *Charter*. Here, the *Charter* has expressly provided for the right to communicate in either official language with some offices of an institution of the Parliament or Government of Canada and with any office of an institution of the Legislature or Government of New Brunswick. The right to communicate in either language postulates the right to be heard or understood in either language.[34]

So the instrumental aspect of language, its communicative function, when detached of its cultural context, would lead to a literal interpretation of a constitutional guarantee to use one's language. The Court neglected the fact that using simultaneous interpretation leads to a distracted judge, who has to listen both to the speaker and to the translation; and consecutive interpretation doubles the time and cost of a trial. Neither represents equal access to the justice system.

It took almost twenty years for the Court to return to the issue, but it eventually reverted to a teleological interpretation of the right to use one's language in court proceedings, albeit with regard to a slightly different right: the right to have a criminal trial in the official language of the accused.[35] The Court made it clear that the "political" nature of language rights had no consequence on their interpretation of the law and that all language rights had to be interpreted according to their object: "Language rights must *in all cases* be interpreted purposively, in a manner consistent with the preservation and development of official language communities in Canada."[36] So it did not matter that the accused was bilingual or not: if he wanted a trial in his language, he had the right to obtain it, as an affirmation of his identity and in the name of an equal access to the court system. Although *Beaulac* did not reverse *Société des Acadiens* on the main issue, the constitutional right to be understood by the court without an interpreter, it did reverse its previous pronouncement on the interpretation rule.

33. Société des Acadiens du Nouveau-Brunswick v. Association of Parents for Fairness in Education, supra, at [53].

34. Idem. at [55].

35. A right guaranteed in s. 530 and 530.1 of the *Canadian Criminal Code*.

36. *R. v. Beaulac* [1999] 1 SCR 768 at [25].

And the new rule resulted in enhancing the right to a trial in the language of the accused:

> The right to a fair trial is universal and cannot be greater for members of official language communities than for persons speaking other languages. Language rights have a totally distinct origin and role. They are meant to protect official language minorities in this country and to insure the equality of status of French and English.[37]

"To protect the official language minorities": the collective underpinning of language rights is thus affirmed clearly, and with it its necessary corollary: the fact that language is linked to culture. Although the right to a trial in one's language is not directly a cultural right, the fact that it exists to ensure equal access to the court's system and also to enhance the status of a minority language, is tribute to the fact that the deeper meaning of language rights goes beyond the mere act of communication. Indeed, the Court mentions explicitly the fact that s. 530 is the affirmation of a collective identity by the accused, so his or her linguistic ability is irrelevant:

> In the present instance, much discussion was centered on the ability of the accused to express himself in English. This ability is irrelevant because the choice of language is not meant to support the legal right to a fair trial, but to assist the accused in gaining equal access to a public service that is *responsive to his linguistic and cultural identity*. It would indeed be surprising if Parliament intended that the right of bilingual Canadians should be restricted when in fact official language minorities, who have the highest incidence of bilingualism (84 percent for francophones [*sic*] living outside Quebec compared to 7 percent for anglophones [*sic*] according to Statistics Canada 1996 Census), are the first persons that the section was designed to assist.[38]

So, as was the case for bilingualism in the legislative process, the right to a trial in one's language must be construed as a response to the affirmation of a cultural identity. If only the communicative aspect had been involved, translation would have ensured proper communication and the right to understand what is going on in Court. The reversal of *Société des Acadiens* rule of interpretation in *Beaulac* has a direct consequence on the way the Court gives meaning and effect to entrenched rights. Culture becomes the "raison d'être" of the rights, so they are given a purpose co-

---

37. Ibid., at [41].
38. Ibid., at [45]. My emphasis.

herent with their deeper object.

Education

Education is a natural field to involve culture, as it is in school that culture is transmitted to the younger generations. So it comes as no surprise that the judicial link between language and culture was made the most strongly with regard to education. As soon as 1984, in one of the first important decisions on s. 23 of the *Charter* involving minority language education rights, the Ontario Court of Appeal adopted the strong language of an expert's report to establish this link:

> The French language school provides a setting within which the Francophone student will have a better opportunity to come to know and to understand and to strengthen and develop their own culture and heritage. . . . The school occupies a central role in the cultural life of the linguistic community. . . . The French language schools must truly be community schools and easily accessible to the general population of the linguistic group they exist to serve. . . . This Commission shares the belief, which is widely held by Franco-Ontarians, that the establishment of French language schools in which the language of both communication and administration is French best meets this . . . need to preserve the language, customs and culture of the Francophone student.[39]

So the inescapable legal conclusion follows:

> S. 23(3)(b) should be interpreted to mean that minority language children must receive their instruction in facilities in which the educational environment will be that of the linguistic minority. Only then can the facilities reasonably be said to reflect the minority culture and appertain to the minority.[40]

S. 23 was interpreted as including the right to homogeneous linguistic schools, but not bilingual or immersion schools. The Courts conclusions also led to include in s. 23 a right to manage and control minority language education, even if the text of s. 23 does not include such a right. For the Court, it was imperative that the minority group itself controls the linguistic and cultural aspect of education in its schools.

But it was in *Mahe* that the Supreme Court of Canada, in the clearest possible language, acknowledged the relationship between language and culture, and derived legal conclusions from

---

39. Reference re Minority Language Education Rights (Ontario) (1984), 10 DLR (4d) 491, at 531–532.
40. Ibid. My emphasis

it:

> The general purpose of s. 23 is clear: it is to preserve and promote the two official languages of Canada, *and their respective cultures*, by ensuring that each language flourishes, as far as possible, in provinces where it is not spoken by the majority of the population. The section aims at achieving this goal by granting minority language educational rights to minority language parents throughout Canada.[41]

And the Court went on to say:

> My reference to cultures is significant: it is based on the fact that any broad guarantee of language rights, especially in the context of education, cannot be separated from a concern for the culture associated with the language. Language is more than a mere means of communication; it is part and parcel of the identity and culture of the people speaking it. It is the means by which individuals understand themselves and the world around them.[42]

The Court could not be clearer: "language is more than a mere means of communication." Drawing on this conclusion, the Court confirmed the conclusions of the Ontario Court of Appeals and read into s. 23, even if its text did not mention it, an ancillary right to management and control of the linguistic and cultural aspects of education. This right could be implemented in various ways, of which a minority language school board is the highest level of control, but it was required by the fact that majorities cannot always consider properly a minority's concerns:

> Furthermore, as the historical context in which s. 23 was enacted suggests, minority language groups cannot always rely upon the majority to take account of all of their linguistic and cultural concerns. Such neglect is not necessarily intentional: the majority cannot be expected to understand and appreciate all of the diverse ways in which educational practices may influence the language and culture of the minority.[43]

The Court cites similar conclusions drawn by the Ontario Court of Appeal[44] and the Court of Appeal for Prince Edward Island, who used even stronger language: "If such were the case [that minority language schools were managed by the majority], a majority language group could soon wreak havoc upon the rights of the minority and could soon render such a right worthless."[45]

41. *Mahe v Alberta* [1990] 1 SCR 342, at [31].
42. Ibid.
43. Ibid., at [52].
44. Re Minority Language Education Rights (Ontario), supra, at 531.
45. Reference Re Minority Language Educational Rights (P.E.I.), (1988), 69 Nfld.

The Court used the same technique when having to decide if an Acadian minority in Prince Edward Island had the right to an elementary school in their community, rather than having to bus the children to a nearby minority language school. In *Arsenault-Cameron*, the Court put new emphasis on the cultural aspect of minority language education rights in these terms:

> It is clearly necessary to take into account the importance of language and culture in the context of instruction as well as the importance of official language minority schools to the development of the official language community when examining the actions of the government in dealing with the request for services in Summerside.[46]

The Court also recognized in that case that cultural needs had to be considered when assessing pedagogical requirements for a minority, and not the pedagogical requirements of the majority: "The pedagogical requirements established to address the needs of the majority language students cannot be used to trump cultural and linguistic concerns appropriate for the minority language students."[47]

The Court thus confirmed the first judge's order to build a minority language school in the town of Summerside. It also emphasized that the determination of the cultural needs of the minority community pertains to its school board and not to the Minister of Education: "Where a minority language board has been established in furtherance of s. 23, it is up to the board, as it represents the minority official language community, to decide what is more appropriate from a cultural and linguistic perspective."[48]

In *Doucet-Boudreau*, the Court confirmed a structural injunction against the government, ordering it to build new schools for the Acadian communities of Nova-Scotia and ordering the government to report on the implementation of the order. Commenting on the necessity to apply diligently language rights, the Court mentioned:

> Thus, particular entitlements afforded under s. 23 can be suspended, for so long as the numbers cease to warrant, by the very cultural erosion against which s. 23 was designed to guard. In practical, though not legal, terms, such suspensions may well be permanent. If delay is tolerated, governments could potentially avoid the duties imposed upon them by s.

& P.E.I.R. 236, at 259.

46. Arsenault-Cameron v Prince Edward Island [2000] 1 SCR 3 at [27].

47. Ibid., at [38].

48. Ibid., at [43]; see also at [51].

> 23 through their own failure to implement the rights vigilantly. The affirmative promise contained in s. 23 of the *Charter* and the critical need for timely compliance will sometimes require courts to order affirmative remedies to guarantee that language rights are meaningfully, and therefore necessarily promptly, protected.[49]

Health Care

Health is another area where the cultural aspect of language can be important. In Ontario, provincial legislation stipulates that designated services in designated areas are to be provided in French.[50] Therefore, a full French hospital, Montfort hospital, was designated in Ottawa, so that not only were health services provided in French, but also that the French minority ran the institution itself and French was the working language. This hospital also acted as an educational center for future doctors and nurses. In the early 1990s, the provincial government, faced with important budgetary deficits, created a Commission to reorganize health services in the province and the Commission recommended the closure of Montfort, and that decision was challenged by way of judicial review. The divisional Court acknowledged the larger role of Montfort within the community:

> Directions which replace a wide variety of truly francophone medical services and training at Montfort with services and training elsewhere in a bilingual setting—however well those bilingual facilities may appear to work in any given case—fail to conform to the principle underlying our constitution which calls for the protection of francophone minority rights. . . . Given the constitutional mandate for the protection and respect of minority rights—an independent principle underlying our constitution, "a powerful normative force"—it was not open to the Commission to proceed on a restructured health services' mandate only, and to ignore the broader institutional role played by Hôpital Montfort as a truly francophone centre, necessary to promote and enhance the Franco-Ontarian identity as a cultural/linguistic minority in Ontario, and to protect that culture from assimilation. We find this is what the Commission did. Accordingly, its directions cannot stand.[51]

The Court of Appeal for Ontario agreed. It ruled that to close the hospital, the government had to adopt a regulation removing

49. Doucet-Boudreau v Nova Scotia [2003] 3 SCR 3 at [29].
50. *French Language Services Act*, RSO 1990 ch. F.32, s. 2, 5 and 7.
51. *Lalonde v. Commission de restructuration*, [1999] OJ 4489 (QL), (Ont. Div. Ct.) at 83–84.

the designation as a French language service provider, and that had not been done; furthermore, no such regulation could be adopted without the government having to show that all reasonable alternative measures had been considered, which it didn't. The Court said that the French Language Services Act should be interpreted in light of the unwritten constitutional principle of protection of minorities and that a French hospital was much more than a mere service provider. The Court states clearly its position:

> Language and culture are not, however, separate watertight compartments. The reality of the matter is, as found by the Divisional Court, that the Commission's directions would reduce the availability and accessibility of healthcare services in French, both directly in the Ottawa-Carleton region and eastern Ontario, and indirectly by imperiling the training of health care professionals, which would in turn increase the assimilation of Franco-Ontarians. Montfort's designation under the F.L.S.A. includes not only the right to healthcare services in French at the time of designation but also the right to whatever structure is necessary to ensure that those healthcare services are delivered in French. This would include the training of healthcare professionals in French. To give the legislation any other interpretation is to prefer a narrow, literal, compartmentalized interpretation to one that recognizes and reflects the intent of the legislation.[52]

Health care involves more than just talking. So even if the Commission had proposed to offer medical services in French in bilingual hospitals, that was not sufficient in the eyes of the Court to justify closing a truly French hospital. Indeed, it ignores the central role that minority language institutions play in the vitality of the community:

> We agree with the Divisional Court, at pp. 65–66, that the language and culture of the francophone minority in Ontario "hold a special place in the Canadian fabric as one of the founding communities of Canada and as one of the two official language groups whose rights are entrenched in the Constitution." If implemented, the Commission's directions would greatly impair Montfort's role as an important linguistic, cultural and educational institution, vital to the minority francophone population of Ontario. This would be contrary to the fundamental constitutional principle of respect for and protection of minorities.[53]

So these ideas, which could well be found in any textbook about linguistic diversity, are now legal conclusions: "language

52. Lalonde v Commission de restructuration (2001), 56 OR (3d) 506, at [162].
53. Ibid., at [181].

and culture are not "separate watertight compartments"; to close a French language hospital, even if some services would be provided within a bilingual setting, would "impair" the institution's role among the minority community, as it is "vital" for her; this runs contrary to the unwritten constitutional principle of protection of minorities. The broad sweep of these declarations cannot be ignored. Should language be viewed as a mere communication tool, again, translation services or partial services within a bilingual institution would suffice to satisfy the rights of Francophone patients; but there is much more to it than only communication, and therefore an institution belonging to the minority cannot be tampered with under Canadian constitutional law.

Broadcasting

Broadcasting represents a way to express a minority's culture. Media are a central part of cultural development in our contemporary world. When Radio-Canada, the French language public radio broadcaster, faced with important budgetary cuts, decided to close down a French language production unit in a minority community in south-western Ontario, the decision was met with a legal challenge. The divisional Court decided that it did not have jurisdiction over the matter and remitted the question to the Canadian Radio-Television Council, who, in the Court's opinion, had exclusive jurisdiction over these matters. Nevertheless, the Court acknowledged the nature and importance of language in these terms:

> Language is more than the sum of its parts—words. It is the vehicle by which ideas, thoughts, history, events, emotions and perspectives are expressed. It is a permanently open door to the ethos of the other; understanding, support, tolerance, development and security. Language sustains the past, the present and the future of the cultural identity of both the individual and his or her community. Its fundamental importance to the survival of the cultural whole cannot be overemphasized with respect to those communities of people whose numbers form a minority of the population of the area in which they live.[54]

The Court let it be known that should it have been considered that the court had had jurisdiction, it would probably have struck down the decision:

> In my view, to undermine the significance of the French lan-

54. *Larocque v Radio-Canada* (2009), 98 OR (3d) 220 at [4].

> guage to isolated francophone communities and to those who, while not francophone, recognize the importance of second language acquisition, is to risk an endorsement of assimilation and the slow but permanent and insidious loss of the French identity in that geographic locale.[55]

And this is because "Based on all of the evidence before me, it is absolutely clear that CBEF serves as a pillar for the francophone community, enabling them to live in French."[56] The Court also draws a clear link between local broadcasting and cultural vitality:

> The reduction in local Windsor content will undoubtedly have a deleterious effect on the sense of sharing, support and intimacy from which this isolated francophone community derives its strength and identity. In my view, expert evidence is not required for such an observation. No matter the language, people rely on local media newspapers, television and/or radio to learn of matters concerning the community in which they live. A reduction of the time or space available to broadcast local affairs will have an impact on the community as a whole.[57]

So decisions concerning broadcasting issues should be led by the unwritten constitutional principle of protection of minorities and take into account the damaging effect a reduction in services would have on an official language minority in Canada; and this conclusion was drawn by the Court without any reference to a legal right, although the *Broadcasting Act* contains some reference to the Canadian linguistic duality.[58]

Conclusion

This brief review of Canadian case law indicates that the courts are sensitive to the link between language and culture and that this link, when acknowledged, makes a difference in the interpretation of language rights. The taking into account of culture leads to a sensitivity to collective rights and to the importance of institutions in the maintaining of a minority language community.

Culture cannot be legislated. It is a living phenomenon. It is constantly created by the people, shifting, malleable to influences, both internal and external. But language can be the subject of legislation. And although legislation has its own limits, although

55. Ibid., *at* [5].
56. Ibid., at [11].
57. Ibid., at [41].
58. *Broadcasting Act*, RSC 1985 c. B-, s. 3.

rights are useless if they are not vigorously pursued and affirmed by right-holders themselves with the help of courageous courts, the legal system nevertheless can play a useful role in the defense of a minority population—that is, if language rights are properly understood and taken for what they truly are. But for that to happen, the Canadian jurisprudence shows that a link must be made between both. It has been made in Canadian law, and it has come as an aid to French speaking minorities throughout the country, breathing life into legal rights, stopping governments from invoking financial or administrative inconvenience to curtail the rights of a national minority. It is to be hoped that this example may be followed by other courts in other constitutional settings or by the same courts with regard to indigenous languages in Canada, when they will be faced with the issue.

Bibliography

Legislation

An Act to Provide that the English Language Shall be the Official Language of the Province of Manitoba, 1890 (Man.), c.14. Available at: http://scc.lexum.org/decisia-scc-csc/scc-csc/en/nav.do

Charter of French Language (Qc.), RSQ 1977 c. C-11. Available at: www2.publicationsduquebec.gouv.qc.ca/dynamicSearch/telecharge.php?type=2&file=/C_11/C11_A.html

Government of Canada. *Constitution Act, 1867,* 30 & 31 Vict. c. 3 (U.K.). Available at: http://laws-lois.justice.gc.ca/eng/

Government of Canada. *Constitution Act, 1871,* 34 & 35 Vict. c. 28 (U.K.). Available at: http://laws-lois.justice.gc.ca/eng/

Government of Canada. *Constitution Act, 1982,* Annex B of the *Canada Act, 1982* (U.K.) c. 11. Available at: http://laws-lois.justice.gc.ca/eng/

French Language Services Act (Ont.), RSO 1990 ch. F.32. Available at: www.e-laws.gov.on.ca/html/statutes/english/elaws_statutes_90f32_e.htm

Inuit Language Protection Act (Nun.), SN 2008 c. 17. Available at: www.canlii.org/en/nu/laws/stat/snu-2008-c-17/latest/snu-2008-c-17.html

Supreme Court of Canada. *Manitoba Act, 1870,* 33 Vict. (Can) c. 4.

Available at: http://scc.lexum.org/decisia-scc-csc/scc-csc/en/nav.do.

Supreme Court of Canada. *Official Languages Act (Can.)*, RSC 1970, c. O-2. Available at: http://scc.lexum.org/decisia-scc-csc/scc-csc/en/nav.do.

Supreme Court of Canada. *Official languages Act (N.-B.)*, RSNB 1973 c. O-1. Available at: http://scc.lexum.org/decisia-scc-csc/scc-csc/en/nav.do.

Supreme Court of Canada. *Official Languages Act (Nun)*, SN 2008 c. 10. Available at: http://scc.lexum.org/decisia-scc-csc/scc-csc/en/nav.do.

Supreme Court of Canada. *Official Language Act (Qc.)*, LQ 1974 c. 22. Available at: http://scc.lexum.org/decisia-scc-csc/scc-csc/en/nav.do.

Cases Cited (SCR = Supreme Court Reports)

Supreme Court of Canada. *Arsenault-Cameron v Prince Edward Island* [2000] 1 SCR 3. Available at: http://scc.lexum.org/decisia-scc-csc/scc-csc/en/nav.do.

Supreme Court of Canada. *Blaikie v Attorney General for Quebec* [1979] 1 SCR 1012. Available at: http://scc.lexum.org/decisia-scc-csc/scc-csc/en/nav.do.

Supreme Court of Canada. *Doucet-Boudreau v Nova Scotia* [2003] 3 SCR 3. Available at: http://scc.lexum.org/decisia-scc-csc/scc-csc/en/nav.do.

Supreme Court of Canada. *Ford v. Quebec* [1988] 2 SCR 712. Available at: http://scc.lexum.org/decisia-scc-csc/scc-csc/en/nav.do

Supreme Court of Canada. *Forest v. Attorney General for Manitoba* [1979] 2 SCR 1032. Available at: http://scc.lexum.org/decisia-scc-csc/scc-csc/en/nav.do.

Supreme Court of Canada. *Jones v. Attorney General for New-Brunswick* [1975] 2 SCR 182. Available at: http://scc.lexum.org/decisia-scc-csc/scc-csc/en/nav.do.

Lalonde v. Commission de Restructuration, [1999] OJ 4489 (Quicklaw) (Ont. Div. Court).

Lalonde v Commission de Restructuration (2001), 56 OR (3d) 506 (Ont. C.A.).

Larocque v Radio-Canada (2009), 98 OR (3d) 220.

Supreme Court of Canada. *MacDonald v. Montreal (city)*, [1986] 1 SCR 460. Available at: http://scc.lexum.org/decisia-scc-csc/scc-csc/en/nav.do.

Supreme Court of Canada. *Mahe v Alberta* [1990] 1 SCR 342. Available at: http://scc.lexum.org/decisia-scc-csc/scc-csc/en/nav.do.

Supreme Court of Canada. *R. v. Beaulac* [1999] 1 SCR 768. Available at: http://scc.lexum.org/decisia-scc-csc/scc-csc/en/nav.do.

Supreme Court of Canada. *Re: Objection by Quebec to a Resolution to Amend the Constitution*, [1982] 2 SCR 793. Available at: http://scc.lexum.org/decisia-scc-csc/scc-csc/en/nav.do.

Supreme Court of Canada. *Reference re Manitoba Language Rights* [1985] 1 SCR 721. Available at: http://scc.lexum.org/decisia-scc-csc/scc-csc/en/nav.do.

Reference re Minority Language Education Rights (Ontario) (1984), 10 DLR (4d) 491. Available at: www.uottawa.ca/constitutional-law/language1.html

Supreme Court of Canada. *Reference Re Minority Language Educational Rights (P.E.I.)*, (1988), 69 Nfld. & P.E.I.R. 236, at 259. Available at: http://scc.lexum.org/decisia-scc-csc/scc-csc/en/nav.do.

Supreme Court of Canada. *Reference Re Secession of Quebec*, [1998] 2 SCR 217. Available at: http://scc.lexum.org/decisia-scc-csc/scc-csc/en/nav.do.

Supreme Court of Canada. *Société des Acadiens du Nouveau-Brunswick v. Association of Parents for Fairness in Education*, [1986] 1 SCR 549. Available at: http://scc.lexum.org/decisia-scc-csc/scc-csc/en/nav.do.

Supreme Court of Canada. *Solski v. Quebec*, [2005] 1 SCR 201; *N'Guyen v. Quebec* [2009] 1 SCR 826. Available at: http://scc.lexum.org/decisia-scc-csc/scc-csc/en/nav.do.

Doctrine

Migneault, Gaetan. *Les Acadiens du Nouveau-Brunswick et la Constitution canadienne*. Moncton: Éditions de la francophonie, 2006.

Royal Commission on Bilingualism and Biculturalism. *Final Report: Book 1—The Official Languages.* Ottawa: Queen's Printer, 1967.

6
Language Rights in Canada
A Political or Judicial Leadership?

André Braen

Language rights in Canada have a very long history.[1] In fact, language was central to French-English relations throughout the pre-Confederation period. Language rights were included in the *Constitutional Act, 1867*[2] and mainly in the *Canadian Charter of Rights and Freedoms of 1982*.[3] However, the judicial enforcement of language rights remains a relatively new phenomenon in Canada, even though its development seemed inevitable. Language rights include the guarantees given to languages themselves and to individuals. In the first case, status and privileges are granted to one or more specific languages, French and English in our case; while in the second case, individuals are given the right to use one or more specific languages in communications with the state. To

1. For the history of languages in Canada, see: Chennells, *The Politics of Nationalism in Canada*; Boberg, *The English Language in Canada*; Martel and Pâquet, *Langue et politique au Canada et au Québec*. According to the 2006 census, there were around 32 million people in Canada and the number of people whose mother tongue is French was about 22 percent of this figure. Most of Francophones live in the province of Quebec although near one million live in the other provinces of Canada. Outside Quebec, English is the common language. In general, census shows that the proportion of Francophones and French continue to decline. More particularly for the linguistic portrait findings coming out from the census, see the Statistic Canada website: www.stat.can.ca.
2. *Constitution Act, 1867* (U.K.), 30–31 Vict., c.3 being Schedule B to the *Canada Act 1982*, (U.K.), 1982, c.11 and reprinted in R.S.C. 1985, App.II, c.5.
3. Part of the *Constitution Act, 1982* being Schedule B to the *Canada Act 1982, supra*, footnote 2.

exist legally, a right or a language guarantee must be recognized by the state that creates or deletes them. To exist materially, a right or language guarantee also requires the state's involvement, and the state must ensure its implementation.[4] In the case of *R v. Beaulac*,[5] the Supreme Court of Canada brought this aspect of language rights to light by confirming that a language right granted to a citizen also involves a corresponding obligation for the state to implement it. For example, what is the use of the right to instruction in the language of the minority if resources to provide such instruction are not available?

Therefore, the courts' involvement was necessary to clarify the scope and the content of language rights contained in Canadian constitutional documents and statutes, and also to identify their objectives and foundations. Court decisions also served to guide or compel government action and even to penalize violations in some cases. However, there are significant limitations on judicial intervention because in a democracy the courts cannot be substituted for a legitimately elected government that legally exercises its powers. Since the state's involvement is a prerequisite in language matters, it must exercise leadership in this area. Nevertheless, in Canada, promoting language rights seems to be more of a judicial work than a political one. Who in Canada really assumes leadership in this matter?

Clarifying Language Rights

Language rights are found in the Canadian constitution[6] and also in federal and provincial statutes.[7] Canada is a federation of provinces and each level of government, federal and provincial, may make law in its areas of jurisdiction.[8] As such, language is not an

4. Braën, "Language Rights," 14–25.
5. (1999) 1 S.C.R. 768.
6. *Constitutional Act, 1867*, sec.133, *Manitoba Act, 1870*, R.S.C., 1970, App.II, sec. 23 and *Canadian Charter of Rights and Freedoms*, sec.16—23. French and English are the two official languages of the Parliament and government of Canada and of the province of New Brunswick, French is the official language of the province of Quebec and English is the language of the 8 other provinces. For an analysis of the constitutional language regime in Canada, see Bastarache ed., *Language Rights in Canada*, 2nd ed.
7. At the federal level, see the *Official Languages Act*, R.S.C. 1985, c.31 (4th Supp.). At the provincial level see the *Official Languages of New Brunswick Act*, S.N.-B. 2002, c.O-05, for Quebec the *Charter of the French Language*, R.S.Q. c.C-11 and for Ontario, the *French Language Services Act*, R.S.O. 1990, c.F-32.
8. Constitutional Act, 1867, sec. 91—95.

enumerated head of power in the *Constitutional Act, 1867*. Rather, language is an area of concurrent jurisdiction and each level of government may make law in its assigned areas of jurisdiction as well as regulate language matters within them as long as, in doing so, enshrined or constitutional rights are not violated. And, in Canada this constitutional review is done by ordinary superior courts.[9]

Since language rights are stated in constitutional or statutory provisions, the role of the courts becomes a determining factor. It is the court that provides a final interpretation of the provisions, which defines their actual meaning and scope, and that penalizes violations, if applicable. For example, Canada's constitution sets out the obligation of the Parliament of Canada and of the Legislative Assemblies of Quebec, Manitoba and New Brunswick to print and publish their laws in French and English.[10] It was decided that this obligation for statutory bilingualism also applies to the printing of legislative enactment, as well as their adoption processes, with the latter requirement being implicit.[11] The obligation for bilingualism also extends to statutory instruments adopted by the government, a minister or a group of ministers, or those who need approval from them before they can be put into force.[12] Other instruments and documents added to statutory material, and that form an integral part of them are also, save exception, subject to this obligation.[13] The penalty for violating this obligation is the invalidation of the document itself.[14] For example, from 1890 up to 1978, the province of Manitoba had published its statutes

9. *Jones v. New Brunswick (A.G.)*, (1975) 2 S.C.R. 182; *Devine v. Quebec (A.G.)* (1988) 2 S.C.R.790, at 807–808. For example and according to sec. 91(27) of the *Constitutional Act, 1867*, Parliament of Canada has exclusive authority to make laws in relation to criminal law including the criminal procedure. So, the Parliament could legislate in respect of language of the criminal proceedings. For a in-depth discussion regarding language and division of powers in Canada, see Office of the Commissioner of Official Languages, *The Equitable Use of English and French Before the Courts in Canada*, 11–14. Also available on the Commissioner of Official Languages' website: www.ocol-clo.gc.ca.

10. Constitutional Act, 1867, sec. 133, Manitoba Act, 1870, sec. 23, Canadian Charter of Rights and Freedoms, sec.18.

11. A.G. Quebec v. Blaikie (No.1), (1979) 2 S.C.R.1016.

12. A.G. Quebec v. Blaikie (No.2), (1981) 1 S.C.R. 312. But see Charlebois v. Saint John (City), (2005) 3 S.C.R.563.

13. *Reference re Manitoba Language Rights (1992)*, (1992) 1 S.C.R. 212; *Sinclair v. Quebec (A.G.)*, (1992) 1 S.C.R. 579. See Leckey and Braën, "Bilingualism and Legislation," 60–78.

14. Reference re Manitoba Language Rights, (1985) 1 S.C.R. 721.

only in English, contrary to sec. 23 of the *Manitoba Act, 1870*. In 1979, the Supreme Court of Canada declared invalid all of this unilingual legislation,[15] but also declared that the application of the rule of law may require that the invalid document continue to apply during the time required for the legislator to correct the situation.[16] According to the court, the purpose of this language guarantee is to ensure full and equal access to the legislator and the law for francophone and Anglophone speakers alike.[17]

In reference to educational matters, section 23 of the *Canadian Charter* gives qualifying parents the right to primary and secondary education for their children in the minority language of the province or territory of residence. The right to minority language instruction is crucial considering the role education plays in the preservation of culture and in the survival of minority language communities all over Canada.[18] The qualifying parents also have the right to have this education provided in educational institutions of the minority and financed with public funds, as long as there are sufficient numbers. The courts determined that section 23 grants to the official language minority of each province the right to manage its own institutions.[19] In the case of *Mahe v. Alberta*,[20] the Supreme Court of Canada clarified that section 23 must not be interpreted as granting three different rights. On the contrary, it consists of variable content with the minimum being the right to education and the maximum being a wider range of institutional requirements for which implementation may vary from a simple school to an individual school system. In this regard, sufficient numbers do not represent a limit that would remove this right. According to the Supreme Court, the quality of education to be provided to the minority is to be on a basis of equality with the majority. And equality does not always mean identity of measures. The protection of a minority language group may require, in addition, the adoption of special provisions designed to ensure the survival of the group's language and cultural characteristics. In this matter, if the recognition of a preferential treatment is

15. Manitoba (A.G.) v. Forest, (1979) 2 S.C.R.1032.
16. Reference re Manitoba Language Rights, supra footnote 14.
17. Ibid.
18. Quebec Association of Protestant School Boards v. A.G. Quebec, (1984) 2 S.C.R. 66.
19. Reference re Education Act (Ont.) and Minority Language Rights, (1984) 47 O.R. 2nd. ed. 1 (Appeal Court, Ontario).
20. (1990) 1 S.C.R. 342.

necessary, it is because that equality has not been achieved.[21]

In general, the courts have opted for a broad, liberal and generous interpretation of language rights.[22] They based this interpretation on the foundations and objects of language guarantees, including the principle of equality and the protection of minorities. They identified contents and elements that are much more favorable to official language minorities. But in other areas, such as legal rights, the courts have, on the contrary, opted for a restrictive interpretation of language rights. For example, and from the outset, it was determined that the constitutional right to use French or English before certain courts does not confer the right to the individual to be understood directly by the judge in the selected language. Asserting that language rights are based on a political compromise, the courts determined that it was not up to them to modify this arrangement. Obviously, this type of literal and restrictive interpretation of language provisions was unfavorable in the eyes of the official language minorities and thus led, for all intent and purpose, to the elimination of the reason for a language guarantee: What is the use of having the right to choose a specific language to speak before a court if there is no guarantee that one will be understood?

The political compromise doctrine by which constitutional language rights ought to be construed narrowly, on account of their origin, seems to have been repudiated in the case of *Beaulac*,[23] where the Supreme Court of Canada said that in all cases, a language right must be given a broad and liberal interpretation in a manner that maintains and expands official language communities. In general then, in interpreting language rights in a liberal manner, Canadian courts have promoted a more generous language rights regime than originally envisioned by the legislation. This liberal and generous approach has been qualified as activist, and rather than having a restrictive and textual interpretation,

---

21. Ibid. See also Arsenault-Cameron v. Prince Edward Island, (2000) 1 S.C.R.3.
22. Braën, *L'interprétation judiciaire des droits linguistiques au Canada et l'affaire Beaulac* (1998) 29 R.G.D., 379.
23. See footnote 5. In the case of *Charlebois v. Saint.John (City)*, *supra* footnote 12, at par.23, Justice Charron speaking for the majority said that a liberal and purposive approach to the interpretation of constitutional language guarantees and statutory language rights should not be adopted in all cases and that this does not mean that the ordinary rules of statutory interpretation have no place. Depending on the case, the contextual and purposive analysis of a statutory rule may remove all ambiguity surrounding its meaning and leave no ambiguity.

courts have relied on the objects and foundations of a language right, particularly the principle of equality and also the necessity to ensure the survival of a minority group's cultural and linguistic characteristics. Therefore, they gave the right a scope favorable to linguistic minorities. In doing so, Canadian courts have clearly established their intent to intervene to protect linguistic minorities and, if applicable, overcome the inadequacies of the legislator.

Implementing Language Rights

Judicial remedy in language matters was made necessary not only to clarify certain constitutional or legislative provisions, but also to counter the state's lack of action, or to at least guide it. For any language right, there is a corresponding obligation for the state to ensure its effective implementation.[24] In this respect, judicial intervention was primarily helpful for implementing school rights in all Canadian provinces, as granted by section 23 of the *Canadian Charter of Rights and Freedoms*.[25] To the extent that the implementation of a legislative framework is required and to the extent that the situation differed from one province to another, even from one region to another within a given province, the court's intervention has allowed the official language minority to determine the parameters of legislative and executive action and even, in some cases, to force administrative action.

In the criminal sphere, the *Criminal Code*[26] allows for trials to be conducted in French and English throughout Canada. In many provinces other than Quebec, conducting trials in French was found to be problematic and the courts hesitated before ordering them to be held in the minority language. The case of *R v. Beaulac* refers to an accused Francophone prosecuted in British Columbia and who requested a trial in his language. The courts of this province rejected his request given the ability of the accused to express himself in English and the practical problem of conducting a trial in French.[27] The Supreme Court of Canada called them to order[28] and in its opinion, if the right exists it is to help official language minorities preserve their cultural identity. With this right comes

24. R v. Beaulac, supra footnote 5.
25. See Power and Foucher, "Language Rights and Education," 364–452. See also Magnet, *Official Languages of Canada*, 137–184.
26. R.S.C. 1985, c. C-46.
27. (1997) 120 C.C.C. 3rd ed. 16.
28. *Supra* footnote 5.

a corresponding obligation for the court to be institutionally bilingual to ensure that both official languages are used fairly. This is a matter of equality and not simply an accommodation for the official minority language.[29]

In the case of Monfort Hospital, the Health Service Restructuring Commission of Ontario recommended to the provincial government that the hospital's function as the only French language hospital in the province should be changed radically: in other words, it should be eliminated. According to the commission, the French-speaking minority in Ontario could use the bilingual services provided by other hospitals in Ottawa. The legality of the government's action was challenged in the courts. It was determined that the Ontario government had no legal obligation to maintain a French language hospital. However, the principle of protecting minorities, which is an unwritten constitutional principle, nevertheless requires the Ontario authorities to consider the special function of the Monfort Hospital for maintaining and developing the francophone minority. And in the decision to close the hospital, that was not done.[30] On appeal,[31] it was also determined that the Ontario government has an obligation to take this aspect into account in exercising its discretionary powers and that in this respect, the government had failed to fulfill its obligations regarding legislation on services in French.[32]

Limitations of Judicial Intervention

There have been many cases that resulted in court proceedings regarding language matters.[33] We have referred to only few of them. Nevertheless, we can confirm from this brief analysis that court remedy has become a significant tool for promoting and developing language rights in Canada. In some ways, the rules that govern the law of supply and demand in this area have been determined in large part by the courts. They have intervened by relying on the equality principle. For example, by deciding that an official language minority had the right to receive education[34] and

29. Ibid. at par.34 and 49.
30. Lalonde v. Commission de restructuration des services de santé, (1999) 48 O.R. 3rd ed. 50 (Div.Court).
31. (2001) O.J. no 4767, 56 RJ.O. 3rd ed. 505 (Court of Appeal).
32. According to *The French Language Services Act*, R.S.O. 1990, c.F.32.
33. For an analysis see Bastarache, ed., *Language Rights in Canada*.
34. Re Minority Language Educational Rights, (1984) 10 D.L.R. 3rd ed. 491; Mahe v. Alberta, (1990) 1 S.C.R. 342; Arsenault-Cameron v. Prince Edward Island,

government services[35] in its primary language, the courts also decided that in this respect, it meant services of comparable quality to those provided to those of the majority language. Today, these rules make it possible to better position the role of French and English within multicultural Canada.[36]

In terms of advantages, the use of judicial remedy has made it possible to overcome the political weakness of linguistic minorities in their communications with both the majority and the government. In essence, the government acts on the basis of its re-election by the majority. Usually, and to play the game of parliamentary institutions, a minority will search for support for its claims from the majority. However, when the political rule ignores such claims, the minority may try to move the debate to a legal arena. In linguistic matters, as in others, the courts have been asked to build social consensus.[37] Furthermore and in a financial context where resources are by necessity limited, expenses for the maintenance and development of a linguistic minority are not well understood by the electorate. In this respect, a court judgment helps the government act in this area or at least provides it with justification. In short, the government itself may sometimes seek judicial activism.

The Canadian courts have clearly established their intent to intervene to better protect linguistic minorities and, if applicable, overcome the inadequacies of the legislator. However, using judicial remedy in linguistic matters also has disadvantages. First of all, judicial remedy is a long and costly process. Often because court intervention addresses specific cases, the exercise must be repeated for other cases. In reaction to a judicial interpretation that is perceived as too liberal and generous, the legislator or government may become resistant. They may hesitate about giving the linguistic minority additional rights for fear they may be expanded in an undetermined manner by the court.[38] Furthermore,

(2000) 1 S.C.R. 3.

35. DesRochers v. Canada (Industry), (2009) 1 S.C.R. 194.

36. Canada has an official policy on multiculturalism. See *The Canadian Multiculturalism Act*, R.S.C. 1985, c.24 (4th supp.) and section 27 of the *Canadian Charter of Rights and Freedoms*.

37. Before the *Canadian Charter of Rights and Freedoms* came into force in 1982, judicial review in Canada was based primarily on the principle of ultra vires and also on federalism grounds. With the regime introduced by the *Charter*, judicial review gains a significant expansion with the agreement of the political actors.

38. Note that in the case of *Beaulac, supra* footnote 5, at par.25, Justice Basta-

using the courts would not overcome the minority's required dynamism. It is primarily its members that are responsible for planning its development. Finally, and through a process of consultation and negotiation with the government, the threat by the minority to use judicial remedy could cause the latter to retreat. In this case, judicial remedy becomes a dysfunctional factor within the process.

Another issue is the significant limitation with judicial remedy, in that it cannot be substituted for legislative or executive action.[39] A language right only exists through its recognition and implementation by the state. Consequently, it seems clear that in a democratic society, the courts of justice cannot retain all of the powers and must rely on representative government to define, promote and apply language rights. If through its inaction, the state allows a linguistic minority to endure an unfavorable situation, it, however, abdicates its role. If the state does not respect its obligations in this area, it could be perceived by the court as an invitation to correct the situation itself. Nevertheless, the courts do not have the expertise required to make decisions about the orientations and policies of a society. This is why it is primarily up to the representatives to exercise the required leadership on linguistic matters, as in all other areas.

Conclusion

Also named "juristocracy,"[40] judicial activism is a live issue not only in Canada, but also in many democratic countries including the United States. Democracy is more than the simple majority rule and it implies an adequate protection of minority rights, and, in regards to Canada, the protection of official language minorities through constitutionalization and judicial review. The language rights policies currently applicable in Canada have been therefore, largely formed by the courts of justice. Given the very nature of language guarantees, the willingness of politicians to transfer policy-making authority from the political sphere to the courts

rache said "the fear that a liberal interpretation of language rights will make provinces less willing to become involved in the geographical extension of those rights is inconsistent with the requirement that language rights be interpreted as a fundamental tool for the preservation and protection of official language communities where they do apply."

39. See Kirby, *Judicial Activism*.

40. Hirschl, *Towards Juristrocracy*.

and the willingness of the latter to respond positively, it could not be otherwise.[41] In short, Canadian courts have become a major forum for dealing with language rights issues, whereas governments in Canada have avoided playing a very active role in in this arena. Language rights are a dividing factor rather than a unifying one, an issue that governments tend to avoid as much as possible, thus dodging their responsibilities. Reinforcing the Canadian identity requires the government to make language a question of principle, rather than hiding behind the judge. However, this objective will only be reached through continuous consultation with their official language minorities and also in exercising true leadership on the matter. Many years ago, the Commissioner of Official Languages for Canada invited the federal government and its institutions to ensure a more proactive management of their obligations with respect to official language communities and the promotion of linguistic duality.[42] The Commissioner called for strong political leadership, clearly committed to the promotion of language rights. The government's answer is yet to come.

Bibliography

Bastarache, Michel, ed. *Language Rights in Canada*, 2nd ed. Cowansville: Editions Yvon Blais, 2004.

Boberg, Charles. *The English Language in Canada: Status, History, and Comparative Analysis*. Cambridge and London: Cambridge University Press, 2010.

Braën, André. *L'interprétation judiciaire des droits linguistiques au Canada et l'affaire Beaulac* 29 (1998): 379.

———. "Language Rights" in *Language Rights in Canada,* edited by M. Bastarache. Cowansville: Ed.Yvon Blais Inc., 1987: 14–25.

Chennells, David. *The Politics of Nationalism in Canada: Cultural Conflict since 1760*. Toronto: University of Toronto Press, 2001.

Hirschl, Ran. *Towards Juristrocracy*: *The Origins and Consequences of the New Constitutionalism*. Cambridge and London: Har-

41. Ibid.

42. Office of the Commissioner of Official Languages, Adam, Annual Report 2005–2006, *Official Languages in Canada: Taking on the New Challenge*, chapter five. Online: www.ocol-clo.gc.ca.

vard University Press, 2004.

———. *Constitutional Theocracy*. Cambridge and London: Harvard University Press, 2010.

Kirby, Michael. *Judicial Activism*. London: Sweet and Maxwell, 2004.

Leckey, Robert and André Braën. "Bilingualism and Legislation" in *Language Rights in Canada*, edited by M. Bastarache. Cowansville: Ed. Yvon Blais, 2004.

Magnet, Joseph E. *Official Languages of Canada*. Cowansville: Ed. Yvon Blais, 1995.

Martel, Marcel and Martin Pâquet. *Langue et politique au Canada et au Québec: Une synthèse historique*. Montréal: Boréal, 2010.

Office of the Commissioner of Official Languages. *The Equitable Use of English and French Before the Courts in Canada*. Ottawa: Minister of Supply and Services, 1995.

———. *Annual Report 2005–2006 of Dyane Adam*, in "Official Languages in Canada: Taking on the New Challenge," Chapter 5. Online: www.ocol-clo.gc.ca, 1995.

Power, Mark and Pierre Foucher. "Language Rights and Education," in *Language Rights in Canada*, edited by M. Bastarache, 2nd ed. Cowansville: Ed. Y. Blais, 2004.

7
The Iberian Languages and Spanish Nationalism

Xosé M. Núñez Seixas

There is a surprising lack of monographic studies concerning the "linguistic ideology" of Spanish nationalism from the nineteenth century to the present day. Language is implicit and ever-present in the discourse and praxis of Spanish nationalism, as a policy for nation-building or as political and cultural discourse, but it has seldom been treated as a topic in its own right.[1] This is partially due to the paradoxically late emergence of explicit linguistic concerns in Spanish nationalism. Until the beginning of the twentieth century, no real menace to the hegemonic Castilian language had been perceived. The other Iberian languages and dialects posed no serious threat, and a practical tolerance of their instrumental use in education was common in nineteenth-century Spain. However, they were not generally included in political demands, subjected to grammatical modernization or regarded as culturally appropriated as instruments for defining a sub-state, public sphere.

Any true linguistic concern at that time among Spanish nationalists could only be found in the Americas. The independence of American colonies from the Spanish monarchy between 1810 and 1826 and the nation-building processes implemented by the intellectual and political elites of the new Latin American states fostered a debate that would last until the beginning of the twentieth century, regarding the idiomatic alternatives and linguistic

1. Mar-Molinero, "The Role of Language in Spanish Nation-Building," 69–87.

variants that should be adopted as new *national languages*. In Argentina and Chile for example, where the temptation to create a new linguistic norm that synthesized popular speech and the inherited linguistic standard was strong, faithfulness to the Castilian norm was generally considered the best instrument for preserving national independence vis-à-vis North American expansionism. Debates centered around the *purity* of the Castilian language, and on where it had been best preserved, as well as on its national appropriation by these new republics, implying that the language would *no longer belong* exclusively to Spain.[2]

In Spain, however, linguistic issues were of no great importance even in civil legislation. Some exceptions began to emerge in the 1860s, and soon after it was mandated that official documents should be written in Castilian or include a translation into Castilian if written in a foreign language or "dialect of the country."[3] The main theorists of nineteenth-century Spanish nationalism were not excessively concerned with the role of language in national identity. Antonio Cánovas del Castillo, a prominent politician at that time who was mindful of the situation with the Hispanic-American republics, stated in his 1882 *Discourse on the Nation* that language in itself was insufficient for defining a nation.[4] Marcelino Menéndez y Pelayo, the main theorist of traditionalist Spanish nationalism, assigned the Castilian language no significant role as marker and origin of the nation: for him the Catholic religion, the monarchy, and Spanish history were the true unifying factors. The linguistic question occupied almost no space in the reform movement (*Regeneracionismo*) that emerged after 1898; nor was it relevant in publications reflecting on Spanish identity at the turn of the nineteenth to the twentieth century, such as *Idearium español* (1898) by the philosopher Angel Ganivet.[5]

Language as a nationality marker entered the scene in the late 1880s, when other Iberian languages began to be promoted as markers of ethnic distinctiveness. At that time, the first polemics arose regarding the feasibility of encouraging the "rise" of the "dialects," a discussion aimed mainly at the Catalan and Galician languages. In 1888 the Spanish public sphere reacted with ab-

---

2. See Sepúlveda, *El sueño de la Madre Patria*, 210–16. See also Marcilhacy, *Raza hispana*.
3. Ley de Registro Civil, 1870.
4. Cánovas del Castillo, *Discurso sobre la nación*, 70–73.
5. See Junco, *Mater Doloros*.

solute astonishment to the first demands that Catalan be given co-official status with Castilian. In 1896 a Valencian legitimist and Carlist, representative to the Spanish Parliament, presented a motion requiring school teachers to have knowledge of the regional language if it was other than Castilian in the place where they taught. This was rejected in light of the risk that large areas of Spain would *continue to remain* ignorant of Castilian and therefore, not *integrate* into civilization. While the diverse languages, dialects, and popular or local forms of speech should be preserved in their natural state as characteristic of the area and included in a heritage of rich diversity that even enhanced Spanish identity, *civilized people* had to speak Castilian.

From 1900 on, state legislation became much more explicit in prescribing that Castilian be the primary and exclusive language for education, public administration, and public life.[6] In 1916 the first Catalan institution of self-government, the Mancomunitat de Catalunya, represented by the Catalan conservative party Lliga, presented a bill in the Spanish Parliament to make Catalan a co-official language in its territory. Though the bill received the support of several traditionalist representatives, it was rejected. In the parliamentary debates that began in 1916, a clear reaction to Catalan demands emerged throughout the political spectrum, from liberal conservatives to reformists, for two main reasons. First, it was seen as a "serious issue" that a nation-state have its own singular corresponding language. Second, linguistic diversity at administrative and official levels would create difficulties for the free circulation of goods and persons within Spanish borders. Moreover, concern regarding the *real* state of schooling in Castilian also became evident. A 1916 memorandum of the Royal Academy of the Spanish Language recognized that in many schools Castilian was not used for teaching and many local government edicts and official documents were not written in the *national language*. Although the "languages and dialects spoken in the intimacy of the home and in individual relations are respectable," the "voice" of the "single and intangible" nation could only be Castilian.[7] Perceptions of Galician and Catalan varied: some considered them languages, while to others they were "forms of speech" or even dialects. Basque was generically regarded as a language because its linguistic uniqueness did not allow it to be reduced to a

6. See Ferrer and Gironés, *La persecució política de la llengua catalana*, 82–90.
7. See the report reproduced in *Estudios Gallegos*, 18.

Castilian "dialect"; instead it was reduced to colloquial functions and considered a peculiar Iberian relic.

The linguistic debate gathered strength in the parliament and the Spanish public sphere, fed by increasingly intense discussion regarding the value that should be assigned to the common language and the *regional languages*. Opposition to the Catalan goal of becoming a co-official language in the governmental, legal, and educational spheres rapidly congealed and was expressed in the popular mobilizations that took place in several Castilian towns between November 1918 and February 1919, in reaction to the Catalan nationalist campaign for autonomy. The main accusations against Catalanism were its *lack of solidarity* with the rest of Spain and its attempt to gain privileges for Catalan manufacturers. Several outspoken anti-Catalanists, such as the Aragonese politician Antonio Royo Villanova, berated Catalan for lacking the universality of Castilian; only the latter could provide a spiritual nexus for unity and the expression of elevated thoughts.[8]

The Spanish Language as Symbol and Expression of the National Character

Defeat by the United States and the loss of Cuba in the war of 1898 marked the definitive end of the Spanish overseas empire, making it necessary to reformulate the constitutive elements of a Spanish national identity. The association of Castilian Spanish with the national character became more frequent as (1) concern over strengthening ties with the young Latin American republics increased, and (2) the greater visibility of Catalanist proposals within the national territory, as seen above, brought language to the forefront as a symbol and key *ethnic marker* of the national past and present.

Examples of this include historian Rafael Altamira, a great theorist of the collective psychology of the Spanish people, who wrote that "the spirit of a people is found in its language."[9] The Basque writer Miguel de Unamuno considered *race*, national spirit, and language to be intrinsically linked: "language creates the spiritual and psychological race, which is the blood of the spirit." Though projected from a Hispanic-American angle, this sense of

8. See Luzón, "De agravios, pactos y símbolos," 119–51, and Medina, *L'anticatalanisme del diari ABC (1916–1936)*.
9. See Altamira, *Psicología del Pueblo Español*, 79–80, as well as his *Historia de España y de la Civilización Española*, 28–29.

race could also be understood from the perspective of internal national integration. Paradoxically, as Unamuno distanced himself from vernacular languages, particularly Basque, he denied for the other languages of Spain what he defended for Castilian: that language was intrinsic to the collective genius of a people. Linguistic substitution he would argue—such as having Basques speak Castilian—in no way weaken the collective personality of those Spaniards whose original mother tongue was not Castilian. In his discourse at the literary contests in Bilbao in 1902, Unamuno stated that the Basque language was dying a natural death, but that this would make it possible for its soul to live on. All of the languages of Spain had merged or would merge into Castilian, the only language that should receive official protection.[10] Castilian was not only the most extensively used language, but supposedly had the most consolidated high literature. It was also considered ontologically superior to the other peninsular languages, including Portuguese. Melded with its land of origin (Castile), its sober and audacious phonetics (five vowels, */h/*, aspirated */j/*) were incomparable in the family of romance languages. It reflected the rugged, austere, adventure-loving Castilian spirit. For much of the literary Generation of 1898, Castile had forged the soul of Spain.

In the early twentieth century, modernized philology emerged in Spain as an academic discipline with ambitious research to establish the bases for the prestige and universality of Castilian. This was aimed at Spain itself and the Americas, in an attempt to avoid creolization of the language and fragmentation of linguistic norms. Much research was carried out on the history of the language, particularly between 1910 and 1936, by the Centro de Estudios Históricos, under the direction of historian and philologist Ramón Menéndez Pidal.[11] He laid the groundwork for intertwining history, language, and race or cultural community, considering the evolution of languages to be somewhat dependent on political factors.[12] Menéndez Pidal was attempting to demonstrate one key idea: that from the unifying *Reconquista* of Spain from the Muslims and throughout the Middle Ages, Castilian had progressively established its hegemony over the other Iberian languages to become the language of the culture. Castilian included

10. See Pérez-Nievas, "Lengua, territorio y conciencia nacional en España (1839–1975)," 249–51, as well as Resina, "'Por su propio bien,'" 137–66.
11. See the exhaustive analysis by Isasti, *La España metafísica*.
12. Sánchez, *Heterodoxos españoles*, 276–356.

elements adopted from all the other peninsular languages. Centuries of interaction between them had indirectly consolidated the propensity toward political unity and expressed certain similar national character traits throughout the Iberian Peninsula. Castilian had absorbed contributions from the "lost" Asturian, Leonese, and Aragonese languages and even from Basque. It had established itself among both high and low classes throughout the Spanish territory. Castile had provided a stable context in which this language could mature. A literary variant of superior prestige had evolved thanks to an expansionist will, yet at the same time it maintained its essence. Thus, Castilian had become *the* Spanish language par excellence.[13] In his 1925 work *Orígenes del español*, Pidal went on to describe how Castilian was phonetically, morphologically, and syntactically a more *audacious* language, the expression of a "rebellious and discordant force that had arisen in and around the Cantabria valleys," reflected in its radical departure from vulgar Latin. Castilian also showcased a "more correct artistic taste, having adopted early on the most euphonic forms of the vowel sounds." The entrepreneurial and universalizing spirit of Castile, the character of its inhabitants and its promising future as the vehicle of a superior civilization had guaranteed the consolidation and expansion of its language.[14]

The work of Menéndez Pidal and his school of thought also involved reaffirming the role of Spanish in the world and the prestige of Spain as the civilization responsible for the linguistic unity of Hispanic America. The Iberian convergence of language and dialects into Castilian was a prelude to the subsequent fusion and harmonization of American dialects of Castilian.[15] The Spanish nation therefore was predestined, or historically inevitable, even prior to the Roman *Hispania*.

These basic concepts fed all the subsequent Spanish nationalist discourse on the "supremacy" of the Castilian language in the decades that followed. Nuances were imposed by the strategic need for Spanish Republicans to reach an agreement with Catalan Republicans. Also, between 1900 and 1936 sub-state nationalist movements began actively promoting, strengthening, and defending their own languages, which were gradually becom-

13. Pidal, *Manual de Gramática histórica española*, 2.

14. Pidal, *Los españoles en la Historia*, 144–52.

15. See Valle, "Menéndez Pidal, la regeneración nacional y la utopía lingüística," 108–36.

ing standardized, particularly in Catalonia. From 1917 on, Spanish nationalist opposition to demands for autonomy reinforced the symbolism of the defense of the Spanish language, primarily against Catalanism and later against Galician and Basque nationalism. This overshadowed other arguments, such as the "lack of solidarity" among sub-state nationalists. After 1931, the linguistic rights of the Castilian speakers living in the autonomous bilingual territories were incorporated into the debate.

As the traditional arguments to justify Castilian hegemony became radicalized, the focus of public debate shifted to the introduction of sub-state languages into the educational system. During the 1923 to 1930 dictatorship of General Primo de Rivera, tough and repressive legislation prohibited the use of languages other than Castilian in school (but not, paradoxically, in literature, advertising, or the press).[16] Well-known Spanish linguists and intellectuals participated in the heated 1931 parliamentary debates on the new Republican Constitution, as well as the debates surrounding the ratification of the Statutes of Autonomy of Catalonia (1932), the Basque Country (1933), and Galicia (1936), which were approved during the short-lived Second Spanish Republic.

The Castilian Right of Conquest and the Other Languages of Spain (1936–1950)

The *New* Spain that emerged in the areas controlled by Franco's rebel army during the Spanish Civil War (1936–1939) sought the complete authoritarian renationalization of Spain and eradication of sub-state nationalisms. This included a policy of linguistic uniformity. It is true that the war period gave rise to a variety of different attitudes regarding the political structuring of the new Francoist state. However, the other languages were generally regarded as connotative of folkloric peculiarities and relegated to marginal and subordinate roles. In his school instruction manual of 1938, Basque writer José-María Salaverría emphasized that the Basque Provinces were the indomitable bastion of the best Hispanic virtues, including their ancient language or *Euskara*;[17] but Basque greatness could only be carried forward in the New Spain. In prior years, Spanish fascism had proclaimed its tolerance (in theory) toward regional languages and cultures, so long as they remained within the sphere of literature about customs and folk-

16. See Fernández de Soto, *Haciendo españoles*, 239–58.
17. Salaverría, *El muchacho español*, 61.

lore.[18] Nevertheless, this "openness" was quickly swept away by the desire to subdue the vanquished.

Public criticism for speaking languages other than Castilian, at least outside the home, was frequent in the Francoist rearguard. The Falangist press and Francoist broadcast stations insisted on the need to speak exclusively in Castilian in the public arena. Some journalists and politicians argued that the Catholic tradition was linked to the vernacular and timidly defended the recognition of regional languages and their reintroduction as an auxiliary language in primary education. This was overpowered by the conviction that linguistic homogenization was a safer bet for the construction of the New Spain. Any official recognition of regional differences, no matter how minor, might be counterproductive. This included even the idiomatic use of the vernacular in private spheres. Spain was hence considered a single nation with a single official language; but one that included several "dialects" and "incomplete" languages. In reserving the public sphere exclusively for Castilian, these other vernaculars became diglossic and were condemned to extinction in the mid-range. [19]

Paradoxically, the legal framework for enforcing monolingualism tended to be fairly lax and circumstantial, not overly imposing. There were several military edicts expressly prohibiting the use of languages other than Castilian in the public sphere and dispositions banning anything but Castilian for titles, regulations, and statutes, but there was no law to establish a general framework for prohibiting the use of minority languages. Linguistic repression was primarily an intertwined network of suspicions, pressures, fear of informants, and arbitrary interpretations by agents in authority.

The official creed imposed during the first years of the Franco regime insisted that all other national languages were nothing but dialects and inappropriate for modern use, especially in public administration and professional activities. Vernacular languages could be tolerated in minor literary genres, such as satire, burlesque theater for popular consumption, or folkloric poetry.[20] Even so, it might be considered suspicious if it had committed the original sin of being used by the "red-separatists" during the Civil War. Clergymen Albino and Ignacio Menéndez-Reigada, in their

18. See several texts in Primo de Rivera *La Falange y Cataluña*.

19. See Seixas, ¡Fuera el invasor!, 306–20.

20. See Massot and Muntaner, *El primer franquisme a Mallorca*, 429–33.

book *Catecismo patriótico español* (1937), wrote that the Castilian language was the only educated language for Spain and the future language of civilization. They described Castilian as the language of Spain but noted the existence of the Galician, Valencian, Majorcan, and Catalan "dialects"; as well as the Basque language, which was "unique but limited to the functions of a dialect due to its linguistic and philological poverty."[21]

The intensity of daily linguistic repression varied from one region to another, corresponding in part to how threatening to the political unity of Spain the particular vernacular was perceived. Curiously, and as it happened in Fascist Italy or Nazi Germany, in the midst of all of this, an academic, scholarly, folkloric, and ethnographic revival of interest in sub-national languages and dialects emerged, although not without a certain propagandistic function.[22] This was manifest in the journal *Revista de Dialectología y Tradiciones Populares*, which was founded in 1944. Research and monographs published by several provincial institutions also helped spark interest, for example, in the Asturian dialect presented as *bable*. Some books and brochures on peasants and folklore were published in Galician. By 1949, around twenty books on religious themes had been published in the Basque language.[23] In Catalonia, several children's and religious theater pieces were performed and select works were reedited in the vernacular.[24] Limited use of vernacular languages could even be found in legal texts, novels, and poetry, as well as local Catholic and Falangist-leaning newspapers during the early 1940s. The various academies of the vernacular languages survived under Francoism in spite of constant hindrances and staffing with members loyal to the regime. The message was clear: regional languages and dialects could survive in a premodern, rural and prestandardized state, and texts could be published in minor literary genres, folklore, and ethnography, but without defining any written standard norm. This was regarded as another way of re-creating the entire range of Spanish traditions. An illustration can be found in the use of the Valencian variant of Catalan during local festivities, particularly the *Fallas* and the literary contests or *Jocs Florals*,

21. Reigada, *Catecismo patriótico español*, 39–41.
22. Extensively on this aspect, see Núñez and Umbach, "Hijacked Heimats," 295–316.
23. de Pablo, "La lingua basca durante la Dittatura franchista," 123–44; Freitas, *A represión lingüística en Galiza no século XX*.
24. See Gallofré, *L'edició catalana i la censura franquista (1939–1951)*.

which were permitted as early as July of 1939.[25]

In the late 1940s the Francoist elites began to "clean up" the image of the regime in order to gain favor with the Western world. This did not extend to changes in the legal framework; it was deemed sufficient to reduce the intensity of daily linguistic repression practices. Peripheral languages did not regain any legal status and education remained exclusively in Castilian. In Catalonia and the Basque Country there were some private and semi-clandestine initiatives to teach Catalan and Euskara from 1943 onward. However, the Francoist regime continued to intervene very intensely to control what was published in sub-state languages through the mid-1960s.

Francoist Spanish Nationalism: The Supremacy of Castilian Over the "Other" Languages (1950–1975)

Francoism made a radical turn back toward a traditional understanding of Iberian languages and their "natural" hierarchies within Spanish nationalism. By the end of the Spanish Civil War (1936–1939) it was no longer possible for these alternative languages to be (re) assimilated due to the prewar efforts at linguistic recovery that had been fostered by the alternative nationalisms. The first objective of Francoist linguistic policy was to place Castilian on the throne of linguistic supremacy, to which it was "inherently entitled." Pre-1936 arguments of intrinsic superiority, greater usefulness, a universal dimension, intellectual prestige, and association with the soul of Castile and the national spirit of Spain were resurrected to crown Castilian as the only official language. The semantic association between minority languages, rural backwardness, localism, and traditionalism was also revived.

Thus a paradox arose during Francoism: On the one hand there was accelerated cultural assimilation of the allophone peripheries into the Castilian-speaking mainstream of Spain, fostered by compulsory education in Castilian for the entire population. The extension of mass media in Castilian, primarily radio and later television, also contributed to extending the standardized knowledge and use of Castilian. In addition to this, urban Catalonia, and especially the Barcelona metropolitan area, the Basque Provinces, the Balearic Islands, and Valencia were strongly affected by internal migration from the rest of Spain, which greatly increased the

25. See Ballester, *Temps de quarantena* and Cortés and Catalunya, "Poesia franquista valenciana," 109–22.

number of monolingual Castilian speakers in these areas.

On the other hand, however, the minority languages did not disappear. From the late 1940s on, clandestine nationalist movements increased initiatives to defend their peripheral languages as the banner of their cause. Each of these minority languages had its own speed and rhythm of recovery in public spheres. As soon as certain official dispositions were relaxed, new publishing initiatives began in Catalonia. In the Balearic Islands and Valencia, culture was the main sphere of action for nationalist groups. The struggle for control of the public spheres also created areas of broad social consensus regarding the Catalan language. Both the quantity and variety of books published in Catalan increased after the 1950s.[26] In the Basque Country, the Catholic Church was the main guardian of the autochthonous language until well into the 1960s. After 1950, a quiet rebirth was evident in the lesser genres of poetry and theater.[27] In Galicia, publishing in the vernacular was virtually monopolized by *Galaxia*, a publishing house created in July 1950 by a group composed of survivors of the nationalist prewar party *Partido Galeguista*. Its impact was qualitatively noteworthy, though quantitatively limited to urban society and the Galician middle class.[28]

Throughout the 1950s and 1960s, the belligerent position of the regime against vernacular languages became more moderated and nuanced. Catalan, Galician, and Basque came to be considered as languages that had contributed to the Spanish cultural heritage and enjoyed a certain literary tradition. Though forbidden in public or educational spheres, they were tolerated for literary expression, but the limited use they were allowed in festivities and commemorations increased. The regime shifted toward a permissive stance regarding the publication of books in regional languages. Literary censorship served as the filter of what was acceptable to publish or disseminate in minority languages. Until 1958, translations from foreign languages to vernacular languages were generally denied license and the genres of greatest intellectual and literary prestige tended to be those most rigorously

---

26. See Crexell, *Català a l'escola*, 35–47; Vallverdú, "Catalanisme i reivindicació lingüística," 229–42.

27. See Tejerina, *Nacionalismo y lengua*, 119–21; Gurrutxaga, *El código nacionalista vasco durante el franquismo*, 183–86, and Sarasola, *Historia social de la literatura vasca*.

28. Seixas, "Galeguismo e cultura durante o Primeiro Franquismo (1939–1960)," 85–103.

censored.[29]

However, exiled Catalan and Galician groups periodically launched initiatives from France or the Americas to denounce the linguistic repression of the Franco regime, which was seeking to improve its standing with international public opinion. Prior to the 1954, and the UNESCO Eighth General Conference in Montevideo, there were bitter words in the Argentine press between journalists close to the Franco regime and exiled intellectuals. A Francoist literary critic stated that the Franco regime was not persecuting the Galician language and that it was not officially prohibited; in fact, several poetry books "and even some novels" had been published in the last decade. He argued that the triumph of Castilian was simply a case of "*a mental horizon* that had broadened in Galicia," where writers now aspired to something more than "outdated ruminating and nostalgia," and that a natural law was being fulfilled. "Local languages tend to merge into the national language. This is a law of culture," and Castilian was a universal language of the future.[30]

The most widely used school handbooks in Francoist Spain clearly minimized the value of regional languages, arguing that they were adequate for literature and intimate communication within a limited scope, but not for modern life, science, or essay due to their lack of contemporary vocabulary. The exceptional linguistic nature of Basque was recognized as a unique part of the national heritage, but was also considered poor for the functions of modern life and expression. However, ambiguity regarding what value to assign the vernacular languages increased as the regime matured. The 1944 handbook *Enciclopedia Práctica* defined a language as "the special manner of speaking of each country. The language of Spain is Castilian, or Spanish." No mention was even made of the other languages or dialects of Spain.[31] In the 1950s, classical arguments of universality, intrinsic phonetic, grammatical, and orthographical perfection, along with its rich literary heritage from the Middle Ages were recommissioned to bolster the superiority of Castilian. The existence of other languages and dialects was recognized, but considered historically inferior. They had been diluted in the triumphal march of Castilian toward he-

29. Gallofré, "Les 'Nuevas normas sobre idiomas regionales' i les traduccions durant els anys cinquanta," 5–17.
30. Mostaza, "El gallego no es un idioma prohibido," 592.
31. Fernández, *Enciclopedia práctica*, 112.

gemony. The 1957 *Enciclopedia elemental* published by the Female Section of the Fascist Falange party stated the following:

> *The Spanish language* is the language of the countries that constitute the *Hispanidad*, that is, our Homeland and the nations that it formed in its civilizing work throughout History; in other words, the twenty Hispanic-American States, the Philippines and our current colonies. . . . It is estimated that more than 100 million human beings have the privilege afforded by destiny and race to express themselves in Spanish, the most opulent and beautiful of all modern languages due to its harmonious phonetics, the most rational orthography of all existing languages, the richness and infinite delicate nuances of its vocabulary, its flexibility and elegance, which allows and even facilitates the weaving of the finest stylistic patterns, and in sum, its literature.
>
> The first romance language or language derived from Latin that was spoken in the Peninsula was not Spanish but rather the more archaic Galician-Catalan, which gave rise to both these languages as well as Portuguese. Then, after a period of Leonese-Aragonese . . . arose the more mature and perfect Spanish, which was first known as *Castilian,* . . . and then, with the Reconquista [of Spain from the Moors], this language gradually permeated the entire Peninsula until it became the emblematic Spanish language in the imperial sense. . . . The Basque language is not a romance language, but an aggregate existing from the times of the Iberian [tribes], and has remained intact largely due to its geographic isolation. . . . Later on, Castilian or Spanish for various reasons formed its own dialects such as Andalusian, Canarian or Extremeño . . . along with the Spanish of the Americas and the Philippines.[32]

Nine years after this, a commonly used school handbook escalated the imprecision with a definition that established a political hierarchy between language (spoken by a nation) and dialect (spoken in a region). It then proceeded to confuse matters by referring to Galician, Catalan, and Basque as languages, in contrast with the Bable, Extremeño, and Andalusian dialects:

> Language.—Language is the manner of speaking of a people or nation. In Spain we speak Spanish or Castilian; in France, French is spoken. . . .
>
> Dialect.—A dialect refers to the specific manner of writing and speaking the official language of a country in certain regions. Dialects lack a literary tradition. . . . In Spain dialects include *Bable* or Asturian, *Extremeño* and *Andalusian*. In contrast, Catalan, Galician and Basque are categorized as languages and

32. Enciclopedia Elemental, 176–78.

Valencian is a dialectical variant of Catalan.[33]

In addition to this, the democratic opposition movement began to equate democracy with political decentralization and the delegitimization of Spanish national discourse and symbolism, which increased the osmosis between the cultural, linguistic, and even political tenets of the peripheral nationalists and the Spanish national left wing. The demand for full co-official status for the regional languages became the banner that was symbolically, but not always pragmatically waved by many who opposed Francoism. This foreshadowed a change in attitude among many Spanish democratic nationalists, in which the vernacular languages came to be seen as part of the heritage and richness of Spain. They were neither subordinate nor hierarchically inferior; nor were they an unavoidable pragmatic concession to a reality that was no longer considered easier to manage by being monolinguistic. However, most left-wing parties did not embrace the equality or symmetry of all the other languages of Spain, except in Catalonia. Castilian was still pragmatically assumed to be the language of common communication, though it was no longer symbolically exalted as such.[34]

With the 1970 General Law on Education, history textbooks moderated and covered over the most generic, organic, historicist, and idealist features of classical Spanish nationalism. However, the stereotypes and values that associated language with national character or collective psychology lingered on in Spanish literature and language textbooks, most of which were produced by disciples of Menéndez Pidal, such as Rafael Lapesa and Fernando Lázaro Carreter. Thus their decisive influence on banal perceptions regarding the coexistence of several languages in Spain endured. Even after 1975, when Francoism died with its dictator, statements in textbooks still claimed that "Castile, restless and ambitious in politics, revolutionary in law, heroic in its epic achievements, was linguistically the most innovative region. Just as its prodigious vitality destined it to be the axis of national enterprises, its dialect would become the language of the entire Hispanic community"; Castilian was the reflection of the "particular temperament of a country."[35]

---

33. Pérez, Enciclopedia intuitiva-sintética-práctica, 89.
34. Núñez Seixas, "Nuevos y viejos nacionalistas," 59–87; Archilés, "El 'olvido' de España," 103–22.
35. Facal, "La nación ocultada," 111–59.

Language and Spanish Nationalism Since 1975

The monopolization of Spanish nationalist discourse by Francoism and the antidemocratic right influenced the entire spectrum of Spanish nationalists or "patriots," particularly during the final years of Franco regime and the transition to democracy, as they sought to appear democratically legitimized. Any explicit affirmation of Spanish patriotism was automatically delegitimized and identified with old-school National-Catholic tenets. This was particularly noticeable in liberal and left-wing circles as well as in the awkwardness that most democratic parties experienced concerning the public use of the word "Spain." Until the mid-1990s, the social and organizational expression of Spanish nationalism was disjointed at best; but it quietly survived in both the right and left wings of the political spectrum. Its broad internal diversity is characteristic of all nationalist ideologies, with the additional special mix of civic tenets and ethno-cultural elements that form the complex and elaborate ideologies found in stateless nationalisms.[36] All manner of political and social actors with their multifarious worldviews and ideological programs can be found rallying round the flag of Spain as the sole and sovereign entity with collective political rights.

With the new territorial framework set forth in the 1978 Constitution, Spanish nationalist discourse had to be reinvented. Explicit Spanish nationalism disappeared from the statements and speeches of most political parties and leaders, with the exception of the far right and post-Francoist conservatives. Defense of the territorial integrity of the Spanish nation by left-wing leaders and intellectuals was never defined as nationalism, but rather "patriotism" or "loyalty to the Constitution" of 1978. Not until the mid-1990s did conservatives begin to wave the banner of explicit Spanish patriotism, which was sometimes equated with "good nationalism."

Spanish patriotic discourse has been present in the public sphere since the 1990s, particularly through mass media, books, and pamphlets. The rearticulation of Spanish nationalism springs from confrontations with stateless nationalisms and is primarily concerned with supporting Spain as a nation, while opposing and stigmatizing minority nationalisms. This is the fruit of a slow process in which the main ideological currents within Spanish

36. See Balfour and Quiroga, *The Reinvention of Spain*, as well as Seixas, *Patriotas y demócratas*; Ibid., "What is Spanish Nationalism Today?," 719–752.

nationalism and patriotic discourse have adapted to the new circumstances of a democratic Spain. It includes:

a) Adaptation to the new political/institutional framework established by the 1978 Constitution and the State of the Autonomous Communities. Renewed Spanish nationalist discourse had to recognize the institutional plurality that had resulted from the pressure of the stateless nationalisms, while also adjusting to political decentralization.
b) The reinvention of a new political and historical legitimacy that side-steps the legacy of Francoism and recent historical memory to make a fresh start at the most basic symbolic level. The need to "forget" the Civil War and the Franco regime in order to coexist with the main actors of the democratic transition made it difficult for many Spanish democratic nationalists to unite around common issues; but one of which was most definitely the defense of the Spanish language.
c) Ongoing challenges to Spanish nationalism by sub-state nationalisms. The continual demands of the latter for increased self-government reaffirm political goals that clearly exceed the boundaries of the 1978 Constitution. Certain persistent ethnocentric tenets in the discourse and praxis of minority nationalisms, along with the terrorist violence that continued throughout the first decade of the twenty-first century have encouraged the resurgence of Spanish patriotic discourse as an ongoing reaction to stateless nationalisms, particularly Basque nationalism.

Spanish nationalism has also had to adapt to the new legal framework that regulates the linguistic question. However, while this legal framework recognizes the full co-official status of the autonomous languages in their respective territories, it also houses a clear legal asymmetry: every Spanish citizen has the *duty* to know Castilian, but only the *right* to use and know the sub-state languages. The Statutes of several Autonomous Communities tend to symbolically reinforce the vernacular as *the* language of the area, which has facilitated a variety of positive discrimination measures in an effort to give the vernacular clear symbolic primacy. Linguistic quotas for primary and secondary education were not established by the central state; they were instead left to be regulated by the autonomous communities. Each of the bilingual autonomous communities has developed its own linguistic policies. The results have also been quite diverse but can be summarized as a notable increase in the vernacular linguistic competence of the population along with increased public presence and symbolic dominance of the minority languages in several fields.

However, social use of vernacular languages has not advanced as notably vis-à-vis Castilian as was expected.

The linguistic question has become one of the most effective symbolic arguments of Spanish nationalism, since its use by the far right and a portion of the post-Francoist right wing as a topic of opposition to the 1978 Constitution. It was present in the reticence of the conservative party Popular Alliance (*Alianza Popular*) to full bilingualism in the autonomous communities and the use of the term *nationality* throughout much of the 1980s. However, in some places the conservative right adopted a neo-regionalist discourse and practice that actually incorporated a number of sub-state nationalist demands regarding language, particularly in Galicia and the Balearic Islands. This discourse has waned since the beginning of twenty-first century.

The patriotic discourse of the Spanish right wing in the Basque Country and Catalonia has criticized the objectives and methods of the linguistic policies implemented by the autonomic governments. During the 1980s and 1990s, some spokesmen insisted on the discriminatory nature of these linguistic and cultural normalization policies, denouncing the "persecution" of Castilian as a first step in the balkanization and fragmentation of the Spanish nation. The frequency, intensity, and aggressiveness of this issue in the Spanish press increased most notably after 1993–1994. Sub-state nationalisms were portrayed as tending toward intrinsically totalitarian positions by emphasizing collective rights and seeking to impose a monolithic culture on citizens. Journalist Federico Jiménez Losantos and Aleix Vidal-Quadras, former leader of the Popular Party in Catalonia and a brilliant polemist,[37] spoke against the linguistic policies of Catalonia's autonomous government in the 1980s. Fairly similar reactions have occurred in Galicia, particularly within fringe groups since 2006.[38]

Although sub-state languages are no longer reduced to "dialects," at least in public discourse, in Spanish conservative nationalism there is still the idea that Castilian is intrinsically superior. While it is no longer based on historicist arguments, the discourse of Spanish neo-patriotism centers around, one, the greater diffusion and universality of Castilian and thus, the greater usefulness of Castilian. Two, the de facto universal knowledge of Castilian

37. See Losantos, *Lo que queda de España*; Vidal-Quadras, *Cuestión de fondo*; Tubau, *Nada por la patria*.
38. See Jardón, *La "normalización" lingüística*.

by the Spanish population, accompanied by the embedded notion of Castilian as the natural language of all Spaniards. And three, the defense of the linguistic rights of Castilian speakers in bilingual territories, giving priority to individual rights over collective ones, and the freedom of choice of language in administration and education for all citizens. All of these points provide Spanish neo-patriotism with a coating of democratic legitimacy vis-à-vis the sub-state nationalisms, which emphasize ethnic, cultural, and supposedly organic, objective factors.

Spanish conservative thinking has also resurrected the old triumphalist argument regarding the invented and artificial nature of the standardized linguistic norms of the minority languages; an argument that has always been leveled against the unified norm of Basque (*euskara batua*), and has begun to affect Galician as well.[39] The new frame of meaning that is being subliminally distilled in these two regions considers the "modern" (middle class, professional, urban) speaker of minority languages as a peripheral nationalist but not a spontaneous, traditional (rural, working class) and natural speaker of the vernacular. Such individuals are seen as conscious deserters of the Castilian language, possibly because they hope to advance in the regional public administration system, secure a regional teaching position, or obtain some other advantage. The defense or practice of minority languages "overburdens" linguistic politics and thus the speakers should be left to choose their language of expression. Again we encounter resistance to positive discrimination in favor of minority languages, mainly from the right though occasionally from the left, as classic liberal arguments are combined with cost-effectiveness issues and other entirely unscientific rationales, such as the supposed incompatibility of simultaneously learning minority languages as opposed to more "useful" foreign languages.

Much of Spanish nationalist or patriotic discourse still venerates Castilian as the defining Spanish national and cultural identity marker and even the greatest contribution of Spain to universal culture, especially through its rich literary legacy.[40] The traditional role of language comes packaged with a sense of economic

39. See Freire, *Las paradojas de la "normalización" del gallego.*
40. See Salvador, *Lengua española y lenguas de España*; Lodares, *El paraíso políglota and id*, and Ibid., *Babel airada*. See also Bueno, *El mito de la cultura*; id., *El mito de la izquierda, España no es un mito.*

utility in an era of globalization,[41] a tool for economic and commercial progress, thanks especially to the fact that Spanish has become the second language de facto in the United States. This overrides the traditional reticence toward Spanglish, which has been considered an unacceptable deformation of the language in the Hispanic context. It is quite contradictory, since in the United States Spanish is considered a second-rate language with very debatable social prestige and no official recognition in any of the fifty states. But this has had an additional meaning in terms of domestic Spanish politics. In a July, 2003 speech in New Mexico, José-María Aznar, the conservative president of the Spanish government, described North American Hispanics as people with multiple identities, in contrast with "societies that exclude" and use languages and cultures as weapons.[42]

Though the discourse on the linguistic question deployed by Spanish democratic nationalism generically recognizes and condemns the repression of minority languages by the Franco regime and the Spanish nation-state in prior periods, there is an underlying conviction that loss of the minority languages was the necessary sacrifice for progress and modernity; therefore, it is not necessary for the speakers of the majority language to continue expressing remorse. The vice president of the Royal Academy of the Spanish Language, Gregorio Salvador, created no small polemic in May 2007 when he stated that the linguistic imposition of Castilian by the Francoist State was wrong yet forgivable, since it resulted in all Spaniards learning and becoming proficient in a universal language. However, the inverse process of imposing minority languages, which are thought useless for relating to a larger world, would be seen as much less forgivable from a normative perspective.[43] A similar argument was proposed in response to the accusations of cultural genocide that are periodically expressed by some Latin American leaders: Castilian was not imposed on the Americas by right of conquest, but as a consequence of its natural superiority and as a vehicle for communication between peoples.

Since 2005, conservative nationalism has renewed its offensive. Bilingualism is accepted only within certain limits, accompanied by express symbolic recognition of the dominance of

41. del Valle and Gabriel-Steehman, "Lengua y mercado," 253–63.
42. *El País*, 7 12, 2003.
43. See *El País*, 11 5,2007.

Castilian. However, there is still room for pragmatic nuancing of discourse and positions by conservatives, especially when addressing the Catalan and Galician electorates or when Catalan nationalist votes are needed in the Lower House of the Spanish Parliament. Some of these tenets have also mobilized part of the left. The new party Unión Progreso y Democracia (UPyD) has managed to find a niche within the political space between the most secular-liberal segments of the conservative electorate and the most disenchanted left-wing voters who are tired of the pseudo-confederate tendencies of the State of the Autonomies. This party has unabashedly fed the polemics regarding the policies of linguistic normalization in the bilingual autonomous communities, particularly Catalonia and Galicia, defending of the rights of Castilian speakers who are "discriminated" against when choosing a language in the spheres of education or citizen interaction with public administrations. This question is especially prominent in the foundational manifesto of UPyD, which clearly states that:

> A State under the Rule of Law needs a common language, and its use is not only a matter of personal choice but also and especially a political instrument for the linguistic structuring of the democracy itself. All the languages of our nation are respectable and worthy of support, but Castilian is also essential as a vehicle for understanding one another and debating questions.[44]

A common language thus becomes a necessary instrument for articulating the large spheres of democratic deliberation and socioeconomic solidarity and cohesion. To possess and privilege a common language therefore becomes a "progressive" demand to the extent that it is thought to be linked to equal rights for all citizens inhabiting the Spanish State.

The Spanish left wing has oscillated between a conception of Spain as a nation of nations, which is a specific reading of the concept of constitutional patriotism, and the idea of a plural Spain proposed early in the millennium by President José Luis Rodríguez Zapatero. Within this idea, the multicultural nature of Spain as a nation that is a sum of cultures, languages and diverse yet complementary identities has been reaffirmed. These matters are felt differently in Catalonia, Galicia, and the Basque Country than in the rest of Spain. In linguistic matters, the left wing in Spain has generally followed the principles of the constitution,

44. See the founding manifesto of UPyD in: www.upyd.es/servlets/VerFichero?id=11223.

with very diverse local and regional expressions: from adamantly Castilianist mayors to leaders thoroughly identified with linguistic normalization for peripheral languages. The left has sought to avoid making language a matter of conflict and to distance it from public debate.

The positions defended by the Socialist leader José Luis Rodríguez Zapatero and his team between 2000 and 2010 regarding the national question do not reflect careful intellectual design, and are theoretically opaque. The central idea appeared in the 2002–2003 manifestos projecting Spain as "a plural and integrating Nation, proud of its diversity and its linguistic and cultural pluralism."[45] Since then, Zapatero has gradually articulated the idea of a plural Spain as the central axis for dialogue on Spain and the Spanish nation, often with elements of carefully calculated identity ambiguity. He describes Spain as a nation, not a pluri-national state; but it is a multicultural nation based on civic values and democratic deliberation, including diverse cultures, capable of hosting multiple versions of collective identities with variable intensity and a legacy of shared historic and cultural roots. Belief in the existence of these roots and the need to bring them to the forefront became patent in the initiatives of the Zapatero administration during its first legislative period (2004–2008), which included celebrating the four hundredth anniversary of the publication of *Don Quijote* in 2005 and promoting the international efforts of the Instituto Cervantes, founded in 1991, to establish a commemorative day for the Spanish language. April 23 was suggested for the Commemorative Day for the Spanish Language to honor the death of Cervantes, rather than the October 12 Día de la Hispanidad. More recently, June 18 was proposed as "E Day" (Español Day) in several cities; commemorative acts take place on that day and a Castilian word is voted by Internet.[46]

The greatest value and essential richness of the identity of Spain would reside precisely in the internal plurality of cultures and languages as expressed in the Declaration of Santillana del Mar, signed by the territorial leaders of the Socialist party in August, 2003. Their definition of Spain as a "shared project of coexistence" echoed words expressed long ago by Ernest Renan and José Ortega y Gasset. It was essentially a more radical reading of

---

45. See PSOE, *Manifiesto socialista para la España autonómica del siglo XXI*, 4, 14 2003.
46. See www.eldiae.es.

the concept of constitutional patriotism and the idea of a *nation of nations*, combined with an anticentralist view of the history of Spain and manifest in a symbolic policy of recognition of linguistic diversity with no debate on the constitutional status of languages. The motto was reframed in April of 2008, when in his inaugural speech before the Spanish Parliament, President Zapatero described Spain as a "united and diverse" nation that "distills its richness from its diversity. . . . A country united by its past but especially by its future."[47] Though this discourse appears to integrate vernacular languages symmetrically and without hierarchy, only one language has universal projection and symbolizes the role and contribution of Spain to world culture.

Some socialist intellectuals and leaders openly rejected the plural Spain formula for lacking a precise statement of elements common to all Spaniards. Thus, the former president of the Madrid region, Joaquín Leguina, expressed fear of a confederal tendency in the State of the Autonomies, fostered by the support of the PSOE for the Statute of Catalonia and warned of the explicit and obvious lack of solidarity of sub-state nationalisms as they defended the compulsory knowledge of their respective languages in their territories. And the jurist Luis Fajardo Spínola stated in 2009 that the State of the Autonomies needed functional reform in order to complete its development while retaining the "expression and representation of what is common"; in other words, the Spanish nation, one of whose most prominent elements is "the common language."[48]

Conclusion

In the final years of the Franco regime, Spanish nationalism began to rather visibly incorporate an acceptance of internal ethnocultural diversity, with variable tolerance toward the co-official nature of the peripheral languages. Nevertheless, problems arose when absolute symmetry of rights and duties among the various languages of Spain was postulated. Although plurality was recognized in the concept of the Spanish nation that democratic Spanish nationalism has integrated more or less ambitiously since the transition to democracy, the actual limits of that recognition in the linguistic sphere were imprecise and ambiguous. It has had

47. See www.la-moncloa.es/Presidente/Discursodeinvestidura/Españaunidaydiversa.htm.

48. Spínola, ¿Hacia otro modelo de Estado?, 217–18.

to adjust to the central role of linguistic demands in the sub-state nationalisms, whose maximum objective was no longer co-official status, but the full social normalization or even (in some cases) official exclusivity of their languages in their territories, on the legitimizing basis of having been persecuted under Francoism. The reticence of sub-state nationalisms toward accepting Castilian as a sociolinguistic reality in their territories, where it is in most cases the mother tongue of the majority of citizens, and as part of their own cultural legacy as a language that was not only seen as something foreign or imposed in the past,[49] constantly interacted with the Spanish nationalist tendency to not consider the vernacular languages as having full and equal rights and duties.

Does democratic Spanish nationalism today cherish and symbolically integrate the vernacular languages, embracing them as part of the Spanish cultural heritage? It does not, or at least not yet. It coexists with them because it must, to maintain the integrity of the nation. This position reflects some of the nostalgia expressed by Manuel Azaña, the president of the Spanish Second Republic, who wished for a homogenizing past like that of France, which might have simplified the governance of Spain. To him, the monarchy and the nineteenth-century liberal state had not finished their work in this area, leaving no alternative but to pragmatically cope with linguistic diversity.[50] Such reticence is also symbolically influenced by the fact that the non-Castilian languages in their current social configuration largely involve processes of standardization and policies of social normalization that have been mostly fostered by sub-state nationalist movements. This explains the persistent differences in the value assigned by Spanish nationalists to "our" regional languages: as Castilianized and more or less rural dialects they would express diversity within unity, rather than the elaborate "inventions" of the "separatists."

Bibliography

Altamira, Rafael. *Psicología del Pueblo Español.* Mardrid: F.Fé, 1902.

———. *Historia de España y de la Civilización Española.* Barcelona: Gili, 1911.

49. The hypothesis could be put forward that the success of the political aims of substate nationalisms will be directly dependent on their ability to coin inclusive and fully civic national projects, whose agende will not be focused on linguistic and ethnocultural claims.
50. Azaña, *Obras completas*, 511–13.

Álvarez Junco, José. *Mater Doloros: La idea de España en el siglo XIX*. Madrid: Taurus, 2001.

Alvarez Pérez, Antonio. *Enciclopedia intuitiva-sintética-práctica*. Valladolid: Miñon, 1964.

Archilés i Cardona, Fernan. "El 'olvido' de España: Izquierda y nacionalismo español en la Transición democrática; El caso del PCE," *Historia del presente* 2, no. 14 (2009): 103–22.

Azaña, Manuel. *Obras completas*. Mexcio: Ediciones Oasis, 1966–68.

Balfour, Sabastian and Alejandro Quiroga. *The Reinvention of Spain: Nation and Identity Since Democracy*. New York: Oxford University Press, 2007.

Ballester, Josep. *Temps de quarantena: Cultura i societat a la postguerra al País Valencià (1939–1959)*. Valencia: Universitat de València, 1992.

Bueno, Gustavo. *España no es un mito: Claves para una defensa razonada*. Madrid: Temas de Hoy, 2005.

———. *El mito de la cultura: Ensayo de la filosofía materialista de la cultura*. Barcelona, Editorial Prensa Ibérica, 1996.

———. *El mito de la izquierda: Las izquierdas y la derecha*. Barcelona: B, Editiones –Grupo Z, 2003.

Cánovas del Castillo, Antonio. *Discurso sobre la nación: Ateneo de Madrid, 6 de noviembre de 1882*. Madrid: Biblioteca Nueva, 1997.

Cortés, Santi and Anna Catalunya. "Poesia franquista valenciana (1939–1943)." *Caplletra* 5 (1988): 109–22.

Crexell, Joan. *Català a l'escola: Les campanyes populars sota el franquisme*. Barcelona: La magrana, 1998.

De Pablo, Santiago. "La lingua basca durante la Dittatura franchista: Repressione, resistenza e identità nazionale." *Storia contemporanea in Friuli* 37, (2007): 123–44.

Del Valle, José. "Menéndez Pidal, la regeneración nacional y la utopía lingüística." In *La batalla del idioma: La intelectualidad hispánica ante la lengua,* edited by José Del Valle and Luis Gabriel-Stheeman, 108–36. Madrid: Iberoamericana, 2004.

Del Valle, Jose and Luis Gabriel Steehman, "Lengua y mercado: El español en la era de la globalización económica." In *La batalla del idioma: La intelectualidad hispánica ante la lengua,* edited by José Del Valle and Luis Gabriel-Stheeman, 253–63. Madrid: Iberoamericana, 2004.

Falange Española Tradicionalista and Sección de las J.O.N.S. *Enciclopedia Elemental.* Madrid: [s.n.], 1946.

Fajardo Spínola, Luis and Joaquin Leguina Herrán. *¿Hacia otro modelo de Estado? Los socialistas y el Estado autonómico.* Cizur Menor: Civitas, 2009.

Fernández Rodriguez, Antonio and Juan Navarro Higuera. *Enciclopedia práctica: Grado medio.* Barcelona: Miguel A. Salvatella, 1946.

Ferrer Gironés, Francesc. *La persecución política de la llengua catalana: Història de les mesures preses contra el seu* ús *des de la Nova Plata fins avui.* Barcelona: Ediciones 82, 1985.

Freire, Andrés. *Las paradojas de la "normalización" del gallego.* February 3, 2014. www.fundacionfaes.org/file_upload/publication/pdf/20130520171105las-paradojas-de-la-normalizacion-del-gallego.pdf

Freitas Juvino, María Pilar. A *represión lingüística en Galiza no século XX: Aprozimación cualitativa á situación sociolingüística de Galiza.* Vigo: Edicións Xerais de Galicia, 2008.

Gallofré i Virgili, María Josepa. *L'edició catalana i la censura franquista (1939–1951).* Barcelona: Publicaciones de l'Abadia de Montserrat, 1991.

Gallofré i Virgili, María Josepa. "Les 'Nuevas normas sobre idiomas regionales' i les traduccions durant els anys cinquanta." 5–17. February 3, 2014. www.raco.cat/index.php/Marges/article/viewFile/109949/157285.

García Isasti, Prudencio. *La España metafísica: Lectura crítica al pensamiento de Ramón Menéndez Pidal (1891–1936).* Bilbo: Euskaltzaindia, 2004.

Gavinet, Angel. *Idearium español.* Buenos Aires, 1940.

Gurrutxaga, Ander. *El código nacionalista vasco durante el franquismo.* Barcelona: Anthropos, 1985.

Ibon Sarasola, José Antonio. *Historia social de la literatura vasca.* Madrid: Akal, 1982.

Jardón, Manuel. *La "normalización" lingüística: Una anormalidad democrática; El caso gallego*. Madrid: Siglo Veintiuno de España, 1993.

Jimenez Losantos, Federico. *Lo que queda de España: Con un prólogo sentimental y un epílogo balcánico*. Madrid: Temas de Hoy, 1995.

Ley de Registro Civil, 1870. www.euskalnet.net/e-abizenak/verano02/c_genealogia.html

Lodares Marrodán, Juan Ramón. *Lengua y patria: Sobre el nacionalismo en España*. Madrid: Taurus, 2002.

———. *El paraíso políglota: Historias de lenguas en la España moderna contada sin prejuicios*. Madrid: Taurus, 2000.

Lopez-Facal, Ramon "La nación ocultada." In *La gestión de la memoria: La Historia de España al servicio del poder*, 111–59. Barcelona: Crítica, 2000.

López García, Ángel. *Babel airada: Las lenguas en el trasfondo de la supuesta ruptura de España*. Madrid: Bibioteca Nueva, 2004.

———. *El rumor de los desarraigados: Conflict de lenguas en la Península Ibérica*. Barcelona: Editorial Anagrama, 1985.

López Sánchez, José María. *Heterodoxos españoles: El Centro de Estudios Históricos, 1910–1936*. Madrid: Marcel Pons: CSIC, 2006.

Mar-Molinero, Clare. "The Role of Language in Spanish Nation-Building." In *Nationalism and the nation in the Iberian Peninsula: Competing and conflicting identities*, edited by Clare Mar-Molinero and Angel Smith, 69–87. Washington, D.C.: Berg, 1996.

Marcilhacy, David, Javier Moreno Luzón and Monique Pinot. *Raza hispana: Hispanoamericanismo e imaginario nacional en la España de la Restauración*. Madrid: Centro de Estudios Político y Constitucionales, 2010.

Massot i Muntaner, Josep. *El primer franquisme a Mallorca: Guerra civil, repressió, exili i represa cultural*. Barcelona: Publicacions de l'Abadiade Montserrat, 1996.

Medina, Jaume. *L'anticatalanisme del diari ABC (1916–1936)*. Barcelona: Publicaciones de l'Abadia de Montserrat, 1995.

Menéndez Pidal, Ramón. *Manual de Gramática histórica española*.

Madrid: Espasa-Calpe, 1989.

———. *Los españoles en la Historia*. Madrid: Espasa-Calpe, 1991.

Menéndez-Reigada, Albino G. *Catecismo patriótico español*. Barcelona: Península, 2003.

Moreno Luzón, Javier. "De agravios, pactos y símbolos: El nacionalismo español ante la autonomía de Cataluña." *Ayer* 63, no. 3 (2006): 119–51

Mostaza, B. "El gallego no es un idioma prohibido." *Criterio* (August 12, 1954).

Núñez, Xosé-Monoel and Maiken Umbach. "Hijacked Heimats: National Appropriations of Local and Regional Identities in Germany and Spain, 1930–1945." *European Review of History* 15, no. 3 (June, 2008): 295–316.

Núñez Seixas, José. *¡Fuera el invasor! Nacionalismos y movilización bélica durante la guerra civil española 1936–1939*. Madrid: Marcel Pons: Ediciones de Historias, 2006.

———. "Galeguismo e cultura durante o Primeiro Franquismo (1939–1960): Unha interpretación." *Trabe de oro* 5, no. 19 (1994): 407–25.

———. "Nuevos y viejos nacionalistas: La cuestión territorial en el tardofranquismo, 1959–1975." *Ayer* 68 (2007): 59–87.

———. *Patriotas y demócratas: El discurso nacionalista español después de Franco*. Madrid: Catarata, 2010.

———. "What is Spanish Nationalism Today?: From Legitimacy Crisis to Unfulfilled Renovation (1975–2000)." *Ethnic and Racial Studies*, 24, no. 5 (2001): 719–752.

PSOE. "Manifiesto socialista para la España autonómica del siglo XXI." April 14, 2003. www.psoe.es/contents/showResource.do?urlRsr=/000000001500/000000001785.pdf.

Quiroga Fernández de Soto, Alejandro. *Haciendo españoles: La nacionalización de las masas en la Dictadura de Primo de Rivera (1923–1930)*. Madrid: Centro de Estudios Políticos y Constitucionales, 2008.

Resina, Juan Ramon. "'Por su propio bien': La identidad española y su gran inquisidor, Miguel de Unamuno." In *La batalla del idioma: La identidad hispánica ante la lengua,* edited by José del Valle and Luis Gabriel-Stheeman, 137–66. Madrid:

Iberoamericana, 2004.

Salvador, Gregorio. *Lengua española y lenguas de España*. Barcelona: Ariel, 1987.

Salaverría, José María. *El muchacho español*. San Sabastián: Librería Internacional [1940?].

Sepúlveda Muñoz, Isidro. *El sueño de la Madre Patria: Hispanoamericanismo y nacionalismo*. Madrid: Fundación Carolina, 2005.

Tejerina Montaña, Benjamín. *Nacionalismo y lengua: Los procesos de cambio lingüístico en el País Vasco*. Madrid: Siglo Veintiuno de España, 1992.

Tubau, Iván. *Nada por la patria: La construcción periodística de naciones virtuales*. Barcelona: Flor de Viento Ediciones, 1999.

Vallverdú, Francesc. "Catalanisme i reivindicació lingüística." In *Catalnisme: História, política y cultura*, edited by Tàboas Pancho, 229–42. Barcelona: Editorial L'Avenç, 1986.

Vidal-Quadras, Aleix. *Cuestión de fondo*. Barcelona: Montesinos, 1993.

Zabaltza Pérez-Nievas, Xabier. "Lengua, territorio y conciencia nacional en España (1839–1975)," Other Thesis, Universidad Pública de Navarra, 2003.

8

Nation-States and Native Tribal Language Vitality

Postcolonial Language Policy in North America and East Africa

Denis Viri

What matters far more than words—what matters far more than any resolution or declaration—are actions to match those words.

—Barack Obama, December 10, 2010

In the long term, the colonization of the Americas by Europeans has had a devastating effect on the continuity of virtually all American Indian languages. In fact, it was government policy, especially during the Indian boarding school era, to use punitive measures to eliminate the use of Native languages and to replace them with English. Ironically, although intended to serve as agents of assimilation, the boarding schools actually had the effect of unifying Native peoples as they witnessed the forced dissolution of the use of their tribal languages.[1] As a result, organized resistance, reinforced by innate cultural resilience, has helped usher in a period that Bonnie and Eduardo Duran refer to as "post-colonial Native America"[2] where American Indian tribes now enjoy governmental self-determination, control of their lands, as well as recently enacted, federally mandated protection of the 210 remaining, but highly endangered American languages.

Upon British colonization of the area now comprising the African nation of Uganda, there were—as was the case in the Amer-

1. Adams, *Education for Extinction*.

2. Duran and Duran, *Native American Postcolonial Psychology*.

icas—a variety of tribal groups speaking forty indigenous languages. The British authorities imposed a system of education that ultimately promulgated English as the language of government and as common medium of communication among peoples from Uganda's diverse language groups. As in the Americas, students were often denigrated for using tribal languages, as such languages were deemed unsuitable for teaching the tenets of Christianity, a primary "justification" for colonizing Africa.[3] Uganda obtained its independence as a sovereign nation in 1962 but continues to faces lingering effects of colonization, including the use of English, which has been incorporated as the official language of the nation. There are continuing efforts to adopt and propagate one African language—namely Kiswahili—as an official language to unite Ugandans linguistically,[4] given that, Uganda's forty tribal languages have thus far thrived within their respective speaking enclaves.

Although American Indian and Ugandan tribal groups share postcolonial freedoms and rights, albeit in somewhat different contexts, they exist within nation-states that act as instruments of national unity in the realms of economic, social, and cultural life. Where a diversity of languages is concerned, the actual exercise of linguistic freedom remains enmeshed in the experience and paradigms born of colonial language policy and practices, which influence contemporary policies and practices within these nation-states. These policies and practices have greatly varying effects on efforts to recognize, revitalize, preserve, and protect tribal languages. Nowhere is the tension more reflected than in the education systems of both Uganda and the United States, systems rooted in assimilative models, dominated by a colonial language, but with recent attempts to introduce policy innovations more accommodating to tribal language vitality.

As nation-states, the United States and Uganda share ideals of national unity with language, a foremost symbol. Although American Indian tribes enjoy a more socially constructed form of postcolonialism within the larger nation state, Ugandan tribes exist within a nation-state that was freed from direct colonial rule only in 1962. However, in both cases, language policy and practice—particularly in the formal education sector—is having a profound effect on the vitality of language diversity in those nations. The

3. Kilson, "The Emergent Elites of Black Africa," 351–94.

4. Muksama, *Getting Ugandans to Speak a Common Language.*

question is whether a nation-state, through its system of education, can truly embrace and even promote linguistic diversity and tolerance as national ideals, or will surviving fundamental tensions embedded in a colonial past remain to undermine it?

Postcolonial Theory

The purpose of this paper is to examine Native language vitality from two aspects within a broader postcolonial framework. This examination will focus upon the agency of education and the related policies of two separate nation states on different continents and its effects on Native language vitality. Insofar as one aspect is socially constructed within critical theory (United States), and the other a literal and direct outcome of national independence (Uganda), this examination will compare and critique processes and statuses, thus informing the broader conceptualization of decolonization and its effects on Native language vitality in the respective postcolonial environments.

The American Heritage Dictionary defines *postcolonialism* in the most literal sense: "of, relating to, or being the time following the establishment of independence in a colony."[5] Alternatively, Duran, Duran, Yellow Horse Brave Heart, and Yellow Horse-Davis offer a processual definition, which include psychological, social, cultural, and physical dynamics and their effects on those colonized by others.[6] As an aspect of critical theory, postcolonialism is a social construct associated with the control of discourse and the deconstruction of Western knowledge forms and ideology that have been imposed on colonized people. This aspect addresses the complex relationship of contemporary cultural identity in formerly colonized peoples and the manner and extent to which those affected articulate and enact their collective identity. The act of a nation colonizing a territory and its population has long been considered an act of aggression, exercised from a position of presumptive superiority of one group over another. The colonizing entity imposes constraints, values, laws, and policies upon a people it considers to be less developed or sophisticated. According to Edward Said, The essence of colonization is power and control and the imposition of a dominant discourse that marginalizes

5. *The American Heritage Dictionary of the English Language.*

6. Duran, Duran, Yellow Horse Brave Heart, "Healing the American Indian Soul Wound," 341–54.

and attempts to eradicate existing cultural identity.[7]

Postcolonialism in the most literal sense relates to the period after which a nation is granted full freedom as an independent state. In the more socially constructed and processual sense, colonized people within an existing nation-state locate a space to redefine and reestablish their cultural identity, often by destabilizing Western styles of thought that have dominated—often for multiple generations—the relationship between the colonizers and colonized. In both instances, control of the discourse that was used to define relationships and to categorize people and processes reverts to the indigenous population who then often must struggle with reorganizing the mechanisms previously used in their subjugation. In critical theory, the most substantial goal of postcolonialism is to clear space for voices that have been previously marginalized or silenced by dominant ideologies, voices that Gayatri Chakravorty Spivak refers to as the "subaltern."[8] In creating space, the subaltern can now speak with a voice that previously had been denied due to their marginalization.

While it is recognized within the paradigm of postcolonialism that the control of both *space* and *discourse* are essential ingredients, there is also the notion that the knowledge bases used to rationalize and support colonization need to be destabilized and replaced with Indigenous knowledge forms.[9] In the American Indian context, control of discourse and destabilization of Western knowledge that has had an adverse effect on Native identity are key themes in the reconstruction of Native identity. Duran and Duran have noted that in the process of being colonized, Native people have suffered an intergenerational "soul wound" that can only be healed through a process of recognizing and confronting the issues embedded in the acts of colonization by a dominant force and to then instigate their own renewed discourse about those acts and their effects on generations of American Indians. According to Duran and Duran, the life ways and culture of American Indians do not deserve to be subjectively compared to the ways and processes of other cultures—especially Western culture—because they are valid in their own right. Thus, Native people are entering a postcolonial era as they define their identity on

7. Said, *Orientalism*, 12.
8. Spivak, "Can the Subaltern Speak?" in *Marxism and the Interpretation of Culture*, 271–313.
9. Smith, *Decolonizing Methodologies*.

their own terms and confront the colonial past that has wrought havoc on Native culture and the psyche of Native people.[10] In addition to various U.S. laws and policies that now allow a degree of self-determination among American Indian Tribes, there are two areas of social-intellectual life where the processes of decolonization appear especially evident—literature, and research and academics.

Colonization, Native Languages, and Education Systems

When a nation colonizes a territory and its people, the control of discourse is usually exerted in the most literal sense, through the imposition of the colonizer's language. The principal agent of this linguistic colonialism is an education system, usually established and controlled by the colonizer and requiring instruction in and use of the colonist's language. In many cases, this imposition is accompanied by deliberate efforts to eradicate or limit the use of native languages. In all cases, the native language becomes marginalized with little or no currency in mainstream realms of business, economy, government, or trade. The colonizer's language usually becomes a "high status" lingua franca, meaning that those who become accepting of and fluent in its use are afforded opportunities and advancement. Those who do not accept or learn the colonizer's language are viewed—often with the complicity of their fellow colonized—as backward and unsophisticated. When a colonizing nation imposes its language, the aims of colonization will be fulfilled through the dominance of discourse and communication.

Once sovereignty is gained by a formerly colonized society there is no automatic reversion to native language. Most previously colonized nations retain the basic form of the education systems established by the colonizers and often adopt the colonial language as an "official" language, especially where multiple native languages were spoken. At the same time, newly emancipated nations, or people seeking reinforcement for cultural identity, grapple with issues of language, recognizing that the colonizer's language has had a profound impact on the development of the society during the colonial period.

As direct colonialism has waned during the latter part of the past century, there has been growing attention to the area of

10. Duran and Duran, *Native American Postcolonial Psychology*.

human rights. A fundamental right contained within the United Nations Statement on Human Rights declared in 1947 the use of one's native language as fundamental.[11] More recently in 2007, the United Nations adopted a Declaration on the Rights of Indigenous Peoples, which emphasizes language rights.[12] The declaration states in Article 13-1:

> Indigenous peoples have the right to revitalize, use, develop and transmit to future generations their histories, languages, oral traditions, philosophies, writing systems and literatures, and to designate and retain their own names for communities, places and persons" and Article 14-1 reads "Indigenous peoples have the right to establish and control their educational systems and institutions providing education in their own languages, in a manner appropriate to their cultural methods of teaching and learning.[13]

The international focus on human and indigenous language rights has grown partially out of the legacy of colonization and its aftermath, especially in developing nations. The assertion of human and linguistic rights is a bold stance on the part of the international community and recognizes the abuses and their aftermath wrought by colonial power exercising dominance over other nations and people. Since language is the foundation of identity and culture, the United Nations, accordingly, have underscored the control over and exercise of native language as an essential human right.

The American Indian Context

There are over five hundred recognized tribal entities within the borders of the United States. Although the effects of colonization by Europeans were collectively experienced, it had greater impact on some tribal groups than others. However, despite intense assimilative pressures over the years, Native America has maintained its marked resistance, and fueled a pan-Indian movement that ultimately won major concessions during the past century in such areas as language preservation and tribal sovereignty.

---

11. "Universal Declaration of Human Rights" Office of the United Nations High Commissioner for Human Rights, accessed March 1, 2011 www.ohchr.org/en/udhr/pages/60udhrintroduction.aspx.
12. "United Nations Declaration on the Rights of Indigenous Peoples" Adopted by the General Assembly 13 September 2007, accessed March 1, 2011 www.un.org/esa/socdev/unpfii/en/declaration.html."
13. Ibid.

Today, American Indian nations enjoy a dependent form of sovereignty within the larger structure of national constitutional governance within the United States. This has allowed them to maintain and manifest their uniqueness within American society while still maintaining a government-to-government relationship with the colonizer that, in itself, serve to both protect and restrict sociocultural and linguistic autonomy. This current status follows many years of effort—often employing forceful and cruel means at the hands of government and religious organizations—to divest American Indians of their cultures and languages. This has only stiffened the resolve and efforts of Native peoples to maintain cultural integrity and fueled the efforts that secured the rights they enjoy in American society today.

The movement toward a "postcolonial" Native America has been hard earned. The voice of Native people is nowhere more evident than in the field of literature, where there has been a renaissance of Native voices during the past forty years. N. Scott Momaday was awarded a Pulitzer Prize for *House Made of Dawn*, and was followed by such Native authors as Paula Gunn Allen, Robert Warrior, Craig Womack, Greg Sarris, Louis Owens, Gerald Vizenor, Leslie Marmon Silko, Sherman Alexie, Simon Ortiz, and Louise Erdrich.[14] These authors fused Native knowledge and insights into mainstream literary traditions, "decolonizing," the Native as previously portrayed in literature and asserting a literary Native identity. In Elvira Pulitano's book, *Toward a Native American Critical Theory,* she notes that oral traditions and Native knowledge forms and epistemologies are reimagined and blended in a literary form that challenges and transforms the mainstream critical theoretical strategies, creating a "site of powerful creative resistance to the dominant conceptual paradigms."[15]

In academics and research, there have been steadily increasing numbers of Native professors and researchers working not only in tribal colleges but also in mainstream academia. In academics and research, the postcolonial paradigm is iterated in a strong movement toward what Linda Tuhiwai Smith refers to as "decolonizing methodologies," where control and voice of research resides with indigenous scholars and the Native communities with which they work. This is necessary to offset the marginalization, allowing Native academics to reinvigorate and

14. Pulitano, *Toward a Native American Critical Theory.*
15. Ibid, 8

ground themselves in Native epistemologies and a worldview in their research and studies.[16]

While federal and state governments have demonstrated greater and more humane respect for Native people and their quest to retain their unique cultural identity during the past fifty years, American Indians remain continually vigilant in their struggle to resist the embedded and often difficult to identify tendency toward cultural homogeneity. A most egregious and current threat is the No Child Left Behind Law,[17] which, while it is intended to foster more equal outcomes for disadvantaged learners, has also imposed standards associated with a presumed body of skills and measures of learning deemed essential for success in the nation-state. The law does not take into account Native epistemologies, bodies of tribal knowledge, or allow assessment of learning in any tribal language, thereby forcing tribal educators and schools to homogenize the curriculum in favor of dominant academic testing and assessment scheme, and away from tribal influences and interests. While equality of results in schooling and learning is indeed a civil rights issue in the United States, there is an overall failure to recognize and honor Native epistemologies and their linguistic implications that are not located in the generally accepted knowledge and academic assessment and performance framework of the nation-state. Robert Patrick assesses the effect of the law: "Federal assimilative efforts therefore remain, cloaked in the language of NCLB, standardized curriculum, and the association between academic achievement and test scores."[18] Lomawaima and McCarty note that the law "standardizes inequality and ensures that existing race- and class-based hierarchies are legitimized and reproduced"[19]

The second case in point is a deeply embedded fervor for the preeminence and dominance of the English language in American culture. While the United States Constitution does not nominate a national language, influential groups—mostly through voter initiatives—have instigated "English Only" laws, which marginalize not only Native languages, but also all languages other than English, in education and in the public sphere. Even states like Arizo-

16. Smith, *Decolonizing Methodologies*.
17. Public Law 107–110, 115 Stat. 1425, The Elementary and Secondary Education Act (The No Child Left Behind Act of 2001) enacted January 8, 2002.
18. Patrick, "Perspectives on Change," 79
19. Lomawaima and McCarty, "When Tribal Sovereignty Challenges Democracy," 298.

na and California with sizeable Native populations have enacted such laws, which have had the effect of disabling Native language retention and revitalization efforts in publically funded schools.[20]

The U.S. constitution recognizes the essential sovereignty of American Indian nations and acknowledges a trust responsibility for the welfare of Native people. In spite of years of deliberate and concerted efforts to obliterate Native culture and language throughout U.S. history, recent efforts led by American Indians have been successful in seeking remediation for the damage caused by these efforts. Recent acts, policies, and presidential executive orders now serve to honor and protect the traditions, knowledge, and languages of Native America. Some of these include the Native American Languages Act, Title I, in 1990,[21] most recently amended by the Esther Martinez Native American Languages Preservation Act of 2006.[22] When this act was passed, Congress declared:

> The status of the cultures and languages of Native Americans is unique and the United States has the responsibility to work together with Native Americans to ensure the survival of these unique cultures and languages.[23]

The act recognizes the right of Indian tribes and other Native American governing bodies to use their ancestral languages as a medium of instruction in all schools funded by the Secretary of the Interior, reflecting the policy to "preserve, protect, and promote the rights and freedom of Native Americans to use, practice, and develop" indigenous languages. Furthermore, the act declares that "the right of Native Americans to express themselves through Native American languages shall not be restricted in any public proceeding, including publicly supported education programs."[24]

The preservation and revitalization of native languages has also been the focus of several other national efforts. The Bilingual Education Act of 1968, also known as Title VII of the Elementa-

---

20. Crawford, *At War with Diversity*.
21. Native American Languages Act. Public Law 101-477, Title 1. October 30, 1990 accessed June 15, 2011 www.nau.edu/jar/SIL/NALAct.pdf
22. Public Law No: 109-394 Esther Martinez Native American Languages Preservation Act of 2006, accessed June 5, 2011 www.gpo.gov/fdsys/pkg/PLAW-109publ394/pdf/PLAW-109publ394.pdf.
23. Ibid.
24. Native American Languages Act. Public Law 101–477.

ry and Secondary Education Act (ESEA),[25] made funding available for programs designed to help English language learners master English. However, the Office of Bilingual Education and Minority Languages Affairs (OBEMLA) that administered Title VII of ESEA no longer exists. Its successor, Title III of the No Child Left Behind Act, does not fund Native American language restoration programs. The Administration for Native Americans (ANA)[26] in the U.S. Department of Health and Human Services is the only federal resource that supports large-scale language preservation and revitalization programs; however, the resources available through ANA are quite limited. In the meantime, a final report of the U.S. Secretary of Education's Indian Nations at Risk Task Force in 1991, developed with substantial community input, identified the maintenance of native languages and cultures as one of its ten primary goals.[27]

In response to the threat of losing hundreds of native languages within the next fifty years, many tribes, tribal schools, and native organizations throughout Alaska, Hawai'i, and mainland United States presently have resorted to operating their own language revitalization or maintenance programs, many depending on their own resources. Although many native languages have already been relegated to linguistic texts with no living speakers, there is now more commitment and action than ever before to protect and maintain in living use those that have survived. Still, the future of most Native American languages is uncertain. Enactment of protectionist measures by the federal government cannot ensure the survival of any language, especially if they remain unfunded, under-funded and/or counteracted by national education policies such as No Child Left Behind. As more American Indians become urban dwellers, the likelihood that they will adopt English as their everyday language increases. If historical patterns of language shift and language loss hold true, the utilitarian value of ancestral languages will also diminish. In spite of laws, proclamations, and the will of Native people to preserve

25. 1967 Bilingual Education Act (or Title VII of the Elementary and Secondary Education Act) (Public Law 90—247).

26. The Administration for Native Americans (ANA) is authorized under the Native American Programs Act of 1974, as amended. It promotes the goal of social and economic "self-sufficiency" of American Indians, Alaska Natives, Native Hawaiians and other Native American Pacific Islanders including Native Samoans.

27. "Indian Nations at Risk."

their languages, the national education system is not only unwilling and unprepared to support Native language revitalization, but is actually working against it.

The Ugandan Context

Lying within East Africa, Uganda was once referred to by Winston Churchill as the "Pearl of Africa."[28] It was a protectorate of the British Empire from 1894 to 1962, which originally encompassed the Buganda Kingdom and eventually lesser kingdoms and tribal areas that constitute present day Uganda. The nation peacefully gained its Independence from Great Britain October 10, 1962. It is a land of multiple tribal groups and over thirty living languages, none of which are dominant in numbers or in tribal land holdings. Luganda is spoken by the largest number of Ugandans at 16.3 percent, Lusoga at 7.8 percent, Runyankore at 7.1 percent, Rukiga at 7.1 percent, and Ateso at 8.3 percent.[29] Another eight languages comprise about 5 percent of the population and the remaining languages are spoken by less than 3 percent of the population. Though literacy rates are generally low at 52 to 57 percent, literacy in some of Uganda's languages is common.[30] Several newspapers are published in local languages, including Buganda, Leb Lango, and Acholi.

Uganda is a constitutional democracy, governed by a president who has held office continuously since 1986. The 1996 constitution of Uganda recognizes fifty-six tribal languages.[31] The language families include Bantu, Eastern Sudanic, Luo, Elgon, Kuliak, and Central Sudanic. Some of these language families also exist in countries adjoining Uganda. Like other countries in Africa, English was introduced by colonizing British who spread the language through missionary work and the educational system. Although English always remained the official language under colonial rule, there were some early, and now later efforts to develop Kiswahili as a practical unifying language. This met with some resistance

28. Churchill, *My African Journey*, 197.
29. Peter, et al, *Language in Uganda*, 80.
30. Muksana, 1991.
31. Position Paper on Ethnic Minority Rights in Uganda. The Equal Opportunities Committee, Parliament of the Republic of Uganda Kampala, Uganda 2007 pg. 5, accessed June 9, 2011 www.aresearchug.org/reports/commissioned research/Ethnic percent20Minorities percent20Position percent20Paper, percent202007.pdf

since it was viewed as a threat to political power.[32] An effort to create another official Ugandan language—Luganda—also failed because of opposition from its speakers.

While Uganda is a diverse linguistic environment, there are mixed feelings about such diversity's influence on national unity, universal education, and literacy, and the pace of development of the country economically. However, current educational policy focuses on the development and use of "local languages" as the medium of instruction in the primary grades (P-4) in all areas of the country where a local language is dominant. English is taught as a subject in these grades and then shifts to the medium of instruction in primary, grade 4. In urban areas with mixed languages, English will serve as the primary medium of instruction. In areas where local languages will be used as a medium of instruction, language boards of native speakers have been established to guide curriculum development. A National Language Board has also been established to oversee issues of language of instruction. In order to promote pan-Africanism, as well as a potential national language, Kiswahili is also a required subject in both primary and secondary schools, but actual instruction has been hindered by a lack of qualified speakers of the language. This latter development does not evoke a sense of urgency.

While there were conflicts between Ugandan tribes and their British colonizers, they did not rule over-oppressively. Although English continued as the official language during the colonial era, the colonial government did consider at one time educating in local languages.

The postcolonial period brought renewed interest in establishing African languages as official languages, but any language suggested created controversy and no immediate decisions were made. Idi Amin declared Kiswahili as a second national language, but it lost its status in the 1995 convention, and then was later restored as the second official language by the National Assembly in 2005. Today, Kiswahili is considered a language that unites Uganda with Tanzania and Kenya where the language is more widely spoken.[33] As former British colonies, these countries have also adopted Kiswahili as an official language. Uganda, like its neighbors, is trying to balance its need to identify itself linguistically as a

32. Mukuthuria, "Kiswahili and Its Expanding Roles of Development in East African Cooperation," 154–165.
33. Ibid.

distinctly African nation while at the same time still adopting and teaching the colonizer's language, which has become associated with advancement and development.

Interestingly, a form of distinctly Ugandan English has evolved, which differs in form and style from Standard English. "Uganglish" has been greatly influenced by the existing native languages of Uganda, giving it distinctive inflections and accent and unique vocabulary.

While the education system was established by the colonizing nation to root the English language in Ugandan societies, a nationally controlled education system has been making major revisions to the system to promote the use of local languages for learning, to promote greater literacy by creating materials in local languages, and by developing orthographies for languages not currently written. Specifically, in the current language policy of the Uganda Ministry of Education and Sports it is stipulated that:

- The mother tongue be used as a medium of instruction in education up to Primary Four (modified to cover only P1-P3)
- The area languages—Luganda, Luo, Runyakitara, Ateso/ Nakarimojon and Lugbara—whose orthographies are ready—be taught as a subject in primary schools and be examinable in PLE.
- That a National Language Advisory Board be established to assist in the development of Uganda languages.
- The language policy is in use in other countries like Nigeria, Ghana, South Africa, Zambia, Malawi, Lesotho, Swaziland, and Zimbabwe.[34]

In enacting the policy, the Ministry of Education and Sports anticipates the following benefits:

- Local languages promote comprehension, accuracy of expression, interest in nature around and increases appreciation of culture, which is important for one's identity.
- Local languages are a tool for socialization that helps to shape people's compatibility with the environment around them. This enhances the participatory methods used in

34. Bukenya, "Teaching in Local Languages Good Policy" *New Vision*, Thursday, March 6, 2008. Accessed February 28, 2011 at www.newvision.co.ug/D/8/459/615142.

the classroom like group participation skills that are effective in achieving learning.

- Local languages create confidence in one's language. This forms the basis for learning other languages. The people who went to school in the 1960s and used this system have a better command of the first and second languages because of this background.
- Local languages are a basis for the formation of an integral part of the philosophy of an individual, which is an important factor for future learning of social studies and other humanities
- Local languages are a bridge between the home and school learning. This enhances the philosophy of teaching from the known to unknown. This helps the child to relate what is at home to what is learned at school.[35]

In implementing the language policy, the Ministry of Education Sports is closely guided by "a broad-minded and a development-oriented approach which has helped to fulfill the ministry's objective of increased access, equity, quality achievement and retention of children in schools"[36]

Comparing American Indian and Ugandan Contexts

The value of examining and comparing these two very different contexts relates to what one can learn from one context that will inform the other. Further, a comparative examination informs the larger field of language policy and practice, as well as offer insight into facets of the construct of postcolonialism within nation-states and "decolonization" as socially constructed or literally occurring as an aspect of national independence.

The most striking aspect of a comparison is the degree of deliberate and affirmative activity on the part of the Ugandan nation-state to promote, celebrate, and secure Native languages. While Uganda has at times demonstrated some ambivalence about adopting a national language, or which language to choose, its education policies now clearly embrace the development of native languages as instructional media with later transition to instruction in English with local languages taught as subjects. While the multilingual nature of Ugandan society has

35. Ibid.
36. Ibid.

been viewed by some as a hindrance in nation building, the policy clearly underscores the primacy of education and literacy, regardless of the language used, as paths to their achievement. In the most literal sense, Uganda has embraced its postcolonial autonomy, exercising its independence, though still continuing to wrestle with some of the artifacts of colonization. Its policies on language education and multilingualism, as they are facilitated within its education system, are evidence of a nation-state representing and responding to social realities within the nation in an effort to address widespread poverty and third world conditions. In terms of space and discourse, and the empowerment of people through the agency of education—the nation-state has realistically addressed a critical component of national identity—its diversity of languages and their anticipated value in national development and social harmony.

Although U. S. policy declarations, acts, and presidential executive orders pertaining to Native language are well crafted and supportive in their rhetoric, they are often disingenuous in practice. There is an underlying ambivalence in U.S. policy toward Native languages and, in particular, toward the role of the educational system in promoting and supporting languages other than English. This is likely rooted in the "melting pot ideology"[37] that continues to pervade American society and its institutions. It may also be linked to the doctrine of "manifest destiny,"[38] a belief popular in the United States that the total of mankind benefits when a superior society expanded its borders, even if it means exterminating, oppressing, and forcing the assimilation of other peoples. Since a government policy of manifest destiny had been explicitly exercised in the past and had previously targeted native languages for extinction, it is difficult to anticipate that such an influential doctrine would altogether disappear. The nation's current embroilment in debates about illegal immigration and the languages immigrants bring, which are perceived to threaten and undermine the integrity of the English language, strongly suggest that these ideologies are far from in a state of dormancy.

The most recent amendment to the Native American Languag-

37. ushistory.org. "What Is the American?" U.S. History Online Textbook, accessed June 15, 2011 at www.ushistory.org/us/29.asp

38. ushistory.org. "Manifest Destiny" U.S. History Online Textbook, accessed June 15, 2011 at
www.ushistory.org/us/29.asp.

es Act includes "preservation" in its title, and acknowledges the loss of many languages and underscores to right of tribal groups to take proactive steps the retrieve and preserve tribal languages. Aside from specific but limited programs targeting these efforts, such as the Administration for Native American Program, there is no active and deliberate emphasis on public education's role in the issue, other than invocations to that effect, affording individual tribal entities their *right* to use, preserve, or restore their languages in the ways they see fit. This is a passive and ambivalent approach on the part of the U.S. nation-state in contrast to Uganda's more affirmative and proactive approach, which is now thoroughly grounded in its education system.

The hallmark of the No Child Left Behind Law is its lack of recognition or regard for the value of Native language and cultural knowledge in learning. The law expresses ambivalence about the capacity of Native people to educate their children for effective participation in society. With respect to the U.S. public education system and its role in the preservation of Native language and enhancement of Native children's learning through culturally responsive teaching, Dr. David Beaulieu notes that there are "significant incongruities between the federal protective statuses regarding language and culture and the implementational realities of NCLB."[39] And, Teresa McCarty observes that as a national policy, NCLB has a "chilling effect on the ability of tribal communities to provide linguistically, culturally, and academically rich curricula for Native students, even in nonpublic, federal, and community– and tribally-controlled schools."[40]

In the socially constructed postcolonial paradigm, the subaltern assumes control over the discourse pertaining to their own condition and destabilizes the Western thinking that defines and influences it. Also, space is created for a revised or renewed discourse to take place. The Ugandan nation state retained a colonial institution—its education system—recognizing its potential power in nation building and development. Through the agency of education, Uganda is investing heavily on its future by employing educational strategies that are believed to be most effective for

39. Beaulieu, "A Survey and Assessment of Culturally-based Programs and Native American Students in the United States." *Journal of American Indian Education*, 50–61.

40. Romero-Little and McCarty, "Language Planning Challenges and Prospects in Native American Communities and Schools."

long-term national development. At the same time, it is acknowledging its linguistic diversity as an asset in the implementation of that strategy. The local languages policy also acknowledges the value of cultural knowledge as it is conveyed through teaching and learning in local languages. The policy is responsive to the realities of Uganda as a multicultural and multilingual nation, suggesting a paradigm of future development that will honor and celebrate these characteristics.

Conversely, the U. S. nation-state, in spite of the findings of considerable research on the subject of bilingualism/multilingualism, abandoned mother tongue education as a long-term development/educational improvement strategy, bowing to a system that embraces the supremacy of the English language, along with standards and accountability measures associated with a homogeneous body of Western knowledge. This has been done in spite of the reality of the considerable linguistic diversity that has always been part of American society. Up until 1972, American Indian nations had control of neither public nor Bureau of Indian Affairs education. However, when tribes were granted that right to contract government schools, they still have to operate the school in accordance with national curricula and standards. Schools that have taught subject matter in the Native language were discouraged because government testing was in English. The teaching of indigenous knowledge was usually relegated to the occasional appearance of a tribal elder to address classes that otherwise studied the standard curriculum and were tested in English. A telling trend was that in order to exercise true self-determination in language and indigenous epistemology, the few schools that were truly organized as "tribal" would accept no funding from government sources and would have to seek and employ educational innovations on their own. Such schools show promise of moving the social construction of postcolonialism and decolonization to deeper dimensions, but the efforts are few and the nation-state fails to encourage or support them.

There have been considerable strides in achieving a degree of governmental autonomy for American Indian tribes and in literature and academics, however, this has all been accomplished in the language of the colonizer. A primary agent of language revitalization is the education system that within it lies "significant incongruities," which only serve to highlight the nation-state's failure to honor, in the most substantial way, its own rhetoric about

Native languages and the role of education where it concerns the language, knowledge base and culture of its first peoples.

Conclusion

The nation-state is a powerful mediator of culture and identity of those who live under its influence. In democracies, the nation-state itself is molded through representation reflecting the attitudes and aspirations of its franchised people. However, in a monolithic entity such as a nation-state, there can also be what Alexis de Tocqueville describes as "tyranny of the majority,"[41] which overrides the interests of minority entities. Voices are not silenced but they can become muffled, unheard and generally ignored, a condition imposed by the franchised over the disenfranchised.

For American Indians, there is substantial evidence of a post-colonial renaissance, where Natives now participate in the public discourse, and where their voices are now enabled in some political, literary and academic domains of American society. However, this renaissance proceeds only partially beyond the state of disenfranchisement that American Indians have experienced since colonization. It is known that a system of education is a most powerful social engine, which can serve to promote, divert, or inhibit the enfranchisement and social identity of people via its treatment of knowledge and the manner and style in which it is imparted. Language is the key element of social identity, providing continuity in the transmission of culture from one generation to the next. While the nation-state has affirmed the rights of American Indians to protect and preserve their languages and cultures, it has greatly inhibited the process by imposing national policies in education that are inimical to their potential influences in schooling. In a special issue of the *Journal of American Indian Education*, the editors go so far as to say that there is "outright discrimination by federal, state, and local government agencies and total disregard for federal laws and court-mandated regulation such as Lau vs. Nichols (1974) and the 1992 Native American Languages Act. These patterns include failure to use tax revenues in support of regenerating heritages and endangered languages across the nation."[42]

41. A. De Tocqueville, A. *Democracy in America, 1835*, available March 2, 2009 at xroads.virginia.edu/~HYPER/DETOC/toc_indx.html.
42. Aguilera, Lipka, Demmert and Tippeconnic, "Special Issue on Culturally

Though a recently created democracy, the nation-state of Uganda exercised its full independence and has enjoyed considerable success in creating a national ethos of decolonization that celebrates many different tribal entities and languages. While national unity is an important goal, the nation-state has invested itself heavily in education and to increasing the literacy rate of its people. In recognition of the power of education and its relationship to national progress and development, the nation-state has chosen a course that honors the role and effectiveness of community language in the education of children. It also promotes literacy within its diversity of languages. As a third world nation, Uganda does have social and economic problems to overcome, but it makes a substantial investment in education, creating greater opportunities and encouragement for participation in the greater discourse leading toward eventual solutions.

The test of the postcolonial paradigm, both in the socially constructed or literal sense, lies in the realization of the aspirations and hopes of the people and the full enfranchisement of those who had formerly been oppressed through colonization. Where investment for the integrity and transmission of culture and language lies with a significant agent of socialization such as the educational system, a simple question must be asked: Is the Native child attending his village school in rural America or East Africa receiving an education that de-marginalizes and empowers him while reinforcing Native identity through full celebration of the home culture and language? All indications are that while the United States has iterated a supportive framework for this postcolonial goal, the actual rhetoric and implementation employed by the nation-state, in terms of education policy, works against it. Conversely, in Uganda, the nation-state not only advocates for a healthy and productive native identity but has put into place definitive processes in education that fully support the aims of reinforcing cultural identity and language.

As a construct, postcolonialism cannot be quantitatively gauged or assessed; however, there are indicators that suggest the functionality and directionality of both the socially constructed and literal forms are based on independence from the colonizer. In either form, the agency of education in the future for-

Responsive Education for American Indian, Alaska Native, and Native Hawaiian Students," 4.

Pulitano, *Toward a Native American Critical Theory*, 16.

mation of children's identity and their ultimate enfranchisement is a certain indicator. In the United States, the greatest advances for Native people have been made in the areas of self-determination and on the literary and academic fronts. Uganda has evolved into a postcolonial society where the nation-state is exercising its independence while celebrating and reinforcing the diversity of the nation. All told, the future of native identity will largely be determined by what happens in the classroom. Native voices, now supported by international resolutions of indigenous rights, have been clear: The vision of the future includes the revitalization, retention, and maintenance of ancestral languages and Native epistemologies that have sustained Native people through periods of colonization. Within the spectrum of movement toward regaining space and control of discourse, Native people in the United States have made remarkable but uneven progress. The nation-state engages, however unwitting or unintentionally, powerful obstacles that are ingrained in its systems and processes. The legacy of colonialism remains a strong undercurrent in the relationship between those who control the dominant discourse and those who seek their voice. The control of space and discourse by Native people is realized only to a limited and contradictory extent within the national ethos. Tribal nations exist in a relationship of dependency within the nation-state rather than a relationship of true independence from it. As Elvira Pulitano notes, there exists an "irony of a discourse of Native postcolonialism" as it is operating in a "condition of colonialism"

Only in December 2010 did President Obama acknowledge before American Indians that words must met with action. Embedded in the meaning of his statement is that the nation-state has failed in honoring and sustaining the will of American Indians to exercise their right to the sanctity of existence within the domains of their own languages, cultures and epistemologies. Rhetoric must also meet reality for American Indians to also be fully enfranchised—in their own terms—to participate in the productive processes and discourse of the U. S. nation-state. Uganda—a tiny country compared to the United States—is, on the other hand, a country plagued with poverty, recent civil strife, challenges to development, and a short history of independence. But Uganda seems to have approached the most significant dimension of a postcolonial society, an affirmative acknowledgement of and support of indigenous language rights, cultures and knowledge forms within the national framework, aided by an education system that has implemented rhetoric with actual practice.

Bibliography

Aguilera, Dorothy, Jerry Lipka, William Demmert, and John Tippeconnic, "Introduction to Special Issue on Culturally Responsive Education for American Indian, Alaska Native, and Native Hawaiian Students" *Journal of American Indian Education* 46 (2007): 4.

Adams, David. *Education for Extinction: American Indians and the Boarding School Experience, 1875–1928*, Lawrence: University Press of Kansas, 1995.

American Heritage Dictionary of the English Language, Fourth Ed. Houghton Mifflin Company, 2006.

Beaulieu, David. "A Survey and Assessment of Culturally-Based Programs and Native American Students in the United States." *Journal of American Indian Education* 45 (2009): 50–61.

Bukenya, G. "Teaching in Local Languages Good Policy" *New Vision*, March 6, 2008. Accessed February 28, 2011 at www.newvision.co.ug/D/8/459/615142.

Churchill, Winston S. L. *My African Journey*. London: Hodder and Stoughton, 1908.

Crawford, James. *At War with Diversity: US Language Policy in an Age of Anxiety*, Clevedon, England: Multilingual Matters, 2000.

De Tocqueville, Alexis. *Democracy in America, 1835*. Accessed March 2, 2009 at xroads.virginia.edu/~HYPER/DETOC/toc_indx.html.

Duran, Eduardo and Bonnie Duran. *Native American Postcolonial Psychology*. Albany, NY: State University of New York, 1995.

———. Yellow Horse Brave Heart, M., and S. Yellow Horse-Davis. "Healing the American Indian Soul Wound." In *International Handbook of Multigenerational Legacies of Trauma*, edited by Y. Danieli, 341–354, New York: Plenum, 1998.

Indian Nations at Risk Task Force. "Indian Nations at Risk: An Educational Strategy for Action: National Education Goals for American Indians and Alaska Natives," Accessed July 6, 2011 www.tedna.org/pubs/nationsatrisk.pdf.

Kilson, Martin. "The Emergent Elites of Black Africa, 1900–1960." In *Colonialism in Africa 1870–1960, Vol. 2, The History and Politics of Colonialism, 1914–1960,* edited by L. R. Gann and Peter Duignan. London: Cambridge University Press, 1970.

Ladefoged, Peter, Ruth Glick, Clive Criper, Clifford H. Prator, and Livingstone Walusimbi. *Language in Uganda* (Ford Foundation language surveys vol. 1). London/New York: Oxford University Press, 1972.

Lomawaima, Tsianina and Teresa L. McCarty. "When Tribal Sovereignty Challenges

Democracy: American Indian Education and the Democratic Ideal." *American Educational Research Journal* 39 (2002): 279–305.

McCarty, Teresa. L. "The Impact of High Stakes Accountability Policies on Native American Learners: Evidence from Research." *Teaching Education* 20 (2009): 7–29.

Mukuthuria, Mwenda. "Kiswahili and Its Expanding Roles of Development in East African Cooperation: A Case of Uganda," *Nordic Journal of African Studies* 15 (2006): 154–165.

Muksama, R.G. *Getting Ugandans to Speak a Common Language: Changing Uganda.* Kampala: Fountain Publishers, 1991.

Obama, Barack. "Remarks by the President at the White House Tribal Nations Conference" December 15, 2010. Last accessed March 1, 2011 at www.whitehouse.gov/the-press-office/2010/12/16/remarks-president-white-house-tribal-nations-conference.

Office of the United Nations High Commissioner for Human Rights. "Universal Declaration of Human Rights." Last accessed July 10, 2011 www.ohchr.org/en/udhr/pages/60udhrintroduction.aspx.

Parliament of the Republic of Uganda Equal Opportunities Committee. "Position Paper on Ethnic Minority Rights in Uganda" Uganda: Kampala, 2007. Accessed July 9, 2011 at aresearchug.org/reports/commissioned-research/Ethnic percent20Minorities percent20Position percent20Paper, percent202007.pdf.

Patrick, Robert. "Perspectives on Change: A Continued Struggle for Academic Success and Cultural Relevancy at an American Indian School in the Midst of No Child Left Behind." *Journal of American Indian Education* 47 (2009): 79.

Pulitano, Elvira. *Toward a Native American Critical Theory.* Lincoln: University of Nebraska Press, 2003.

Romero-Little, Mary Eunice and Teresa L. McCarty. "Language Planning Challenges and Prospects in Native American Communities and Schools." Arizona State University Language Policy Research Unit, 2006. Accessed June 5, 2011 epsl.asu.edu/epru/documents/EPSL-0602-105-LPRU.pdf.

Said, Edward. *Orientalism*, New York: Vintage Books, 1979.

Smith, Linda. T. *Decolonizing Methodologies: Research and Indigenous Peoples.* London: Zed Books, 1999.

Spivak, Gayatri Chakravorty."Can the Subaltern Speak?" In *Marxism and the Interpretation of Culture*, edited by Nelson and Lawrence Grossberg, 271–313. Urbana, IL: University of Illinois Press, 1988.

United Nations General Assembly. "United Nations Declaration on the Rights of Indigenous Peoples" September 13, 2007, accessed July 10, 2011 at www.un.org/esa/socdev/unpfii/en/declaration.html.

ushistory.org. "Manifest Destiny," U.S. History Online Textbook, Accessed June 15, 2011 at www.ushistory.org/us/29.asp.

"What Is the American?" U.S. History Online Textbook, Accessed June 15, 2011 at www.ushistory.org/us/29.asp.

9
Giving Language Rights Meaning
Revitalizing Basque, Navajo, and Other Indigenous Languages and Cultures

Jon Reyhner

The Basques are the indigenous people of Europe, with a language and culture dating back tens of thousands of years to the Upper Paleolithic Era before the arrival of the Indo-European languages that later spread across the continent. As indigenous people they share many characteristics with other indigenous peoples worldwide. First and foremost they have managed to survive with a distinct culture despite their lands being overrun by Roman, Arabic, Spanish, and French armies. They have held on to their unique language and culture despite repeated government efforts at repression, especially in the schools educating their children. As that repression has lessened in recent years they have been faced with the onslaught of the forces of globalization and popular media, especially movies and television, in the "world languages" of Spanish, English, and French. English is not just a worldwide language of commerce and diplomacy, it is as Basque writer Iran Zaluda notes, "the only language that allows any literature to be known worldwide: it is the passport to The World Republic (that is to say market) of Letters."[1]

In an increasingly urban, globalized, and capitalist world that favors economic utility, geographically restricted minority languages and cultures are often seen as rural, backward, and of little use. But this modern world is also increasingly one of the

1. Zaldua, "Eight Crucial Decisions," 100.

lonely crowd and bowling alone[2] where supportive belief systems and social networks that serve key human needs are being lost. Extended families give way to modern nuclear families and age-specific peer groups replace cross-age groupings that allow the transmission of traditional time-tested values across generations. When an Ojibwe[3] high school student on the Red Lake Reservation in Minnesota shot and killed a teacher and seven students in 2005, Navajo Nation president Joe Shirley emphasized how the breakdown of long-established cultures helped make such a tragedy possible:

> I believe these kinds of incidents are evidence of natives losing their cultural and traditional ways that have sustained us as a people for centuries. . . .
>
> Even on the big Navajo Nation, we, as a people, are not immune to losing sight of our values and ways. Each day we see evidence of the chipping away of Navajo culture, language and traditions by so many outside forces.
>
> Because we are losing our values as a people, it behooves native nations and governments that still have their ceremonies, their traditions and their medicine people, to do all they can to hang onto those precious pieces of culture. That is what will allow us to be true sovereign native nations. This is what will allow our people to stand on our own. The way to deal with problems like this one is contained in our teachings.[4]

Political conservatives usually want to promote traditional and family values, however they also in Spain, France, and the United States and elsewhere tend to follow a "one nation, one language" ideology that sees a single national language as unifying a nation despite a history of revolutionary and civil wars, as in the American, French, and Russian Revolutions and the English, American, and Spanish Civil Wars where many on both sides of these conflicts spoke the same languages and in contradiction to more stable multilingual countries like Switzerland. Languages, like flags, become superficial symbols of unity and replace the basic concepts that democracies are built on, including liberty and justice for all. This display of ethnocentric nationalism that tramples minority rights is shortsighted in our increasingly globalized world. In a world democracy, English, Spanish, and French speakers would certainly be calling for minority rights as their

---

2. See e.g., Riesman, Glazer and Denney, *The Lonely Crowd* and Putnam, *Bowling Alone*.
3. Also known as Ojibwa, Anishenabe or Chippewa.
4. Joe Shirley Jr. "Another Viewpoint," 5.

concerns for their languages and cultures would be swamped by speakers of Chinese and Hindi. Democracies that do not protect minority rights can be as tyrannical as dictatorships.

Language Repression

Responding to an antibilingual education "English for the Children" initiative, Proposition 203 on Arizona's November 2000 ballot Navajo Nation president Kelsey Begaye declared in a press release that the "preservation of Navajo culture, tradition, and language . . . is the number one guiding principle of the Navajo Nation."[5] He wrote,

> The Navajo Way of Life is based on the Navajo language. By tradition, the history of our people and the stories of our people are handed down from one generation to the next through oral communication. Naturally, the true essence and meanings for many Navajo stories, traditions and customs cannot be fully transmitted, understood or communicated as told through non-Navajo languages.[6]

In four of Arizona's fifteen counties a majority of voters were against Proposition 203, and three of those counties comprised large portions of the Navajo Nation, the largest Indian Nation in the United States in area and second largest, after the Cherokee, in population. Ironically, it was Spanish speaking immigrants from Latin American countries that were targeted by this law, and its negative effects on efforts to revitalize indigenous languages was just collateral damage. The fear and anger against the rising tide of Spanish-speaking immigrants to the United States threatening to make "white" Americans the new minority can be seen in books like Victor Davis Hanson's *Mexifornia* where "Mexico has now invaded America" destroying the "inheritance from our hardworking and creative forefathers."[7]

Linguicism (language prejudice) has a long history in countries around the world. In Spain it goes back to at least 1766 when the president of the Council of Castile prohibited printing books in any language other than Spanish and two years later King Charles III declared that "teaching will only be carried out in Spanish."[8] Across the border in France, in the push for equality during the

5. Begaye, "Guest Commentary," 4.
6. Ibid.
7. Hanson, *Mexifornia*, 31 and 150.
8. As quoted in Ametzaga, "Introduction to a Political History of the Basque Language and Literature," 42.

French Revolution, the Basque language was seen as retrograde and antirevolutionary. In the late nineteenth century, social Darwinist thinking mistakenly applied ideas about biological evolution, especially natural selection leading to the survival of the fittest, to the development of civilizations with American Indian, Basque, and other indigenous languages and cultures being seen as dying vestiges of a less civilized past. An example of this attitude can be seen Karen Stocker's 2005 study titled *I Won't Stay Indian, I'll Keep Studying*. Stocker found in Costa Rica a challenge shared by indigenous peoples worldwide where "the label *Indian* had connotations of backwardness and even inferior intellect. . . . Being Indian automatically set students up for being treated as inferior" and that "for most students from the [Indian] reservation, projecting an Indian identity seemed incompatible with school success."[9] Indigenous peoples are often faced with a false dichotomy where they are told they must choose the modern world and the national language or remain "savage" or at least "backward" less educated second-class citizens.

To speed the development of supposedly backward, savage people, their children were taught the national language of their country and punished for speaking their Indigenous language. Punishment for speaking Basque in schools in the late nineteenth and early twentieth centuries included the "iron ring," comparable to the "Welsh Knot" used in Wales, to punish students for speaking Welsh. One Basque student recalled, "when I was young I had to wear in several occasions the iron ring, that in this case had thorns in order to cause a wound in the finger. This way I learned Spanish. The student who took the ring could not play with the others and rambled alone by the schoolyard, far from all, since the only way to take off the ring was to accuse to another boy of having spoken in Basque."[10] At the end of the week the student with the Welsh Knot or the iron ring would receive corporal punishment. These efforts at minority language suppression can lead to resistance. Basque author Bernardo Atxaga writes about being punished in school for speaking Basque, as have many American Indians and other indigenous peoples, but instead of abandoning it, it became his household language.[11] A

9. Stocker, *I Won't Stay Indian*, 2.
10. Ametzaga, "Introduction to a Political History of the Basque Language and Literature," 41.
11. Atxaga, "The Cork and the Anchor."

countervailing force to globalization is localization, the desire to be of a particular place and to know one's particular heritage. For Atxaga, writing in Basque is "an act of love, . . . commitment . . . autonomy, . . . an aesthetic act, and act of renovation and modernity."[12]

Parallel to the repression of minority languages and cultures in Spain under the dictator Francisco Franco was the post–World War II era in the United States when a conservative majority in the U.S. Congress began to eliminate American Indian reservations as a final act of forced assimilation. However repression can stimulate resistance. The Basque, like other indigenous peoples, have both resisted and accommodated the forces that intersected their lives from the ancient Romans to the modern Spanish and French. They largely adopted Catholicism and their language has incorporated foreign words, however its grammar has resisted change. Author Mark Kurlansky found for the Basque and other groups "political repression produces cultural revival."[13] Ironically, the relaxation of repression can have the opposite effect as Deborah House notes in her study, *Language Shift among the Navajos.*[14] No longer having to fight for cultural and linguistic survival people can relax and start letting it slip away as mass media and popular culture drowns out their Indigenous voices. Kurlansky writes, "The promotion of the Basque language remains the goal of most [Basque] nationalists,"[15] however, the effectiveness of that promotion beyond mere rhetoric can be in doubt for Indigenous peoples generally.

Language Revitalization

Countering repressive efforts of national governments were various efforts at cultural revival. A Basque renaissance began with Floral Games in 1879 that included Basque literary competitions, games, folk singing, and oral poetry.[16] Private schools were set up to teach Basque but under Franco after the Spanish Civil War they were suppressed. However, the many refugees from that war elsewhere in Europe and in North and South America worked to keep their language alive outside of Spain. One effort was to

12. Ibid., 86.
13. Kulansky, *The Basque History of the World*, 158.
14. House, *Language Shift among the Navajos.*
15. Kulansky, *The Basque History of the World*, 331.
16. Conversi, *The Basques, the Catalans and Spain*, 51.

translate the classics of world literature into Basque to show that it was "capable of expressing anything written in any human language."[17]

To develop a written form that all Basque could read and understand some standardization was needed. The Basque dialects in the south and north of Basque country varied enough to cause difficulty understanding each other. To standardize the language for written purposes central dialects were used to make it the most understandable for those both in the south and north.[18] Creation of a Basque written corpus helped give it prestige against the rural backward stereotype that most Basque and other speakers of Indigenous languages suffer under.

After World War II, the human rights movement epitomized by the foundation of the United Nations in 1945 and calls for self-determination and minority civil rights led to a reversal of the termination policy in the 1960s in the United States and ushered in self-determination that facilitated the establishment of American Indian locally controlled schools starting with Rough Rock Demonstration School in 1966 and Navajo Community College in 1969 that sought to include Navajo language and culture as part of their curriculum. Lionel Bordeaux, President of Sinte Gleska (Tribal) College in South Dakota, noted that the founders of tribal colleges, "foresaw the need to preserve the Indian culture so cultural preservation is really the foundation of tribal colleges."[19] In 2011 there were thirty-six small tribal/Indigenous colleges in the United States and one in Canada.[20]

In Spain, the post-Franco Spanish Constitution of 1978 in article 3.3 declared, "the richness of the different linguistic modalities of the Spanish state is a cultural heritage that will be the object of special respect and protection" and in 2007 a Council and an Office of Official Languages of the Ministry of Territorial Policy was created to give attention to linguistic rights. However University of Navarre professor Asier Barandiaran concludes, "its effectiveness has been nil."[21] With more success, the Basque re-

17. Ametzaga, "Introduction to a Political History of the Basque Language and Literature, 52.

18. Ibid., 55.

19. Bordeaux, "Higher Education from the Tribal College Perspective," 11–18.

20. See the American Indian Higher Education Consortium's web page at www.aihec.org/.

21. Barandiaran, "Linguistic Policy and Controversies Relating to Basque in the Historic Community of Navarre (2000–2009)," 329.

gional government promotes Basque literature through a subsidy to the Basque Writers Association and prizes, but authors seeking wider readership are drawn to international languages, especially Spanish but also English.

In the United States when conservatives began pushing to making English the Official Language of the country in the 1980s, Indigenous peoples of the United States, led by Native Hawaiians who saw their recently established Hawaiian language immersion schools threatened, lobbied successfully to get a Native American Languages Act passed in 1990 that made it U.S. policy to "preserve, protect, and promote the rights and freedom of Native Americans to use, practice, and develop Native American languages."[22] However, that policy has led to only few million dollars of funding for language revitalization projects. More funding was provided for American Indian programs by the Bilingual Education Act passed in 1968, which was mostly to support transitional bilingual programs to help Spanish-speaking students learn English. However in 2001 with the signing of the No Child Left Behind Act, the efforts of the government turned to promoting English language acquisition with no Native language support.

Globalization, Liberalism, and the Onslaught of Modernity

Like the many other indigenous peoples who have moved off their traditional lands, often to cities to find jobs, the Basques have undergone a diaspora that has led them to the United States and other countries across the globe. They, like indigenous peoples worldwide, are survivors, having faced repression and even genocide off and on throughout their history. For the Basque, the death of Franco in 1975 accelerated the easing of three and a half decades of repression, leading in 1979 Basque Statue of Autonomy and a subsequent increase in the number of schools teaching Basque and in Basque. The 1982 Law for the Normalization of the Use of Euskara [Basque] led to new publishing houses for Basque writers, something most indigenous peoples can only hope for today. For Miren Agur Meabe, writing in a minority language shows "*pride in the language and respect for one's neighbor*, pride and respect based on the principles of equality and solidarity, and not on assimilation."[23] According to Iban Zaldua "There is no doubt that

22. Title I, Sec. 104(1) of Public Law 101-477, October. 30, 1990, Native American Languages Act. Retrieved www2.nau.edu/jar/SIL/NALAct.pdf

23. Meabe, "Five Reasons for Writing in the Language of the Neighborhood,"

the nationalist movement [since the 1950s] turned the Basque language into one of the main faces of contemporary Basque identity. . . . Race and religion, which had been the pillars of the first nationalist movement, were pushed into the background."[24]

However the liberalization Spain has undergone since the Franco's death that led to a Basque revival also has its downside. Mark Kurlansky notes in his *Basque History of the World,* today more than government repression it is television, movies, and other modern mass media that are threatening the Basque language, a sentiment echoed by American Indian elders. As Koldo Izagirre argues, "the triumph of liberalism may well end up harming Basque, because modern liberal thought places no special emphasis on a sentimental attachment to a minority language."[25] Liberals tend to look at individual rather than group rights. The eminent sociolinguist Joshua Fishman notes that group rights need to be respected and to "view local cultures (all local cultures, not only their own) as things of beauty, as encapsulations of human values which deserve to be fostered and assisted (not merely 'preserved' in a mummified sense)."[26] He asserts,

> The denial of cultural rights to minorities is as disruptive of the moral fabric of mainstream society as is the denial of civil rights. Civil rights, however, are focused on the individual, while cultural rights must focus on ethnocultural groups. Such groups have no recognized legal standing in many Western democracies where both establishment capitalist thought and anti-establishment Marxist thought prophesies the eclipse of culturally distinct formations and the arrival of a uniformized, all-inclusive "modern proletarian" culture.[27]

Fishman argues for the need to recognize "cultural democracy" and to see efforts to preserve and restore minority languages as societal reform efforts that lead to the appreciation of the beauty and distinctiveness of other cultures as well as one's own. He emphasizes that efforts to restore minority languages should be "facilitating and enabling" rather than "compulsory and punitive."

Language restoration efforts face a difficult path. Deborah House notes in her study *Language Shift among the Navajos* that

94.

24. Zaldua, "Eight Crucial Decisions," 94.
25. See Izagirre, *Incursions en Territorio Enemigo* as quoted in Landa, "Identity, Language, Creation."
26. Fishman, *Reversing Language Shift*, 33.
27. Ibid., 70.

Navajos, like other Indigenous peoples, "are faced with the dilemma of how to create an authentic yet viable Navajo identity in an irreversibly modern world."[28] There is in fact a danger that Indigenous and other minority groups can in fact define themselves as the "white man's shadow," as opposite everything that the materialistic and individualistic Euro-American man is perceived as being.[29] They can also become repressive themselves if they gain power. A permanent Council to support the Basque language was established in 1995 and declared that it is "unacceptable for anybody to attack our language, the most fundamental element of the identity of the Basque Country and heritage we all share as citizens."[30] Such as call can be seen as a suppression of free speech and dissenting points of view, which can lead discrimination against anyone who does not fall in line with language revitalization efforts. House, who took Navajo Studies classes and taught at the Navajo tribal college in the 1990s, found there:

> non-Navajo students (Anglo, Hispanic, and others) were encouraged to disparage their own upbringing and cultural experiences. Furthermore, their language, literature, religion, family life, and ethnic identities are routinely, and at times painfully, denigrated and devalued by Navajo and non-Navajo instructors, administrators, and other students.[31]

House found that while much was spoken about the importance of revitalizing Navajo language and culture at Diné College, much less was actually being done. The ideal Navajo lifestyle that was promoted in some Diné College classes of "sheepherding and growing a small garden, living in a hogan, and driving a team of horses" was not really viable for most Navajos, especially considering the great increase in Navajo population over the last century.[32]

Healing the Wounds of Colonialism

Sally Midgette writes, "I have heard several Native Americans speak feeling about their sense of rootlessness and despair, and how they recovered when their grandmothers taught them to speak Tolowa, or Navajo, and they regained a sense of themselves

---

28. House, *Language Shift among the Navajos*, xxvii.
29. Ibid. See also Simard, "White Ghosts, Red Shadows," 333–369.
30. Ametzaga, "Introduction to a Political History of the Basque Language and Literature," 66.
31. House, *Language Shift Among the Navajos*, 38.
32. Ibid., 87.

and their heritage."[33] Interviewing Navajo elders in their own language, Northern Arizona University professor of modern languages Evangeline Parsons Yazzie found, "Elder Navajos want to pass on their knowledge and wisdom to the younger generation. Originally, this was the older people's responsibility. Today the younger generation does not know the language and is unable to accept the words of wisdom."[34] She concluded, "The use of the native tongue is like therapy, specific native words express love and caring. Knowing the language presents one with a strong self-identity, a culture with which to identify, and a sense of wellness."[35] A Navajo elder told her,

> You are asking questions about the reasons that we are moving out of our language, I know the reason. The television is robbing our children of language. It is not only at school that there are teachings, teachings are around us and from us there are also teachings. Our children should not sit around the television. Those who are mothers and fathers should have held their children close to themselves and taught them well, then our grandchildren would have picked up our language.[36]

In a similar study a Navajo elder lamented,

> television has ruined us. A long time ago, they used to say, don't do anything negative or say anything negative in front of children. It doesn't take that long for a child to catch onto things like this. Therefore a mother and a father shouldn't use harsh words in front of the children. . . . These days . . . they see movies with people having sex in them and they're watching. In these movies they shoot each other. . . . Movies are being watched every day, but there is nothing good in it.[37]

As indigenous children learn English or other "national" languages and cultures through the media and in schools, they increasingly become separated from their heritage, and some cannot speak to their grandparents. One of Yazzie's informants told her, "Older people who speak only Navajo are alone."[38] Many American Indians see language as the key to their identity, and they question whether one can be Cherokee, Navajo, Crow, Seminole, and so forth without speaking their tribal language.

---

33. Midgette, "The Native Languages of North America," 39.
34. Yazzie, "A Study of Reasons for Navajo Language Attrition as Perceived by Navajo Speaking Parents," 3.
35. Ibid.
36. Ibid., 135.
37. McCauley, *"Our Songs Are Alive,"* 242.
38. Yazzie, "A Study of Reasons for Navajo Language Attrition as Perceived by Navajo Speaking Parents," 4.

In the 1970s the all-Navajo Rock Point Community School Board concluded "that it was the breakdown of a working knowledge of Navajo kinship that caused much of what they perceived as inappropriate, un-Navajo, behavior; the way back, they felt was to teach students that system."[39] Kinship through family and clans, for the Navajo and other tribes, establishes rules for interacting in a respectful manner. To counteract this breakdown the Rock Point School Board established a Navajo-English bilingual program in their school that emphasized Navajo Social Studies and the Navajo beliefs about kinship, The Rock Point bilingual program was modified and transported to the Window Rock Public School where it was found the Navajo immersion students showed more Navajo adult-like behavior than the Navajo students not in the immersion classes.[40]

Many American Indian leaders have expressed their support for their indigenous languages. At the 2005 annual meeting of the National Indian Education Association, Cecelia Fire Thunder, then president of the Oglala Sioux at Pine Ridge, testified, "I speak English well because I spoke Lakota well. . . . Our languages are value based. Everything I need to know is in our language." She declared that language is more than communication: "It's about bringing back our values and good things about how to treat each other." Sisseton Wahpeton tribal college president William Harjo LoneFight declared, "When people spoke Dakota, they understood where they belonged in relation to other people, the natural world, and to the spiritual world. They truly knew how to treat one another."[41] Northern Cheyenne educator Richard Littlebear found,

> Our youth are apparently looking to urban gangs for those things that will give them a sense of identity, importance, and belongingness. It would be so nice if they would but look to our own tribal characteristics because we already have all the things that our youth are apparently looking for and finding in socially destructive gangs.[42]

He writes how,

> If we could transfer the young people's loyalty back to our own tribes and families, we could restore the frayed social

39. Holm and Holm, "Rock Point," 178.

40. Holm and Holm, "Navajo Language Education," 141–167.

41. as quoted in Ambler, "Native Languages," 8.

42. Littlebear, "Some Rare and Radical Ideas for Keeping Indigenous Languages Alive," 4.

> fabric of our reservations. We need to make our children see our languages and cultures as viable and just as valuable as anything they see on television, movies, or videos.[43]

A study of Hopi Indians in Arizona linked language loss to "un-Hopi" behavior by youth that included "substance abuse, gang membership, and domestic violence" and a decline in Hopi traditional values of hard work and humility.[44] A study of Hawaiian language immersion programs found that families "valued the program's emphasis on Hawaiian culture as much as its focus on the language" because students learned respect and other values.[45]

Language Revitalization and Academic Knowledge

There is a pervasive idea that time spent in school with indigenous languages will hold students back from learning the academic subjects that are critical for success in the modern world. However, evidence from indigenous language immersion schools from around the world indicate students who are taught in their indigenous language, even when they enter school not knowing it, are not held back. In fact in many cases teaching ethnic minority students in the national language, even when they only speak a dialect of it at home, have a history of substandard educational performance as is the case with the New Zealand Māori, Canadian and Australian Aboriginals, Native Hawaiian, Native Alaskans, and American Indian children. [46] As in the case of other studies of bilingual education, Jasone Cenoz, professor of research methods in education at the University of the Basque Country, finds,

> International evaluations indicate that the [test] results of the BAC [Basque Autonomous Community], where the minority language is the most common language of instruction, are at least the same and even higher than in similar education contexts which are monolingual.[47]

---

43. Ibid., 5.
44. Nicholas, "'How Are You Hopi if You Can't Speak It?' An Ethnographic Study of Language as Cultural Practice Among Hopi Youth," 58.
45. Luning and Yamauchi, "The Influences of Indigenous Heritage Language Education on Students and Families in a Hawaiian Language Immersion Program," 46. For more examples of the effect of language revitalization on student behavior see Reyhner, "Indigenous Language Immersion Schools for Strong Indigenous Identities," 138–152.
46. See e.g., Barrington, *Separate But Equal* and Reyhner and Eder, *American Indian Education*.
47. Cenoz, *Towards Multilingual Education*, 108.

She finds "bilingual education is compatible with successful academic development" and it is important to Basque as a language of instruction and not just teach it as a separate subject. These students taught in Basque can also achieve "a good command of Spanish."[48] She concludes,

> The maintenance and promotion of a minority language, Basque in this case, contributes to the maintenance of linguistic and cultural diversity. There are important ecological, historical, economic, cultural and emotional reasons to go on protecting and promoting Basque and giving Basque children the opportunity to learn and use Basque along with other languages in schools which aim at multilingualism and multiliteracy.[49]

It is clear that well-planned and implemented indigenous language revitalization programs can get children speaking their Native language without hurting their learning academic subject matter as well as national and world languages.

However, it is not enough just to teach children their indigenous language, they also need to be taught subjects in that language. Experience with Māori language revitalization indicates that seven years teaching in Māori starting in preschool will give students a command of their Native language that can survive their becoming fluent in the national language.[50] However, ironically, if language revitalization programs are successful in their ultimate goal that Joshua Fishman stresses of getting the language transmitted again in the family and students start coming to school again speaking their indigenous language, then waiting to fifth grade, as many Hawaiian immersion schools do to introduce the national language will most likely hold these students back from fully participating in the wider society. Effective language revitalization and bilingual education programs need to fit local situations, and no one model is adequate to address the needs of different communities.

Language Rights as a Basic Human Right

The United Nation's 1948 Universal Declaration of Human Rights declares in Article 26 that "Parents have a prior right to choose

---

48. Ibid.

49. Ibid., 239. See also Elorza and Muñoa, "Promoting the Minority Language Through Integrated Plurilingual Language Planning," 85–101.

50. Hill and May, "Exploring Biliteracy in Māori-Medium Education," 161–183.

the kind of education that shall be given to their children."[51] According to the U.S. State Department's website:

> The protection of fundamental human rights was a foundation stone in the establishment of the United States over 200 years ago. Since then, a central goal of U.S. foreign policy has been the promotion of respect for human rights, as embodied in the Universal Declaration of Human Rights. . . . Because the promotion of human rights is an important national interest, the United States seeks to:
>
> - Hold governments accountable to their obligations under universal human rights norms and international human rights instruments;
> - Promote greater respect for human rights, including freedom from torture, freedom of expression, press freedom, women's rights, children's rights, and the protection of minorities.[52]

In Article 29 of the UN's Convention on the Rights of the Child entered into force in 1990, "States Parties agree that the education of the child shall be directed to. . . . The development of respect for the child's parents, his or her own cultural identity, language and values" as well as "for the national values of the country in which the child is living, the country from which he or she may originate, and for civilizations different from his or her own." Only Somalia and the United States have not ratified this Convention.[53]

Despite the lukewarm support of the United States, the UN continues to advance human rights efforts.[54] The UN declared 1993 the International Year of the World's Indigenous People and then UN Secretary General Boutros Boutros-Ghali wrote in his foreword to the 1994 book *Voices of Indigenous Peoples: Native People Address the United Nations* that half the world's languages stopped being spoken in the twentieth century and,

> The modern world will therefore prove to have been a great destroyer of languages, traditions, and cultures. The latter are being drowned by the flood of mass communications.

---

51. United Nations, "Universal Declaration of Human Rights, 1948." Retrieved www.un.org/en/documents/udhr/
52. U.S. Department of State, "Human Rights." Retrieved www.state.gov/g/drl/hr/.
53. United Nations, *Convention on the Rights of the Child*, G.A. Res. 44/25, November 20, 1989, entry into force November 2, 1990, in accordance with Art. 49. Retrieved www2.ohchr.org/english/law/crc.htm.
54. See Mertus, *The United Nations and Human Rights* and Mertus, *Bait and Switch*.

> . . . Today, cultures which do not have powerful media are threatened with extinction. We must not stand idly by and watch that happen. . . . Allowing native languages, cultures, and different traditions to perish through "nonassistance to endangered cultures" must henceforth be considered *a basic violation of human rights*.[55]

On September 13, 2007 the United Nations adopted the Declaration on the Rights of Indigenous Peoples, which includes language rights. Only Australia, Canada, New Zealand and the United States voted against this declaration. However, since then all four of these countries have reversed their positions. On December 16, 2010, President Barack Obama declared,

> And as you know, in April, we announced that we were reviewing our position on the U.N. Declaration on the Rights of Indigenous Peoples. And today I can announce that the United States is lending its support to this declaration.
>
> The aspirations it affirms—including the respect for the institutions and rich cultures of Native peoples—are one we must always seek to fulfill. And we're releasing a more detailed statement about U.S. support for the declaration and our ongoing work in Indian Country. But I want to be clear: What matters far more than words—what matters far more than any resolution or declaration—are actions to match those words. . . . That's the standard I expect my administration to be held to.[56]

Article 13-1 of the declaration reads "Indigenous peoples have the right to revitalize, use, develop and transmit to future generations their histories, languages, oral traditions, philosophies, writing systems and literatures, and to designate and retain their own names for communities, places and persons" and Article 14-1 reads "Indigenous peoples have the right to establish and control their educational systems and institutions providing education in their own languages, in a manner appropriate to their cultural methods of teaching and learning."[57]

The post-World War II human rights efforts associated with the United Nations have recognized the right of self-determination, which includes local self-government, for Indigenous groups

---

55. Boutros-Ghali, "Foreword," in *Voices of Indigenous Peoples*, 13–14.

56. Obama Announces Support for UN Indigenous Rights Declaration, Voice of America News. Retrieved www.voanews.com/english/news/usa/Obama-Announces-Support-for-UN-Indigenous-Rights-Declaration-112008964.html

57. United Nations Declaration on the Rights of Indigenous Peoples, adopted by General Assembly Resolution 61/295 on September 13, 2007. Retrieved www.un.org/esa/socdev/unpfii/en/drip.html

and the right to maintain and revitalize their languages and cultures in and out of schools. Language and cultures are the markers of human identity that define the lifeways and values of groups. The destruction of languages and cultures leads to a rootlessness that leaves children directionless in a world that offers myriad hedonistic dead ends of drugs and materialism. As the late American Indian activist Vine Deloria, Jr. (Standing Rock Sioux) wrote in his book *God Is Red*, "A society that cannot remember and honor its past is in peril of losing its soul."[58] Efforts at indigenous culture and language revitalization are integral to group survival and have an important place in modern society. The United States's longest serving Commissioner of Indian Affairs (1933–1945) John Collier concluded in his *The Indians of the Americas* that modern Americans "have lost that passion and reverence for human personality and for the web of life and the earth which the American Indians have tended as a central, sacred fire."[59] Later in his memoir *From Every Zenith* he wrote, "*Assimilation*, not into our [modern American] culture but into modern life, and *preservation* and *intensification of heritage* are not hostile choices, excluding one another, but are interdependent through and through."[60]

Bibliography

Ambler, M. "Native Languages: A Question of Life or Death." *Tribal College* 15, no. 3 (2004): 8–9.

Atxaga, Bernardo. "The Cork and the Anchor." In *Writers In Between Languages: Minority Literatures in the Global Scene*, edited by Mari Jose Olaziregi. Reno: Center for Basque Studies, 2009: 49–63.

Barandiaran, Asier. "Linguistic Policy and Controversies Relating to Basque in the Historic Community of Navarre (2000–2009)." In *A Legal History of the Basque Language (1789–2009)*, edited by X. Irujo and I. Urrutia. Donostia-San Sebastián: Eusko Ikaskuntza/Society for Basque Studies, 2011: 313–343.

Barrington, John. *Separate But Equal?: Maori Schools and the Crown 1867–1969*. Wellington: Victoria University Press, 2008.

58. Vine, *God Is Red*, 276.
59. Collier, *The Indians of the Americas: The Long Hope*, 17.
60. Collier, *From Every Zenith: A Memoir*, 203.

Begaye, Kelsey. "Guest Commentary: President Begaye Addresses English Only Proposition," *The Navajo Hopi Observer* 19, no. 37 (2000): 4.

Bordeaux, Lionel. "Higher Education from the Tribal College Perspective." In *Opening the Montana Pipeline: American Indian Higher Education in the Nineties*, edited by Deborah LaCounte and Patrick Weasel Head, 11–18. Sacramento, CA: Tribal College Press, 1991.

Boutros-Ghali, Boutros. "Foreword." In *Voices of Indigenous Peoples: Native People Address the United Nations*, edited by Alexander Ewen, 13–14. Santa Fe, NM: Clear Light Publishers, 1994.

Cenoz, Jasone. *Towards Multilingual Education: Basque Educational Research From an International Perspective*. Bristol: Multilingual Matters, 2009.

Collier, John. *From Every Zenith: A Memoir*. Denver, CO: Sage Books, 1963.

———. *The Indians of the Americas: The Long Hope*. New York: W.W. Norton, 1947.

Conversi, Daniele. *The Basques, the Catalans and Spain: Alternative Routes to Nationalist Mobilization*. Reno: University of Nevada Press, 1997.

Deloria, Jr., Vine. *God Is Red: A Native View of Religion*. Golden, CO: Fulcrum, 1973/1994.

Elorza, Itziar and Immaculada Muñoa. "Promoting the Minority Language Through Integrated Plurilingual Language Planning: The Case of the Ikastolas." In *Teaching Through Basque: Achievements and Challenges*, edited by Jasone Cenoz, 85–101. Clevedon, UK: Multilingual Matters, 2008.

Fishman, Joshua A. *Reversing Language Shift: Theoretical and Empirical Foundations of Assistance to Threatened Languages*. Clevedon, UK: Multilingual Matters, 1991.

Hanson, Victor David. *Mexifornia: A State of Becoming*. San Francisco: Encounter Books, 2003.

Hill, Richard and Stephen May. "Exploring Biliteracy in Māori-Medium Education: An Ethnographic Perspective." In *Ethnography and Language Policy*, edited by Teresa L. McCarty, 161–83. New York: Routledge, 2011.

Holm, Agnes and Wayne Holm. "Rock Point, A Navajo Way To Go to School: A Valediction," *ANNALS, AAPSS*, 508 (1990): 170–184.

———. "Navajo Language Education: Retrospect and Prospects," *Bilingual Research Journal* 19 no. 1 (1995): 141–167.

House, Deborah. *Language Shift Among the Navajos: Identity Political and Cultural Continuity*. Tucson, AZ: University of Arizona Press, 2002.

Irujo Ametzaga, Xabier I. "Introduction to a Political History of the Basque Language and Literature," *Tinta* (Spring 2009): 31–69.

Kulansky, Mark. *The Basque History of the World*. New York: Penguin Books, 1999.

Landa, Mariasun. "Identity, Language, Creation: An Autobiographical Vision (Translated by Andrés Krakenberger)." In *Writers In Between Languages: Minority Literatures in the Global Scene,* edited by Mari Jose Olaziregi. Reno: Center for Basque Studies, 2009: 65–74.

Littlebear, Richard. "Some Rare and Radical Ideas for Keeping Indigenous Languages Alive." In *Revitalizing Indigenous Languages*, edited by Jon Reyhner, Gina Cantoni, Robert N. St. Clair and Evangeline Parsons Yazzie, 1–5. Flagstaff, AZ: Northern Arizona University, 1999.

Luning, Rebecca J. I. and Lois A. Yamauchi. "The Influences of Indigenous Heritage Language Education on Students and Families in a Hawaiian Language Immersion Program," *Heritage Language Journal* 7, no. 2 (2010): 46–75.

McCauley, Elizabeth A. *"Our Songs Are Alive": Traditional Diné Leaders and a Pedagogy of Possibility for Diné education*. Ed.D. dissertation, Northern Arizona University, 2001.

Meabe, Miren Agur. "Five Reasons for Writing in the Language of the Neighborhood." In *Writers In Between Languages: Minority Literatures in the Global Scene,* edited by Mari Jose Olaziregi. Reno: Center for Basque Studies, 2009, 75–87.

Mertus, Julie A. *The United Nations and Human Rights: A Guide for a New Era*. New York: Routledge, 2005.

———. *Bait and Switch: Human Rights and U.S. Foreign Policy*. New York: Routledge, 2004.

Midgette, Sally. "The Native Languages of North America: Structure and Survival." In *American Indian Studies: An Interdisciplinary Approach to Contemporary Issues,* edited by Dane Morrison, 27–45. New York: Peter Lang, 1977.

Nicholas, Sheilah E. "'How Are You Hopi if You Can't Speak It?' An Ethnographic Study of Language as Cultural Practice Among Hopi Youth." In *Ethnography and Language Policy,* edited by Teresa L. McCarty, 53–75. New York: Routledge, 2011.

Obama Announces Support for UN Indigenous Rights Declaration, Voice of America News. Retrieved www.voanews.com/english/news/usa/Obama-Announces-Support-for-UN-Indigenous-Rights-Declaration-112008964.html.

Putnam, Robert. *Bowling Alone: The Collapse and Revival of American Community*. New York: Simon & Schuster, 2000.

Reyhner, Jon. "Indigenous Language Immersion Schools for Strong Indigenous Identities." *Heritage Language Journal* 7, no. 2 (2010): 138–152.

Reyhner, Jon and Jeanne Eder. *American Indian Education: A History.* Norman, OK: University of Oklahoma Press, 2004.

Riesman, David, Nathan Glazer and Reuel Denney. *The Lonely Crowd: A Study of the Changing American Character*. Connecticut: Yale University Press, 2001. First published in 1950.

Shirley, J. Jr. "Another Viewpoint: Red Lake Tragedy Points to Loss of Traditional Ways," *Navajo Hopi Observer* 25, no. 13 (2005): 5.

Simard, Jean-Jacques. "White Ghosts, Red Shadows: The Reduction of North American Indians." In *The Invented Indian: Cultural Fictions and Government Policies,* edited by J. A. Clifton, 333–69. New Brunswick, NJ: Transaction Publishers, 1990.

Stocker, Karen. *I Won't Stay Indian, I'll Keep Studying*. Boulder: University Press of Colorado, 2005.

United Nations. *Convention on the Rights of the Child,* G.A. Res. 44/25, November 20, 1989, entry into force November 2, 1990, in accordance with Art. 49. Retrieved www2.ohchr.org/english/law/crc.htm.

United Nations. *Declaration on the Rights of Indigenous Peoples*, G.A. Res. 61/295. September 13, 2007. Retrieved www.un-.org/esa/socdev/unpfii/en/drip.html.

United Nations. "Universal Declaration of Human Rights, 1948." Retrieved www.un.org/en/documents/udhr/.

U.S. Department of State. *Human Rights, 2010*. Retrieved www.state.gov/g/drl/hr/

Yazzie, Evangeline Parsons. *A Study of Reasons for Navajo Language Attrition as Perceived by Navajo Speaking Parents*. Ed. D. dissertation, Northern Arizona University, 1995.

Zaldua, Iban. "Eight Crucial Decisions (A Basque Writer is Obliged to Face)." In *Writers In Between Languages: Minority Literatures in the Global Scene*, edited by Mari Jose Olaziregi, 89–112. Reno: Center for Basque Studies, 2009.

10
"Not Mere Documentation"
Indigenous Languges at the Threshold

Eleanor Nevins

> Every language reflects a unique world-view with its own value systems, philosophy and particular cultural features. The extinction of a language results in the irrecoverable loss of unique cultural knowledge embodied in it for centuries . . .
>
> —FAQ, Endangered Languages, UNESCO

> Native identities are traces, the *différance* of an unnameable presence, not mere statutes, inheritance, or documentation, however bright the blood and bone in the museums. Native identities must be an actuation of stories, the commune of survivance and sovereignty.
>
> —Gerald Vizenor, "Fugitive Languages"

The dueling epitaphs with which I begin my paper stand here for the problem of divergent understandings of the relationship between indigenous languages and identities, and the implications of these for indigenous language advocacy. Both quotes express a sort of affiliation with indigenous peoples, and both imply opposition to forces that disempower them. Yet the two statements, one from UNESCO and the other from a prominent Anishinaabe/Chippewa author and literary critic, sit uncomfortably next to one another. The first presents indigenous languages in relation to concepts like "worldview," "value system," "philosophy," and "cultural knowledge;" all of which suggest broad commensurability with mainstream institutions; but also imply that the uniqueness posed by indigenous languages is a source of value, and that their placement at the brink of extinction poses a global public loss. The second quote problematizes mainstream terms of recognition: "not mere statutes, inheritance, or documentation" and locates Native voices elsewhere, in an "unnamable presence," or in "traces" that require radical acts of reinterpretation in order to be perceived. Importantly for problems of indigenous language advocacy, the two conflict in the role each attributes to documentation, and in the possibilities and limitations for recognition of indigenous voices therein.

For this analysis the tension between these two statements should be kept in mind and approached from yet a third perspective, built from work in linguistic anthropology, concerning the discursive mediation of contemporary indigenous communities in relation to encompassing sociopolitical orders. The UNESCO quote is to be viewed as representative of the rhetoric of "language endangerment" and "language maintenance," while the Gerald Vizenor quote prompts us to be uncomfortable with received notions and mindful that there are other ways of locating indigeneity (and by extension indigenous languages). In the course of the paper that follows it will be established that, while the concern with saving endangered languages seems on the surface of things to be "about" languages, when viewed from the standpoint of local indigenous communities, language endangerment and its "solution" in maintenance programs are about much more than language. They inevitably comprise a particular domain of discourse production (usually in schools or culture centers) alongside many others in a community (extended families, public ceremonies, indigenous media), which sometimes conflict and compete with one another in the politically charged process of establishing terms for mediating that locality as an indigenous one within encompassing sociopolitical orders.

Drawing upon three years of work, from 1996 to 1999, as an ethnographer of communication among members of the White Mountain Apache tribe on the Fort Apache reservation, language endangerment and maintenance is approached by asking what is revealed when we shift our focus from "languages" to "social contexts of language use"? When viewed from this perspective, maintenance programs are often the mirror opposite of what they claim to be. That is, rather than representing continuity and maintenance of indigenous pedagogies and relations of speaking, they instead enact a very specific kind of transformation to the pedagogies and social relations entailed in schooling and language standardization. Such changes may in fact be sought after by some, but for others they may present uncomfortable disjunctures that go unrecognized by outside "language experts," like linguists, curriculum developers, and language planners. And, because language programs confer specific forms of institutionally accredited authority on an otherwise contested political field, they are seldom free of political controversy. These and other social contextual dimensions of language maintenance within indigenous communities are crucial to the meaning and purpose of language programs. However, they are obscured by endangerment rhetoric. The purpose of my previous ethnographic work[1] was to draw out some of the social contextual dimensions of indigenous language issues as the basis of a qualified criticism of endangerment rhetoric and the documentation and maintenance programs based upon it. In this paper, the qualification of that criticism will be further developed. It is not my intention to cast language endangerment discourse as a noble cause to be blindly embraced, or false consciousness to be rejected, but rather to cast it as a mobilizing discourse with global reach that provides terms of mediation among a diverse assemblage of interested parties. In what follows, I first present and problematize endangerment as a rhetoric of mobilization with almost inevitable disjunctures between the diverse communities of practice (linguists, educators, granting agencies, indigenous community members, publishers) it is used to mediate. But then, this will be tempered by placing endangerment within its own conflictual sociohistorical setting. I note that as a framework for local-national or local-global mediation, a concern to "save indigenous languages" is more amenable to the expression of political agency and strategies of self-determination by indigenous peoples than previous assimilationist policies or contemporary "English-Only," or other monoglot standard, political discourses. I conclude by suggesting strategies for specifying and refining indigenous language advocacy in relation to the goal of community empowerment, by making accommoda-

1. Nevins, "Learning to Listen," 269–88; id., "'They Live in Lonesome Dove,'" 191–215; id., "The Bible in Two Keys," 19–32; Nevins and Nevins, Forthcoming. "'They Do Not Know How to Ask.'"

tion in research methods and project design for alternative claims and meanings for indigenous languages by differently positioned members of the communities involved.

The (Inevitable) Problems with Endangerment as a Global Mediating Discourse

"Language endangerment" as a phrased circulated in public life, has a hybrid existence as part of a scientific discourse spoken by university accredited language experts and as a rhetoric of mobilization that has been used to consolidate resources for university-based linguistic field and archival work, as well as educational programs in indigenous communities.[2] Language endangerment makes use of an analogy with species endangerment in order to render the problem as a "crisis" recognizable by the same public constituents concerned about the former. As a rhetoric of mobilization, it operates by defining a crisis, identifying a global public stake in the crisis, and specifying certain instrumentalities for addressing that crisis that can be funded, accounted for, and reported upon. Not surprisingly, linguists have taken the lead in defining the problem and shaping programs to address it. They present indigenous languages at a threshold between life and death, and if death is inevitable, between entering endangered languages into the record by linguists for posterity, or "losing"[3] them. Linguistic documentation, in the form of writing grammatical descriptions and dictionaries, is the first priority for many such programs. This is based upon the rationale that documenting endangered languages is multi-functional, in that documentation serves the scientific community and is a useful first step toward developing indigenous language literacy programs. Funding agencies, including national governments in the United States, Mexico, New Zealand, Canada, Brazil, Australia, international organizations like UNESCO, and independent foundations such as Hans R Foundation, Terralingua, the Endangered languages fund, and the Max Plank Institute all sponsor projects addressing language endangerment. Within academia, the past twenty years has seen an explosion of scholarship devoted to language endangerment

2. For treatments of language endangerment discourse within a political economy framework, see the collection of essays assembled by Duchêne, Allexandre and Heller, (eds), *Discourses of Endangerment*.
3. This meaning of "lost" noted by Moore, "Disappearing, Inc.," 296–315.

and maintenance: conferences, articles, edited volumes, books.[4]

With languages so much in focus as items in crisis, and with linguists playing such an important role in defining remediation efforts, it is tempting to overlook the social context in which the concern to preserve indigenous languages finds expression. This is reflected in the predominant focus on linguistic documentation in programs addressing problems of language endangerment. But surely indigenous language endangerment, when you think about plausible causes and attempted remedies, cannot purely, or even primarily, be a linguistic problem. That is, whether or not a language falls out of use has very little to do with its grammatical structure and lexical inventory. Rather, the play of local vernaculars in the histories of colonial encounters, and in contemporary discursive means that the members of indigenous communities that articulate with wider social contexts and networks, are at least equally, if not more, germane?

Bubbling up among the burgeoning literature on language endangerment and maintenance are an increasing number of accounts of programs that occasion controversy, disjuncture or have unintended consequences in the communities they are intended to benefit.[5] Some of my own work on Western Apache language issues addresses community ambivalence surrounding language programs with which I, as an outside "language expert" was involved.[6] I argue that ambivalence is almost inevitable, and emerges from the complexity of indigenous communities, whose historical placement often entail multiple and sometimes conflicting sources of authority through which claims upon indigenous languages are made. For example, in the Fort Apache speech community, extended family homes versus schools provided two very different ways of knowing the Apache language. Similarly, Traditionalists and Apache Independent Christians made overlapping and conflicting claims on Apache language as public religious speech. Community ambivalence in response to language programs is often simply overridden by language experts, disre-

4. Bradley and Bradley, *Language Endangerment and Language Maintenance*; Evans, *Dying Words*; Grenoble and Whaley, *Saving Languages*; Harrison, *When Languages Die*; Nettle and Romaine, *Vanishing Voices*; Tsunoda, *Language Endangerment and Language Revitalization*.

5. Hill, "'Expert Rhetorics' in Advocacy for Endangered Languages?" 119–133; Hofling, "Indigenous Linguistic Revitalization and Outsider Interaction," 108–116; Wilkins, "Even with the Best of Intentions ..."

6. Nevins, "Learning to Listen."

garded on the rationale that the problem of endangerment is too urgent to allow for distractions from the programmatic goals of documentation and maintenance.[7] I counter that it is exactly in that ambivalence that the stake community members have in indigenous or heritage languages can be found.

Disjuncture, ambivalence, and resistance figure as noise only against the rather narrow definition of the problem of language loss and maintenance that emerges from the concerns of linguistic documentation. By contrast, within the field of linguistic anthropology there is an emerging body of ethnographic work that addresses language shift and maintenance,[8] and in terms of collaboration between scholars of indigenous languages and community members.[9] Work in linguistic anthropology presents indigenous languages at a different sort of threshold. Rather than precariously poised between life and death, documentation and loss, indigenous languages are poised at the threshold of indigenous communities and encompassing sociopolitical orders. At this threshold between communities, indigenous languages are inflected with value, power, and meaning, and language documentation is one of the processes by which indigenous communities are represented within the institutions of the dominant society. By focusing attention on the complex and sometimes contentious social processes attending language shift and maintenance, such work provides a necessary complement to documentation work and language planning.

Indigenous language endangerment as a public issue circulates within indigenous communities as well as with wider public audiences. Through the notion of endangerment (at least in part), the local vernaculars of historically colonized peoples have become key symbols of indigeneity and in this way, have been conferred with value at the threshold of indigenous communities and encompassing political orders. As such they have multiple and diverse claimants. However, the threshold occupied by indigenous languages is not limited to language documentation and mainte-

7. Loether, "Language Revitalization and the Manipulation of Language Ideologies," 238–55; Walsh, "2002 Teaching NSW's Indigenous Languages Lessons from Elsewhere." Prepared for the Aboriginal Curriculum Unit of the NSW Board of Studies.

8. Hill and Hill, "Speaking Mexicano"; Collins, *Understanding Tolowa Histories; Meek, We Are Our Language*; Kulick, *Language Shift and Cultural Reproduction*.

9. Morgan, *The Bearer of This Letter*; Collins, "Our Ideologies and Theirs," 256–270.

nance efforts, but is evident in many other contexts of everyday life, including enactments of family, of belonging to place, and in uses of indigenous language idioms to enact everyday global orientations through, for example, recontextualization of mass media or the Christian Bible. Language programs are not launched in a social vacuum, but within an already dynamic discursive field. One way or another, language programs are impacted by others in the community that have a stake in claiming authority in the language, whether language program developers are aware of it or not.

The Shifting Value of Indigenous Languages

Here we are looking at language endangerment not only as a set of facts about the world, but also as a discourse about language, with its own set of entailed assumptions, relations of authority, and sources of institutional reproduction. Language endangerment discourse mobilizes public and institutional support and sets some of the terms for the mediation of indigenous communities within encompassing state, national, and international social orders. And while the object conjured in the imagination for some by the phrases "indigenous community" or "endangered language" are of out-of-the-way places, or left-by-the-wayside peoples, in fact both concepts are inextricably bound to a historical imagination of colonialism and claims to land within a cosmopolitan, global framework.[10] Engaging with one's social world with an indigenous identity or by speaking an indigenous language (understood as such), implies a particular kind of globally oriented location.

Global indigeneity, manifest in international forums as well as in local communities, has become a focus of recent anthropological inquiry. Merlan[11] and Niezen[12] trace the emergence of indigeneity as a relational concept to twentieth-century international political arenas accompanying the two world wars. Concerns about indigenous language endangerment as a crisis that requires intervention, are reflexes of this fairly recent sea of change. Definitions of indigeneity arose alongside a more general ethical debate in which liberal democracies began to redefine aspects of their own internal social diversity, and these definitions informed

10. Biolsi, "Imagined Geographies." *American Ethnologist* 32(2): 239–259.
11. Merlan, "*Indigeneity*." Current Anthropology 50, no. 3(2009): 303–333.
12. Niezen, *The Origins of Indigenism*.

new legal provisions to accommodate social difference represented in the term.

Prior to the world wars, the liberal democratic settler states (United States, Canada, Australia, New Zealand) had official assimilation policies, in which indigenous languages and cultural practices were marginalized, stigmatized, and repressed. Perhaps most disempowering for Native communities was the forced dismantling of social institutions, as children were taken away from their families for school, ceremonies were banned, and large-scale exchange events, like the potlatch, were outlawed.[13] Prominent symbols of the assimilationist regime were boarding schools, designed to remove children from the socializing effects of their families and communities.[14] In addition to the marginalizing ideological underpinnings of the boarding school system, oversight of administrators and teachers was often lacking, with the predictable effect (though not without exception) of widespread physical and emotional abuses. Traumas endured during the boarding school period are still within the living memory of some elders in contemporary indigenous communities.

Coinciding with the emergent internationalism surrounding the two world wars, world political bodies like the League of Nations and later the United Nations became a forum in which critical scrutiny was brought to bear upon the repression of ethnic minorities. Concerns about the treatment of indigenous peoples were articulated alongside discussions of the deplorable working conditions of the world's poor by global labor organizations. These concerns converged in a global discourse of human rights—culminating in the 1948 United Nations Universal Declaration of Human Rights. As a result, liberal democracies made different kinds of legal accommodations for their own internal social differences and minorities.

Elaborated from human rights, we see the subsequent formulation of language rights and the application of these in different ways toward indigenous and other minority language communities.[15] In principal at least, language rights include some form of

---

13. However, assimilation, although posing severe constraints, also can be approached as a framework of mediation that was actively negotiated by Native Americans and other indigenous peoples. See Bartelt, "American Indian Discourses of Assimiliationism," in *Language and Literature*. 17(1992):59–75.

14. Reyner, *American Indian Education*.

15. Paulson, "Language Policies and Language Rights" Annual Review of Anthropology 27 (1997): 73–87.

recognition of indigenous and minority languages and often some kind of accommodation, either in the form of allowing people to access public institutions and participation in political life via their native tongue, or to ameliorate the effects of a history of oppression and repression by supporting and valorizing minority languages in some official capacity.

Indigenous rights and language rights are actively in play on the world stage today and still negotiated, an example being the United Nations Declaration on the Rights of Indigenous Peoples, only recently endorsed (with elaborate disclaimers and qualifications) by the United States and Canada.[16] Within contemporary national politics, indigenous (and minority) language advocates continue to have opponents in "English-only," or other political movements that pair what Silverstein terms a "monoglot-standard" language ideology[17] with advocacy for restrictions on minority language instruction in public schools. The state of Arizona (which surrounds the Fort Apache reservation) is a very good example of this dynamic.

Just following my field term in 2000, an English-Only political movement was successful in passing proposition 203,[18] also known as the "Unz initiative," which not only withdrew state funding for bilingual education, but also mandated exclusive instruction in English for state-funded schools. More recently, in 2010 Arizona passed SB2281, which "prohibits a school district or charter school from including in its program of instruction any courses or classes that . . . are designed primarily for pupils of a particular ethnic group." An aspect of this legislation required the retraining or removal of any teacher who speaks English with "a heavy accent,"[19] which one might have if one's first language were a Native American language, or a Native American variety of English.[20] Add to this a notorious piece of legislation passed in 2010, Immigration law S.B. 1070, [21] which mandates police search-

16. IPS Arctic Council Indigenous Peoples Secretariat. "Qualified UNDRI Support" www.arcticpeoples.org/index.php?option=com_k2&view=item&id=367:qualified-undrip-support&Itemid=2,(Last accessed, February 21, 2011).

17. Silverstein, "Monoglot 'standard' in America," 284–306.

18. Crawford, "Proposition 203: Anti-Bilingual Initiative in Arizona." www.languagepolicy.net/archives/az-unz.htm. (Posted 2001).

19. Jourdan. "Arizona Grades Teachers on Fluency."

20. Bartelt, Penfield-Jasper and Hoffer, (eds.) *Essays in Native American English*.

21. "Native American Tribes Say they won't Enforce Immigration Law."

es of those who might be suspected of being illegal immigrants, and requiring any possibly suspected people to carry papers documenting their residency status in order to avoid arrest. The law was designed to target Mexican immigrants, but drew opposition from the Inter Tribal Council of Arizona whose members refused to enforce it, and who described it as an assault on tribal sovereignty, and anticipated that implementation would inevitably increase police harassment of Native Americans as well. Portrayals of minority languages and peoples in such a political climate by their opponents can be derogatory and poorly informed. Linguists and other accredited language experts, in the face of these sorts of political movements, are often allies of linguistic minorities. They use their authority and expertise to correct erroneous characterizations, combat stigma, and promote the public support of indigenous and other minority languages.[22] Language endangerment and language rights discourses, as mobilizing rhetoric, operate in state and national arenas against what in the present context is an unintentionally ironic majoritarian "nativism."

Outside of Arizona, United States national statistics reveal a situation stacked against Native languages. According to a 2007 report released by the Department of Education, for 87 percent of Native American fourth graders and eighth graders, reading and language arts are delivered entirely in English. Of students who identify themselves as Native Americans 39 percent of 4th graders and 40 percent of 8th graders said they "never" have exposure to a Native American language at home.[23] In the face of political opponents whose ideologies and policies are reminiscent of the assimilationist regime, and a school system in which Native Languages are already drastically underrepresented, many linguists view support for indigenous languages as a moral commitment linked to their occupational expertise. A survey of book publications and mission statements of granting institutions for field linguistics makes it clear that indigenous language endangerment is a strongly felt course of social relevance for linguistic study.

We can think of public arguments about language endangerment as a mobilization strategy. By drawing an analogy between linguistic diversity with biological diversity, and endangered languages with endangered species, it creates a recognizable identity

22. For example, Fishman, "In Praise of the Beloved Language."

23. Zehr, "Native American Students Flag Holes in Instruction," Education Week, no. 27 (2008).

for the problem of language loss and helps make the case for the necessity of intervention and consequent institutional support. And while it is fair to say that the vast majority of linguists and indigenous language educators are in favor of supporting indigenous languages, the form that this support might take is less well defined if it is to be designed to be maximally relevant within indigenous communities (as opposed to the documentary concerns of linguistics).

Distinguishing Indigenous Community Dynamics from National Politics

In an article entitled "'Expert Rhetorics' in Advocacy for Endangered Languages: Who Is Listening and What Do They Hear?" [24] Jane Hill argues that there is a gulf between language endangerment as the advocacy rhetoric of language experts, and ways that heritage languages are discussed and understood within many Native American communities. Not only does the disjunction pose problems of coordination and mutual understanding, but the hyperbolic terms in which the "expert rhetoric" of language endangerment casts Native languages, for example, as "treasures" that should be saved for the benefit of the public at large, can pose conflict for the bearers of those languages, who often have quite different reasons for wanting to maintain a local language. Similarly, Paiute intellectual property rights scholar, Debra Harry, argues that defining forms of indigenous knowledge in terms of an imagined or legislated "public domain" can run counter to self-determination efforts by indigenous community members.[25] Because linguists situate themselves as expert advocates for linguistic diversity[26] amidst national and international political discourses, and because local indigenous communities articulate with, but are not identical to these discourses, it is perhaps inevitable but also rather awkward that language documentation and maintenance programs can occasion controversy and ambiv-

24. Hill, "'Expert Rhetorics' in Advocacy for Endangered Languages," *Journal of Linguistic Anthropology* 12(2): 119–133.

25. Harry, "Acts of Self-Determination and Self-Defense," 87–98.

26. "Diversity, " much like "indigeneity," stands in for accommodating difference in the mediation of communities within national and international orders, but the "meaning" of diversity and entailments for how to account for and support it, differs according to institutional and contextual placement, a point made by Urciuoli, Bonnie, 2010. "Entextualizing *Diversity*," *Language and Communication* 30, no. 1(2010): 48–57.

alence among members of the communities they are intended to benefit. It is not at all unusual for heritage language research and educational programs to be actively sought after and vigorously supported by some, but also subject to critique, intervention, and various forms of foot-dragging by other members of an indigenous community, most of whom also voice concern about language loss.

Community critiques, controversies, and interventions into indigenous language programs tend to be both underreported and poorly understood in the language endangerment literature. In many accounts of language programs, such things are treated obliquely, as obstacles to be negotiated or overcome to clear the way for the "real work" of documentation and maintenance. Given the embattled placement of most indigenous languages relative to majority languages, some linguists advocate avoiding community controversies on the rationale that one should not "air dirty laundry," or that muddying the advocacy narrative with social complications would only hamper public support for those fragile efforts that are underway. My answer to this concern is that the very cause and perpetuation of language shift, as well as the legacy of any documentation or maintenance effort, is a matter of social complication, top to bottom. Nothing could be more misleading than understanding language shift as a strictly linguistic problem. It would also be misleading to equate community critiques of language programs with statements of opposition to indigenous languages, as these are wielded within "English-only" movements or other monoglot standard rhetorics within state and national politics. Rather, I argue that community critiques and ambivalence emerge from the inevitable internal diversity of indigenous communities and that in fact, a space for their expression is opened up by certain paradoxes accompanying the notion of indigeneity as a relational concept.

Paradoxes of Indigeneity

Indigeneity positions communities with respect to a history of colonial disruption and of partial encompassment within the colonizing society on unfavorable or unfair terms. What were disrupted were communication networks, established and different means of making a living, and moral associations to land, among other things. The notion of indigeneity implies inclusion of that form of alterity from the colonial order found in the colonized community. So local practices and forms of authority that pose an alternative to the mainstream would by implication appear to be germane (even if they exist in uneasy tension with mainstream ways of recognizing difference, e.g., formulations of ethnicity and race). This is part of why elders and ceremonial specialists are often accorded the status of "cultural expert." However, inclusion in wider publics and extensions of government and private grant funding require packaging indigenous ways of doing things in terms recognizable within mainstream institutions.[27] The result is a sort of necessary paradox in which in order to be recognized as "indigenous," the alterity presented by indigenous ways of doing things must be objectified and made comprehensible within familiar institutional terms. When the local language is recontextualized as an indigenous language within institutions like schools and culture centers, the manner in which it is presented can run counter to those ways of speaking that provide an alternative that the notion of indigeneity would otherwise seem to privilege.

Also, it is worth keeping in mind that schools and other educational offices generate political asymmetries of their own, and that in communities where an indigenous language is still spoken, there are often others, such as elders or religious and political leaders, invested with authority to speak and teach from alternate sources that may continue to be relevant. In fact, the continuing use of an indigenous vernacular across multiple contexts of social life may be a good predictor of the likelihood of community critiques and interventions into school-based indigenous language programs. As will be shown below, the implication of this is not that linguists should leave communities alone, but that they must realize the partiality of their own view of language and model of language pedagogy. Furthermore, while language programs may be sought after by some members of an indigenous community, the form programs take is negotiated within a dynamic field of social relationships in which contending claims to indigeneity and indigenous languages are relevant.

Francesca Merlan describes internationalist public discourse surrounding indigeneity, which here is extended to include "language rights" and "saving endangered languages," as both enabling and constraining empowerment efforts in indigenous communities. The following applies readily to indigenous language programs:

---

27. A point argued by Povenelli, in *The Cunning of Recognition*.

> In bringing matters of recognition as well as social participation and economic support onto the terrain of the state, the liberal democracies extended their administrative and bureaucratic functions to regulate them. Many forms of regulation are, almost by definition, different from the range of usual community practices, and the resulting regulatory systems are both enabling and constraining, may stimulate opposition, and may bear the unmistakable stamp of the liberal political cultures that house them.[28]

Public concern for language endangerment enables members of indigenous communities to mobilize support from various quarters of the mainstream public in order to bring wanted resources into their communities. Language documentation and maintenance programs are a means for combating the stigma that had been attached to indigenous vernaculars under the previous assimilationist regime (and which continue in "English Only" movements), and for valorizing indigenous languages as "heritage languages," linking communities to a shared past on a particular landscape. However, after the grammar has been written, and curricula composed, teachers trained, assessment plan devised, the resultant "regulatory system" bears the stamp of a political culture (down to the micro-politics of classroom pedagogy[29]) that runs counter to other pedagogic practices that distribute authority across other community domains (elders, extended families, ceremonial leadership), and that pose their own morally and symbolically weighted claims upon indigeneity.

The process of mediation is more complex than can be captured with a dichotomy between "outsider linguists, language planners" and "insider community members." While "outside experts" are almost always involved in some capacity, an important part of the institutional elaboration of indigenous language efforts has involved university training, research, and program development conducted by members of indigenous communities. Language rights, and language endangerment mobilizing rhetorics provide the rationale for programs through which members of indigenous communities obtain accreditation for themselves and their efforts, and can include linguistic documentation and school-based indigenous language education efforts.[30] Language

28. Merlan, Francesca. "Indigeneity Local and Global," 316.
29. See, for example, Phillips, *The Invisible Culture*.
30. In North America, good examples are: the American Indian Language Development Institute (AILDI) www.u.arizona.edu/~aildi/; Northwest Indian Language Institute (NILI) pages.uoregon.edu/nwili/.

programs often include community members with university accreditation working alongside other community members who derive their authority from other sources, such as their status as elders, family members, or ceremonial leaders. The difference can be a source of conflict and creativity, and is worth paying attention to.

Ethnography and Intellectual Pluralism

I propose that it would be clarifying to broaden the mobilizing concern to "save indigenous languages" from that of documentation to community empowerment. Ultimately, if empowerment is the concern, the center of gravity must shift to emergent subaltern voices, including both university-trained members of indigenous communities and the voices of other indigenous persons as well. I strive to present something other than an expert claim in the present argument and in my ethnographic work. In the pursuit of finer grain accuracy in tracing terms of mediation, I utilize ethnography to match up locally relevant concerns with globally recognizable terms, and provide for their distinction from one another. I try to establish terms of social reflexivity necessary in order to open the project of "saving endangered languages" to an expectation of indigenous intellectual pluralism.

There is an irreducible complexity to indigenous communities in their relation to global orders that has consequences for community responses to language maintenance programs. One consequence is that there is often a relativity to terms and phrases like "language loss," "heritage language," and what it would mean to "save the language;" a relativity in which the meanings held by a linguist or language teacher may be at odds with those held in other quarters of the community. An often unintended and unrecognized consequence of many language maintenance programs is that they redefine the language they are intended to stabilize. They do this by decontextualizing it from relations of speaking and authority within extended families, ceremonies and other community contexts, and recontextualizing it within the authority relationships and practices of schools, culture centers and museums. Some of the controversies that often surround language programs within indigenous communities reflect struggles over authority to impart and define the language across this disjuncture.

Failure to recognize the nature of such struggles serves to

reinforce the naturalization of schools and museums as sites of knowledge and learning over alternatives (e.g., elders in extended families) in the local community. When built into language work, attention to the relativity of social perspectives can offer an alternative to the naturalization of mainstream discourses (modeling indigenous languages as quasi-national standard languages) and practices (school pedagogies), and the local political asymmetries they entail. If indigenous community empowerment is the goal, then community critique and intervention are valuable opportunities to modify and reinterpret language programs in their relation to voices authorized from other sources and for recognizing multiple ways in which language is very much at stake in the mediation of the local community within wider polities. The goal then, is not to discredit language programs but to specify their placement (often an important and dynamic one) within their respective social fields in indigenous communities.

Language Advocacy as Cultural Encounter

A key argument here is that indigenous languages exist at the threshold between indigenous communities and surrounding social orders and figure importantly into community definition at that juncture. Therefore, concerns with saving or supporting indigenous languages are articulated at the same threshold, and have a complicated relationship with local communicative practices because they are often dually articulated through historically imposed institutions like schools, on the one hand, and across generations in extended families, on the other. My concern is to set this as the frame within which to analyze not only the play of indigenous language issues in institutions (like schools) that clearly articulate with state, federal, and international discourses, but to also recognize ways in which community members employ language in methods relevant to local notions of indigeneity to pose alternate definitions of community, centered in family, place and often in religious discourse.

Therefore, following Webb Keane's[31] treatment of missionary work and Thomas Nevins'[32] treatment of ethnography, I treat language work conducted by university accredited experts (indigenous-identified or not) in indigenous communities as a form of encounter between people enmeshed in contrasting sociocultural

31. Keane, "Christian Moderns: Freedom and Fetish in the Mission Encounter."
32. Nevins, "Between Love and Culture."

orders, or ways of enacting social relations. Language documentation and its use to develop materials for teaching vocabulary and grammar in schools is just one way of objectifying language. I draw attention to different modes of objectifying language and reflecting upon it, such as the names, stories, songs, inside jokes, teasing routines, "good words" and prayers that figure into the daily life and ceremonial life of extended families. Differences in objectifying and reflecting upon language across familial and school contexts are enmeshed in different pedagogical practices, ethics of speaking and differential attributions of authority to speak and teach the language. Ethnography, attuned to the multiplicity of contemporary indigenous communities, and mindful of the specificity and partiality of schools and culture centers, can help reframe the "noise" of community critique, ambivalence, and intervention in response to language programs into alternate claims to authority and attempts to define community that are themselves germane to indigenous community empowerment and the ongoing relevance of indigenous languages.

Such an approach demands that we abandon considerations of languages and cultures as static, bounded off entities that require purification. Rather, the play of language use in both extended family environments and school language and culture programs is thoroughly hybrid in the sense that both settings provide means for engagement with local precedents and global discursive flows, albeit in different ways. It should also be clear that I am not claiming that schools and culture centers make a sort of false claim upon an indigeneity that is more properly attributed to homes and families. However, schools and culture centers, because they articulate most closely with government regulating functions, are more likely to be recognized and supported in maintenance programs as sites of language learning. The "taken for granted" quality of knowledge as embodied in state formal education settings tends to obscure articulations of indigenous languages and communities in other contexts and terms. Ethnographic methods of linguistic and cultural anthropology would be a helpful addition to maintenance and other advocacy efforts to bring consideration of the inevitable (for reasons discussed above) intellectual pluralism of indigenous communities into language advocacy and planning.

As a very brief example, I present my work undertaken from 1996 to 1999 among residents of the Fort Apache reservation. As an outsider, and as a researcher interested in changes in ways of using Apache and English, a threshold of sorts surrounded me[33] as I moved through the community—a threshold that differently positioned people interpreted and addressed in different ways. Within the politically prominent family with whom I worked most closely, senior family members responded to my request to learn to speak Apache by directing me to learn how to make bread (which in political families is more than a performance of domesticity, but a perpetual readiness for visitors), and to become an aware participant in the life of the extended family. This involved being attentive enough to get the jokes, learn the stories, and to realize when I was being teased or being invited to help tease someone else (younger than me). On the other hand, my supervisors in educational offices of the tribe paired me with fluent speakers and paid me to create curricular materials for the schools, for which an overriding concern was to make a product that would foster in students pride in their indigenous heritage by presenting their language in terms that compared favorably with materials students were otherwise using for their English classes. In both home and school contexts, discourses about *Ndee bik'ehgo yati'*, the Apache language, were prominent, but cast in different terms. My work in the language program elicited assistance and criticism within my extended family relations, and by paying attention to the terms of these, I was able to trace the differences between pedagogies and language ideologies, addressed to a language researcher,[34] between these two different contexts. Attending to these differences helped to explain some of the successes of longstanding programs, and illuminated political controversies concerning the language program with which I was involved.

I also want to stress that community attention to language issues is not just addressed to domesticating the global, but also involved in making alternate claims to global relevance. For example, schools, mass media, and Christianity are all sites of engagement with encompassing social orders on the Fort Apache reservation as is true for many indigenous communities. The imputed authentic indigeneity of one's voice is often at stake in self and community definitions at such junctures, but figured differently across different social contexts.[35] At all three "sites," it is plausi-

33. Ibid.

34. Nevins, "Learning to Listen."

35. For Apache creative engagements with mass media, see Nevins, "They

ble to trace extensions and transplants of institutions from the dominant society: for example, through schools, satellite network programming, and churches. Within these transplants there are strong interpretive pressures to draw contrasts and comparisons between Apache and English languages through terms established in the institutions of the encompassing society. However, educational, mass media, and Christian discursive materials are also taken up and recontextualized[36] within the discursive practices of extended families and neighborhoods, and their meanings transformed in their reception and use within the terms of discursive precedents established therein. Apache appropriations of titles from mass media discourse for use as official place names for newly constructed neighborhoods are one such example.[37] They are produced as inside jokes, whose meaning is widely recognized among reservation residents, and they are posted on official green and white signs along highways, where they stand as examples of wit and participation in global media observable by reservation residents and outsiders. For example a street sign labeled "Jurassic Park" can be recognized by a person driving through the reservation on her way somewhere else. It is recognizable as a movie title and as an unexpected way of naming a place, even if our traveler does not "get" the particular joke about the neighborhood that reservation residents recognize in the name. As Rumsey puts it, "the effect is not simply to indigenize the exogenous but also to exogenize the endogenous."[38] The characterization is also an apt one for the many varieties of Apache religious discourse, much of it using Apache language idioms to make claims upon the Christian Bible.[39] Contending ways of figuring the Bible in relationship to Apache traditional religion are enacted across conflicting Apache religious identities and circulated with local and

---

Live in Lonesome Dove," 2008; For the emergence of the status of community "language expert" as a result of mission and school translation projects, see Samuels, "Bible Translation and Medicine Man Talk," *Language in Society* 35, no. 4(2006): 529–57; For claims to Apache Christianities as indigenous religious identities, see Nevins, and Nevins, "'We Have Always Had the Bible,'" 2009.

36. Bauman, "Poetics and Performance as Critical Perspectives on Language and Social Life."; Silverstein, "The Natural History of Discourse," 1–17; Spitulnik, "The Social Circulation of Media Discourse and the Mediation of Communities."

37. See Nevins, "They Live in Lonesome Dove."

38. See Rumsey, "The Articulation of Indigenous and Exogenous Orders in Highland New Guinea and Beyond," 62.

39. See Nevins, "The Bible in Two Keys," 2010.

more extended communities in mind. In this manner, attention to language use at the threshold of communities, it is possible to establish and elaborate ethnographically the dynamic local-global social field in which indigenous languages and acts of language use have meaning. These considerations are where ongoing stakes in local vernaculars, as indigenous languages, are claimed, and alongside school programs, they bear directly upon processes of maintenance and expressions of political agency.

Conclusion

Indigenous language endangerment and maintenance discourses provide terms through which historically colonized communities mediate relations to encompassing sociopolitical orders. Language rights and the concern to "save endangered languages" represent an improvement in the status of indigenous peoples in comparison with assimilationist policies of the late nineteenth and early twentieth centuries, and provide terms for ongoing affiliations with sectors of the mainstream public against the contemporary assimilationism of "English Only" and other monoglot standard majoritarian political movements. However, language maintenance programs are often met with ambivalence, critique and intervention by members of the communities they are designed to benefit. I propose that community ambivalence is misrecognized by language planners as noise, as statements of disaffiliation (or a failure of commitment) with respect to the language itself, or as factors external to language such as "factionalism."

I argue that such misrecognition is due to two shortcomings. First, the problem of language loss and maintenance is defined too narrowly with too much emphasis on the products of linguistic documentation. The latter are treated as discrete, community-internal properties that need to be "reinserted" through maintenance programs. If we instead view indigenous languages in their relational, mediating role as representations of indigeneity in the context of broader sociopolitical orders, the field in which people have conflicting stakes in them is brought into focus.

And secondly, there is a failure on the part of many language experts to take the internal diversity of indigenous communities into account, in which members orient to global social orders in more than one way. On the one hand, they are engaged with the representations of their indigeneity within mainstream institutions like schools and culture centers. On the other hand, they also articulate with more extended communities at sites of discourse production defined through alternate relations of authority, such as extended families[40] and locally authored religious activities.[41]

The difference between mainstream and alternate ways of authorizing indigeneity can be paradoxical and conflictual. This is because the notion of indigeneity implies a representation of what is "altern" about a colonized community, but the representations most readily recognized (and supported) by outsiders are those that are couched within mainstream institutional forms. Thus, researchers and language experts are positioned ambivalently in relation to other forms of authority, especially that of elders within extended family networks. The notion of indigeneity would seem to mandate the latter's inclusion and exertion of control; nevertheless, forms of support are rationalized through a regime they do not control, one that is based upon accreditation and program assessment. When the placement of language programs with respect to the multiple articulations of indigenous communities is attended to, expressions of ambivalence, resistance or critique are not noise, but voices we have thus far failed to hear, and which are likely to be important for understanding and refining ongoing language advocacy efforts.

As the two quotes with which this paper began illustrated, there is dissonance between indigeneity as a term in ethno-national discourses and the place that it holds as a link in a historical chain of events between a colonizing national entity and an indigenous socio-cultural order based on other terms. Some kind of alterity, that "unnamable presence" described by Vizenor, looms in the very premise of indigeneity; but, as he indicates, has a complicated relationship to documentation efforts. Therefore, the nature of my critique of language endangerment as a discourse is to place qualifications and limits upon it, limits drawn from recognizing alternate voices, pedagogies, and claims upon language in indigenous communities. For many language programs that have stood the test of time, this process of attending to community critique and accommodating community intervention is already familiar in practice, but not built into the explicit theories informing programs and planning. My aim is to build an expectation of indigenous intellectual pluralism into lan-

40. As in uses of place names and stories by Basso, *Wisdom Sits in Places*.
41. Nevins and Nevins, "We Have Always Had the Bible," 2009.

guage program design and into wider strategies for community empowerment. By defining indigenous languages as a "matter of concern,"[42] endangerment discourse most directly supports linguistic documentation and school maintenance programs, but it also sets new conditions for innovation that extend beyond the purview of linguistic experts. My intention is to open up the discussion of language maintenance to allow for the fact that language programs figure importantly in community empowerment, but not always in ways their designers anticipate or intend. The present effort is an attempt to enable recognition of community responses and interventions into maintenance programs, not as noise or obstacles to progress, but as relevant to indigenous community empowerment more broadly conceived.

Bibliography

Bartelt, Guillermo. "American Indian Discourses of Assimiliationism." *Language and Literature.* 17 (1992): 59–75.

Bartelt, Guillermo, Susan Penfield-Jasper and Bates Hoffer, eds. *Essays in Native American English*. San Antonio: Trinity University Press, 1982.

Basso, Keith, H. *Wisdom Sits in Places: Language and Landscape Among the Western Apache.* Albuquerque: University of New Mexico Press, 1996.

Bauman, Richard and Charles Briggs. "Poetics and Performance as Critical Perspectives on Language and Social Life," *Annual Review of Anthropology* 19 (1990): 59–88.

Biolsi, Thomas. "Imagined Geographies: Sovereignty, Indigenous Space, and American Indian Struggle." *American Ethnologist* 32 no. 2: 239–59.

Bradley, David and Maya Bradley. *Language Endangerment and Language Maintenance: An Active Approach*. New York: Rutledge, 2002.

Collins, James. *Understanding Tolowa Histories: Western Hegemonies and Native American Responses.* New York: Routledge, 1998.

———. "Our Ideologies and Theirs." In *Language Ideologies: Prac-*

42. Latour, "Why Has Critique Run Out of Steam," 2004.

tice and Theory, edited by Bambi B. Schieffelin, Kathryn A. Woolard, and Paul.V, Kroskrity. 256–270. New York: Oxford University Press, 1998.

Crawford, James. "Proposition 203: Anti-Bilingual Initiative in Arizona."www.languagepolicy.net/archives/az-unz.htm (Posted 2001).

Duchêne, Allexandre and Monica Heller, eds. *Discourses of Endangerment: Ideology and Interest in the Defense of Languages.* London: Continuum, 2007.

Evans, Nicholas. *Dying Words: Endangered Languages and What They Have to Tell Us.* Wiley-Blackwell, 2009.

Fishman, Joshua. *In Praise of the Beloved Language: A Comparative View of Positive Ethnolinguistic Consciousness.* Mouton de Gruyter: The Hague, 1996.

Grenoble, Lenore and Lindsay Whaley. *Saving Languages: An Introduction to Language Revitalization.* Cambridge: Cambridge University Press, 2005.

Harrison, K. David. *When Languages Die: The Extinction of the World's Languages and the Erosion of Human Knowledge.* Oxford: Oxford University Press, 2008.

Harry, Debra. "Acts of Self-Determination and Self-Defense: Indigenous Peoples Responses to Biocolonialism." In *Rights and Liberties in the Biotech Age: Why We Need a Genetic Bill of Rights,* edited by Sheldon Krimsky and Peter Shorett. Lanham, MD: Roman and Littlefield, 2005: 87–98.

Hill, Jane H. "'Expert Rhetorics' in Advocacy for Endangered Languages: Who is Listening and What do They Hear?" *Journal of Linguistic Anthropology* 12 no. 2 (2002): 119–133.

Hofling, Charles Andrew. "Indigenous Linguistic Revitalization and Outsider Interaction: The Itzaj Maya Case," *Human Organization* 55, no. 1 (1996): 108–116.

IPS Arctic Council Indigenous Peoples Secretariat. "Qualified UNDRI Support" at www.arcticpeoples.org/index.php?option=com_k2&view=item&id=367:qualified-undrip-support&Itemid=2 (Last accessed, February 21, 2011).

Jourdan, Miriam. "Arizona Grades Teachers on Fluency State Pushes School Districts to Reassign Instructors with Heavy Accents or Other Shortcomings in Their English." *Wall Street*

Journal, April 30, 2010.

Keane, Webb. *Christian Moderns: Freedom and Fetish in the Mission Encounter.* Berkeley, CA: University of California Press, 2007.

Latour, Bruno. "Why Has Critique Run Out of Steam: From Matters of Fact to Matters of Concern," *Critical Inquiry* 30 (Winter 2004): 225–48.

McCarty, Teresa and Ofelia Zepeda. "Amerindians." In *Handbook of Language and Ethnic Identity*, edited by Joshua Fishman. Oxford: Oxford University Press, 1999: 197–210.

Meek, Barbara. *We are Our Language: An Ethnography of Language Revitalization in a Northern Athabascan Community*. Tuscon: University of Arizona Press, 2010.

Merlan, Francesca. "Indigeneity: Local and Global," *Current Anthropology* 50, no. 3 (2009): 303–333.

Moore, Robert. "Disappearing, Inc.: Glimpsing the Sublime in the Politics of Access to Endangered Languages," *Language & Communication* 26 (2006): 296–315.

Morgan, Mindy J. *The Bearer of This Letter: Language Ideologies, Literacy Practices, and the Fort Belknap Indian Community*. Lincoln: University of Nebraska Press, 2009.

Nevins, M. Eleanor. "Learning to listen: Confronting two Meanings of Language Loss in the Contemporary White Mountain Apache Speech Community" *Journal of Linguistic Anthropology* 14 (2004): 269–88.

———. "They Live in Lonesome Dove: Media and Contemporary Western Apache Place-naming Practices," *Language in Society*, 37 (2008): 191–215.

———. "The Bible in Two Keys: Traditionalism and Apache Evangelical Christianity on the Fort Apache Reservation" *Language and Communication* 30 no. 1 (2010): 19–32.

Nevins, M. Eleanor and Thomas J. Nevins. "'They Do Not Know How to Ask': Pedagogy, Storytelling and the Ironies of Languages Endangerment on the Fort Apache Reservation." In *Telling Stories in the Face of Danger,* edited by Paul Kroskrity. Tulsa: University of Oklahoma Press, in press.

Nevins, Thomas J. "Between Love and Culture: Misunderstanding,

Textuality and the Dialectics of Ethnographic Knowledge," *Language and Communication* 30, no. 1 (2010): 58–68.

Nevins, Thomas J. and M. Eleanor Nevins. "'We Have Always Had the Bible': Christianity and the Composition of White Mountain Apache Heritage," *Heritage Management* 2, no. 1 (2009): 11–33.

Nettle, Daniel and Suzanne Romaine. *Vanishing Voices: The Extinction of the World's Languages*. Oxford: Oxford University Press, 2002.

Niezen, R. *The Origins of Indigenism: Human Rights and the Politics of Identity*. Berkeley: University of California Press, 2003.

Paulson, Christina Bratt. "Language Policies and Language Rights," *Annual Review of Anthropology* 27 (1997): 73–87.

Phillips, Susan. *The Invisible Culture: Communication in Classroom and Community on the Warm Springs Indian Reservation*. Long Grove, IL: Waveland Press, Inc., 1992.

Povinelli, Elizabeth A. *The Cunning of Recognition: Indigenous Alterities and the Making of Australian Multiculturalism*. Durham, NC: Duke University Press, 2002.

Reyner, Jon and Jeanne Eder. *American Indian Education: A History*. Tulsa: University of Oklahoma Press, 2006.

Rumsey, Alan. "The Articulation of Indigenous and Exogenous Orders in Highland New Guinea and Beyond." In *Taja: The Australian Journal of Anthropology* 17, no. 1(2009): 47–69.

Samuels, David. "Bible Translation and Medicine Man Talk: Missionaries Indexicality and the 'Language Expert' on the San Carlos Apache Reservation," *Language in Society* 35, no. 4 (2006): 529–57.

Silverstein, Micheal. "Monoglot 'Standard' in America: Standardization and Metaphors of Linguistic Hegemony." In *The Matrix of Language: Contemporary Linguistic Anthropology*, edited by Brenneis, D. and Macauley. Boulder: Westview, 1996: 284–306.

Silverstein, Michael and Greg Urban. "The Natural History of Discourse." In *Natural Histories of Discourse*, edited by Michael Silverstein and Greg Urban. Chicago: University of Chicago Press, 1996: 1–17.

Spitulnik, Debra, "The Social Circulation of Media Discourse and the Mediation of Communities," *Journal of Linguistic Anthropology* 6 (1997): 161–87.

Tsunoda, Tasaku. *Language Endangerment and Language Revitalization: An Introduction*. Moutin de Gruyter, 2006.

Wilkins, David P. "Even with the Best of Intentions ... : Some Pitfalls in the Fight for Linguistic and Cultural Survival (One view of the Australian Experience)," in *As linguas amazônicas hoje: Les langues d'Amazonie aujourd'hui* Éd. sci. Francisco Queixalos et O. Renault-Lescure, 2000.

UNESCO, United Nations Educational, Scientific and Cultural Organization. Frequently Asked Questions, Endangered Languages, www.unesco.org/new/en/culture/themes/cultural-diversity/languages-and-multilingualism/endangered-languages/faq-on-endangered-languages/. Accessed July 2011.

Urciuoli, Bonnie. "Entextualizing Diversity: Semiotic Incoherence in Institutional Discourse," *Language and Communication* 30, no. 1(2010):48–57

Zehr, Mary Ann. "Native American Students Flag Holes in Instruction," *Education Week,* June 25, no. 27 (2008).

Index

F

J

M

R

S

T

List Contributors

André Braën
University of Ottawa
Faculty of Law, Civil Section

Pierre Foucher
University of Ottawa
Faculty of Law, Civil Law Section

Peter Gerrand
Monash University
School of Languages, Cultures and Linguistics

Xabier Irujo
University of Nevada
Center for Basque Studies

Viola Miglio
University of California, Santa Barbara
Barandiarán Chair of Basque Studies

Eleanor Nevins
University of Nevada, Reno
Faculty of Anthropology

Xosé Manoel Núñez Seixas
University of Santiago de Compostela
Contemporary History Department

Jon Reyhner
Northern Arizona University
College of Education, Department of Educational Specialties

Iñigo Urrutia
University of the Basque Country
Faculty of Law, Administrative Law Section

Fernand de Varennes
Murdoch University
School of Law

Denis Viri
Arizona State University
Center for Indian Education

www.ingramcontent.com/pod-product-compliance
Lightning Source LLC
LaVergne TN
LVHW091031080826
845145LV00002B/446